# Chinese

# Chinese

Carol Bowen

Carole Handslip

Kathryn Hawkins

Deh-Ta Hsiung

Wendy Lee

Jenny Stacey

Rosemary Wadey

*p*

This is a Parragon Publishing Book
This edition published in 2003

Parragon Publishing
Queen Street House
4 Queen Street
Bath BA1 1HE, UK

Copyright © Parragon 2001

ISBN: 0-75258-831-1

Printed in China

**Note**

Tablespoons are assumed to be 15 ml. Unless otherwise stated,
milk is assumed to be full-fat, eggs are medium
and pepper is freshly ground black pepper.

# Contents

**Introduction  8**

**Appetizers  20**

Crispy Wontons with Piquant Dipping Sauce **22**
Crispy Seaweed. . . . . . . . . . . . . . . . . . . . . . **23**
Spinach Meatballs. . . . . . . . . . . . . . . . . . **24**
Spring Rolls. . . . . . . . . . . . . . . . . . . . . . . . **25**
Pork Pancake Rolls . . . . . . . . . . . . . . . . . **26**
Lettuce-Wrapped Minced Meat. . . . . . . . . **27**
Steamed Cabbage Rolls. . . . . . . . . . . . . . **28**
Rice Paper Parcels . . . . . . . . . . . . . . . . . . **29**
Deep-Fried Prawns . . . . . . . . . . . . . . . . . . **30**
Sesame Prawn Toasts . . . . . . . . . . . . . . . **31**
Deep-Fried Spare Ribs. . . . . . . . . . . . . . . **32**
Pork with Chilli & Garlic Sauce. . . . . . . . . . **33**
Pork Dim Sum . . . . . . . . . . . . . . . . . . . . . **34**
Barbecue Spare Ribs . . . . . . . . . . . . . . . . **35**
Barbecue Pork (Char Siu) . . . . . . . . . . . . . **36**
Pot Sticker Dumplings . . . . . . . . . . . . . . **37**
Steamed Duck Buns . . . . . . . . . . . . . . . . **38**
Chinese Omelette. . . . . . . . . . . . . . . . . . . **39**

**Salads & Pickles  40**

Sweet & Sour Tofu Salad. . . . . . . . . . . . . **42**
Sweet & Sour Cucumber . . . . . . . . . . . . . **43**
Chinese Hot Salad . . . . . . . . . . . . . . . . . **44**
Oriental Salad. . . . . . . . . . . . . . . . . . . . . **45**
Pickled Vegetables. . . . . . . . . . . . . . . . . . **46**
Hot & Sour Duck Salad . . . . . . . . . . . . . . **47**
Cucumber & Beansprout Salad . . . . . . . . . **48**
Broccoli, Pepper &
  Almond Salad . . . . . . . . . . . . . . . . . . . **49**

**Soups  50**

Mixed Vegetable Soup . . . . . . . . . . . . . . . **52**
Vegetarian Hot & Sour Soup . . . . . . . . . . **53**
Chinese Cabbage Soup . . . . . . . . . . . . . . **54**
Wonton Soup . . . . . . . . . . . . . . . . . . . . . **55**
Spinach & Tofu Soup. . . . . . . . . . . . . . . . **56**
Beef & Vegetable Noodle Soup . . . . . . . . . **57**
Noodles in Soup . . . . . . . . . . . . . . . . . . . **58**
Mushroom & Cucumber Noodle Soup . . . . . **59**
Fish Soup with Wontons . . . . . . . . . . . . . **60**
Seafood & Tofu Soup. . . . . . . . . . . . . . . . **61**
Shrimp Dumpling Soup . . . . . . . . . . . . . . **62**
Crab & Ginger Soup. . . . . . . . . . . . . . . . . **63**
Three-Flavour Soup . . . . . . . . . . . . . . . . . **64**
Curried Chicken & Sweetcorn Soup . . . . . . **65**
Prawn Soup. . . . . . . . . . . . . . . . . . . . . . . **66**
Peking Duck Soup. . . . . . . . . . . . . . . . . . **67**
Clear Chicken & Egg Soup. . . . . . . . . . . . **68**
Chicken Soup with Almonds . . . . . . . . . . . **69**
Lamb & Rice Soup. . . . . . . . . . . . . . . . . . **70**
Pork & Szechuan Vegetable Soup . . . . . . . **71**

## Fish & Seafood 72

Trout with Pineapple . . . . . . . . . . . . . 74
Fish with Black Bean Sauce . . . . . . . . . . . 75
Crispy Fish with Chillies . . . . . . . . . . . . 76
Braised Fish Fillets . . . . . . . . . . . . . . 77
Mullet with Ginger . . . . . . . . . . . . . . 78
Fish in Szechuan Hot Sauce . . . . . . . . . . 79
Steamed Snapper with
  Fruit & Ginger Stuffing . . . . . . . . . . 80
Spiced Scallops . . . . . . . . . . . . . . . . 81
Stir-fried Prawns & Vegetables . . . . . . . . 82
Seafood Combination . . . . . . . . . . . . . 83
Szechuan Prawns . . . . . . . . . . . . . . . 84
Sizzled Chilli Prawns . . . . . . . . . . . . . 85

Prawn Stir-fry with Lemon Grass . . . . . . . 86
Shrimp Fu Yong . . . . . . . . . . . . . . . . 87
Cantonese Prawns . . . . . . . . . . . . . . 88
Sweet & Sour Prawns . . . . . . . . . . . . . 89
Baked Crab with Ginger . . . . . . . . . . . . 90
Squid in Oyster Sauce & Vegetables . . . . . . 91
Fried Squid Flowers . . . . . . . . . . . . . . 92
Fish & Ginger Stir-fry . . . . . . . . . . . . . 93

## Poultry Dishes 94

Chinese Chicken Salad . . . . . . . . . . . . 96
Chicken with Beansprouts . . . . . . . . . . . 97
Kung Po Chicken with Cashew Nuts . . . . . 98
Chicken with Yellow Bean Sauce . . . . . . . 99
Peanut Sesame Chicken . . . . . . . . . . . 100
Braised Chicken . . . . . . . . . . . . . . . 101
Chicken with Pepper . . . . . . . . . . . . . 102
Spicy Peanut Chicken . . . . . . . . . . . . 103
Chicken Fu Yong . . . . . . . . . . . . . . . 104
Chilli Chicken . . . . . . . . . . . . . . . . 105
Szechuan Chilli Chicken . . . . . . . . . . . 106
Chicken Chop Suey . . . . . . . . . . . . . . 107

Chicken with Mushrooms . . . . . . . . . . . 108
Crispy Chicken . . . . . . . . . . . . . . . . 109
Chicken with Celery & Cashew Nuts . . . . . 110
Stir-fried Duck with Broccoli & Peppers . . . . 111
Aromatic & Crispy Duck . . . . . . . . . . . 112
Duck in Spicy Sauce . . . . . . . . . . . . . 113
Honey & Soy Glazed Duck . . . . . . . . . . 114
Duck with Mangoes . . . . . . . . . . . . . 115

## Meat Dishes 116

Lamb Meatballs in Soy Sauce . . . . . . . . 118
Hot Lamb . . . . . . . . . . . . . . . . . . 119
Stir-fried Lamb with Sesame Seeds . . . . . . 120
Five-Spiced Lamb . . . . . . . . . . . . . . 121
Lamb in Garlic Sauce . . . . . . . . . . . . 122
Oyster Sauce Beef . . . . . . . . . . . . . . 123
Beef & Pak Choi . . . . . . . . . . . . . . . 124
Spicy Beef & Broccoli Stir-Fry . . . . . . . . 125
Beef & Chilli Black Bean Sauce . . . . . . . . 126
Peppered Beef Cashew . . . . . . . . . . . . 127
Chinese Beef . . . . . . . . . . . . . . . . . 128
Crispy Shredded Beef . . . . . . . . . . . . 129
Sweet & Sour Pork . . . . . . . . . . . . . . 130

Spare Ribs with Chilli . . . . . . . . . . . . 131
Deep-Fried Pork with a Soy
  Dipping Sauce . . . . . . . . . . . . . . 132
Fish-flavoured Shredded Pork . . . . . . . . 133
Red Spiced Beef . . . . . . . . . . . . . . . 134
Pork with Plum Sauce . . . . . . . . . . . . 135
Stir-fried Pork with Vegetables . . . . . . . . 136
Braised Pork & Tofu . . . . . . . . . . . . . 137

## Vegetable Dishes 138

Vegetable Chop Suey . . . . . . . . . . . . 140
Sweet & Sour Vegetables . . . . . . . . . . . 141
Stir-fried Mixed Vegetables . . . . . . . . . . 142
Braised Bamboo Shoots . . . . . . . . . . . 143
Golden Needles with Bamboo Shoots . . . . . 144
Chinese Braised Vegetables . . . . . . . . . 145
Stir-fried Cucumber with Ginger & Chilli . . 146
Stir-fried Beansprouts . . . . . . . . . . . . 147
Beansprouts with Peppers . . . . . . . . . . 148
Vegetables in Black Bean Sauce . . . . . . . 149
Vegetable & Nut Stir-fry . . . . . . . . . . . 150
Chinese Green Bean Stir-fry . . . . . . . . . 151
Stir-fried Greens . . . . . . . . . . . . . . . 152
Tofu & Vegetables with Black Bean Sauce . . 153
Vegetable & Tofu Casserole . . . . . . . . . 154

Stir-fried Mushrooms, Cucumber &
  Smoked Tofu . . . . . . . . . . . . . . . 155
Deep-fried Tofu with Chinese Five Spice . . 156
Braised Vegetables with Tofu . . . . . . . . . 157
Aubergine in Chilli Sauce . . . . . . . . . . 158
Spicy Aubergines . . . . . . . . . . . . . . . 159

Aubergine in Black Bean Sauce . . . . . . . . . **160**
Spicy Mushrooms . . . . . . . . . . . . . . . . . . **161**
Money Bags . . . . . . . . . . . . . . . . . . . . . . **162**
Steamed Vegetable Cabbage Rolls . . . . . . . **163**
Creamy Cabbage & Leeks . . . . . . . . . . . . **164**
Lemon Chinese Leaves . . . . . . . . . . . . . . . **165**
Chinese Leaves Stir-fried in Soy & Honey . . **166**
Lentil Balls with Sweet & Sour Sauce . . . . . **167**

Crisp Fried Pak Choi with Almonds . . . . . . **168**
Broccoli with Ginger & Orange . . . . . . . . . **169**
Broccoli in Oyster Sauce . . . . . . . . . . . . . **170**
Garlic Spinach . . . . . . . . . . . . . . . . . . . . **171**
Spinach with Straw Mushrooms . . . . . . . . **172**
Chinese Potato Chips . . . . . . . . . . . . . . . **173**

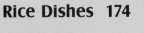

## Vegetable Dishes continued

Chinese Fried Rice . . . . . . . . . . . . . . . . . . **176**
Vegetable Fried Rice . . . . . . . . . . . . . . . . **177**
Fragrant Steamed Rice
    in Lotus Leaves . . . . . . . . . . . . . . . . . **178**
Green Fried Rice with Spinach . . . . . . . . . **179**
Egg Fried Rice with Chilli . . . . . . . . . . . . **180**
Egg Fried Rice . . . . . . . . . . . . . . . . . . . . **181**
Egg Fu Yong with Rice . . . . . . . . . . . . . . **182**
Special Fried Rice . . . . . . . . . . . . . . . . . . **183**
Fried Rice with Prawns . . . . . . . . . . . . . . **184**
Chicken & Rice Casserole . . . . . . . . . . . . **185**
Special Fried Rice with Cashew Nuts . . . . . **186**
Fried Rice & Prawns . . . . . . . . . . . . . . . . **187**

Rice with Crab & Mussels . . . . . . . . . . . . **188**
Fried Rice with Pork, Tomatoes,
    Peas & Mushrooms . . . . . . . . . . . . . . . **189**

## Rice Dishes 174

Chow Mein . . . . . . . . . . . . . . . . . . . . . . **192**
Fried Vegetable Noodles . . . . . . . . . . . . . **193**
Mixed Vegetable Chow Mein . . . . . . . . . . **194**
Transparent Noodles with
    Yellow Bean Sauce . . . . . . . . . . . . . . . **195**
Homemade Noodles with
    Stir-fried Vegetables . . . . . . . . . . . . . . **196**
Transparent Noodles with Prawns . . . . . . . **197**
Seafood Chow Mein . . . . . . . . . . . . . . . . **198**
Curried Prawn Noodles . . . . . . . . . . . . . . **199**
Singapore-Style Rice Noodles . . . . . . . . . . **200**
Cantonese Fried Noodles . . . . . . . . . . . . . **201**
Chicken Noodles . . . . . . . . . . . . . . . . . . **202**

Chicken on Crispy Noodles . . . . . . . . . . . **203**
Pork Chow Mein . . . . . . . . . . . . . . . . . . **204**
Beef Chow Mein . . . . . . . . . . . . . . . . . . **205**
Fried Noodles with Mushrooms
    & Pork . . . . . . . . . . . . . . . . . . . . . . . **206**
Lamb with Transparent Noodles . . . . . . . **207**

## Noodle Dishes 190

Sweet Fruit Wontons . . . . . . . . . . . . . . . **210**
Banana Pastries . . . . . . . . . . . . . . . . . . . **211**
Mango Dumplings . . . . . . . . . . . . . . . . . **212**
Sweet Rice . . . . . . . . . . . . . . . . . . . . . . . **213**
Honeyed Rice Puddings . . . . . . . . . . . . . **214**
Mango Mousse . . . . . . . . . . . . . . . . . . . **215**
Poached Allspice Pears . . . . . . . . . . . . . . **216**
Chinese Custard Tarts . . . . . . . . . . . . . . . **217**
Ginger Lychees with
    Orange Sorbet . . . . . . . . . . . . . . . . . . **218**
Chinese Fruit Salad . . . . . . . . . . . . . . . . . **219**

## Desserts 208

## Index 220

# Introduction

Chinese cuisine was known to and appreciated by a small elite of westerners privileged to travel to the East, but for a long time it was virtually unknown outside China. Chinese settlers in San Francisco first introduced America to the pleasures of their cuisine, especially during the years of the Gold Rush and the building of the Pacific Railroad. However, it was not until much later in the twentieth century that Chinese cuisine found its way to Britain and other parts of Europe. Once it had found a foothold, however, there was no turning back, as its popularity rocketed across the world. Even then, it remained very much in the realm of restaurants and professionals and it is only comparatively recently that western cooks have started preparing Chinese dishes at home.

## CHINESE CUISINE

The nature of Chinese cuisine has been shaped by two very different elements – one practical and the other philosophical and religious. For the majority of Chinese peasants, life was bitterly harsh. They were at the mercy of natural disasters, from floods to failed harvests. Not only was food often in short supply, but fuel with which to cook it was always a scarce commodity. That a cuisine of international renown should have developed from such an unpromising and uncompromising situation is a remarkable example of ingenuity and imagination.

The perennial shortage of fuel brought about the development of fast-cooking techniques, the best known of which is stir-frying. Slicing, chopping, dicing and shredding food into very small pieces meant that it could be cooked more quickly and required less wood for the fire. Filling foods, such as rice and wheat products, depending on what grew best locally, were used to satisfy the appetite or sometimes just to appease hunger. Even when they were available, meat, fish and fresh vegetables had to be used sparingly. Consequently, if only a small portion of a savoury sauce was all there was to flavour a bland bowl of rice, it needed to be packed full of delicious tastes. A careful use of herbs and spices and the development of flavourings, such as soy, hoi-sin and fermented bean sauces, was the practical – and happy – solution to this problem.

Of course, not everyone in China was poor and the influence of the wealthy and aristocratic is also reflected in modern Chinese cooking. One of the first and certainly one of the most important appointments made by a new Emperor of China was the court chef. No mere cook, he was an exalted person with the heavy responsibility of ensuring that food served in the royal household kept its members physically and spiritually fit and healthy. There was also a natural sense of rivalry with his predecessors and each new chef worked to outdo the skills of previous ones and constantly sought new flavours, ingredients and recipes. Consequently, a kind of haute cuisine grew up in Peking, China's one-thousand-year-old capital, and in other parts of the North.

The second major influence on Chinese cuisine is connected with the philosophical and religious belief that everything in the universe is balanced and harmonious. As Yin balances Yang, day balances night and man

balances woman, so with food, the textures, colours and flavours should balance each other to create a harmonious whole. Harmony is achieved through contrast, so a crispy dish is served with one that has a creamy texture, and a spicy dish is accompanied by a mild, sweet-tasting one. Balance of the four basic flavours – sweet, sour, bitter and salty – may even be encompassed in a single dish.

## REGIONAL COOKING

China is a huge country, covering an area of over 9,500 million square kilometres (3,700 million square miles), larger than the United States. The terrain varies widely from the high Tibetan Plateau to the flat flood plain of the Yangtze River. Climate varies accordingly, too, so it is hardly surprising that there are many distinctive regional styles of cooking.

## Northern China – Shantung and Honan

This region, stretching to the borders of Inner Mongolia, is dry and quite arid. Wheat, rather than rice, is the staple ingredient, giving rise to all kinds of noodles, breads, pancakes, steamed buns and dumplings. Cooking methods tend to be simple, mainly roasting and boiling, and strong-tasting dipping sauces are characteristic. Sesame seeds, now widely used throughout China, were first introduced in the North by invading Tartars and the seeds and oil still feature prominently there. An abundant supply of seafood is to be found on the coast, and the Yellow River is a source of excellent freshwater fish. Sweet-and-sour carp is a speciality. Fine grapes and peaches are grown in Shantung, which is also the homeland of pak choi.

China's capital is now more accurately written as Beijing in English characters, but in cookery terms will probably remain Peking for decades. Its style of cooking is elegant and light, rather than rich. From time to time the city was invaded by Tartars and the Moslem traditions of Central Asia have had their effect on Peking cuisine, not least in that this is one place in China where pork is not the most commonly eaten meat.

## Southern China – Canton

Cantonese cuisine is the best known in the West because the first immigrants to America and Europe came from there. The province of Kwangtung has an excellent climate for agriculture, producing a plentiful supply of fresh vegetables throughout the year. These feature in Cantonese dishes, usually quickly stir-fried and served with a little additional sauce. Sugar cane, tangerines, mandarins, oranges and loquats grow in the semi-tropical valleys and these are often combined with meat and poultry in a sweet-and-sour sauce.

Fish and seafood are abundantly available and Cantonese dishes feature prawns, crab, abalone or scallops. Crab or lobster and ginger is a classic combination. Steaming is a favourite method of cooking, although the region is also famous for char siu roasting, a process in which the meat, often pork, is marinated for a long period and then roasted very quickly. Dim sum, small steamed parcels, which in China are usually served as an afternoon snack in tea houses, originated in Canton. Fish-flavoured meat, that is using oyster sauce and other flavourings normally associated with cooking fish to prepare meat, is also a speciality of the region. Spices tend to be aromatic rather than hot, and light soy sauce is preferred to dark because it affects the colour of other ingredients less. Other popular Cantonese sauce are plum, hoi-sin, oyster and black bean. Cantonese cuisine is very sophisticated and varied. This results partly from an influx of chefs from the royal household in 1644, when the Ming Dynasty was overthrown, and partly from Canton's role as the first major Chinese trading port open to foreign influences.

## Western China – Szechuan and Yunnan

A fertile mountain-ringed basin, Szechuan is a prosperous region famous for producing robustly spiced dishes which feature chillies, hot pepper oil, sesame paste and Szechuan peppercorns. Pungent vegetables, such as onions and spring onions, are extensively used.

Not all Szechuan food is hotly spiced, however. The region is also known for a method of cooking meat and vegetables in a clear broth, flavoured with wine and spices, until it has reduced to a thick, rich sauce, and for prolonged dry-frying, which results in crisp, well-coloured dishes.

Both Szechuan and its southern neighbour Yunnan are well known for food preservation techniques, which include salting, smoking, drying and pickling. Szechuan hot pickle and Yunnan cured, smoked ham are local specialities.

## Eastern China – Fukien, Kiangsu and Chekiang

This region is rich in fruit and vegetables for, lying on the Yangtze delta, it is one of the most fertile in China. Wheat and rice are both grown, as well as corn, potatoes, peanuts and soya beans. Freshwater fish are widely available and Kiangsu and Chekiang are well known for seafood. Kiangsu, north of the river is famous for dumplings, noodles and pork dishes, too. South of the river lies Chekiang and the style of cooking here is known as Kiangche, a combination of the two provinces' names. Food is sophisticated and has absorbed many influences from other parts of China, not least because both Hangchow and Nanking have been the capitals of China in the past. Duck dishes and spare ribs are specialities. This region also produces the best rice wine in China, in Shaoxing.

The huge port of Shanghai has a culinary style all of its own which is characterized by richness and elegance. As a major trade port in the nineteenth century, it absorbed many foreign influences, which can be seen in the use of ingredients such as butter, milk and lard. To the south, Fukien makes good use of its agricultural land and abundant seafood in a style strongly influenced by its Cantonese neighbour.

## The Chinese Meal

Family meals also observe the Chinese approach to a life of harmony and balance. Three or even four generations gather peacefully together to share the food, with everyone taking only what they need from the communal selection of dishes placed on the table. To select an especially delicious piece of food with the chopsticks and offer it to someone else is a mark of both respect and affection. All the savoury dishes, including soup, are placed on the table at once. Individual portions are never served. Family meals do not usually include a dessert; these are usually served only at banquets and on very special occasions. Fresh fruit may be eaten at the end of the meal and sweet snacks are often eaten between meals.

The choice of dishes for any meal should reflect balance through contrast. The same main ingredients are to be avoided and a hot and spicy dish should be served with a sweet-and-sour dish, for example. The number of dishes served at a family meal depends on the number of people. An easy rule of thumb is to serve one dish per person although, of course, everyone will share all the dishes, plus soup and rice or noodles. It is always wiser to increase the number of dishes, rather than to increase the size of individual dishes, as this produces far greater variety. It is sensible to avoid too many dishes that require last-minute attention.

A formal dinner has more strictly observed rules. The number of guests is usually twelve or fourteen, always an even number, and the same number of dishes as people are served. Appetizers, perhaps one cold and three hot dishes, are served first, followed by soup. A main course of, say, six dishes follows, with rice or noodles. Finally, two desserts complete the meal. Balance and harmony are, again, essential to the Chinese meal and dishes are always garnished in different ways.

# The Chinese Store-cupboard

*Many Chinese dishes can be prepared with ingredients commonly used in the West – spring onions, garlic, peppers, peanut oil, many herbs, fish and meat. Some more unfamiliar and exotic ingredients may need an explanation. They will usually be available from Chinese foodstores, some health-food shops and some supermarkets.*

**Baby Corn Cobs** have a sweet flavour and a crunchy texture. They are available fresh, frozen and canned.

**Bamboo Shoots** are mild-flavoured and widely available in cans. Drain and rinse thoroughly before use. Fresh shoots can sometimes be found in Chinese foodstores. They can be stored in fresh water in a covered jar in the refrigerator for up to 1 week.

**Basil** is a popular herb in Asian cooking and a number of different varieties are used.

**Bean Sauce** may be black or yellow and is made from crushed, salted soya beans mixed with flour and spices, such as ginger and chilli, to make a thick paste. It is used both as a flavouring during cooking and as a condiment. It is sold in cans and jars and once opened, should be stored in the refrigerator.

**Beansprouts** from mung or soya beans are widely available from supermarkets. Canned and frozen sprouts are also sold, but these are not usually so crisp as fresh. You can sprout your own beans very easily.

**Black Beans** are salted fermented soya beans, available in packets or cans.

**Cardamom** is an aromatic spice, available in two forms – small green pods and large black pods. Use the green variety for Chinese cooking.

**Cashews** are often used to provide extra flavour and texture, particularly in chicken dishes.

**Chilli Bean Paste** is a fermented bean paste mixed with hot chillies and other seasonings. It can vary from mild to fiery hot.

**Chilli Oil** is a hot, red oil flavoured with chillies and sometimes containing chilli flakes. Use it sparingly. You can make your own by infusing a few dried chillies in a small bottle of oil for several days.

**Chilli Sauce** is widely used as a dipping sauce and a flavouring in cooking. Made from chillies, vinegar, sugar and salt, it is extremely hot.

**Chillies** may be red or green and vary in size, shape and spiciness. As a rule, dark green chillies are hotter than pale green or red ones, but this is not invariably the case. Thin, pointed chillies tend to be hotter than short, blunt ones. Dried chillies are usually hotter than fresh. Take care when handling chillies, as the juice stings, and always wash your hands thoroughly afterwards. For a milder taste, remove and discard the seeds before using the chilli.

**Chinese Five-Spice Powder** is a distinctive mixture of star anise, fennel seeds, cloves, cinnamon and Szechuan pepper. It is very pungent and should be used sparingly. It is different from Indian five-spice powder.

**Chinese Leaves** are widely available in two different varieties. One has a pale green, tightly wrapped elongated head, rather like a Cos lettuce, and the other is shorter and fatter with yellow or green leaves.

**Chinese Pancakes** are made from flour and water, with no added seasoning. They are available fresh and frozen. Thaw frozen pancakes before use.

**Coriander** is also known as Chinese parsley. It has a distinctive flavour and also makes an attractive garnish. Tearing rather than chopping the leaves results in a more subtle flavour.

**Garlic** is a primary seasoning in Chinese food. It may be chopped, crushed or pickled, depending on how strong you wish the flavour to be. Store in a cool, dry place, but not in the refrigerator.

**Ginger** has an unmistakable, sharp, pungent taste. Fresh ginger root is widely used in savoury dishes and stem ginger in sweet ones. Ground dried ginger is not an adequate substitute. Look for plump, unwrinkled roots, then peel and grate, shred, slice or chop before using.

**Hoi-sin Sauce** is made from soy beans, sugar, flour, vinegar, salt, garlic, chillies and sesame seed oil. Available in cans or bottles, it will keep in the refrigerator for several months.

**Lemon Grass** is an aromatic herb with a strong, lemon flavour. It is available fresh, bottled or dried as a powder. Chop or slice the lower part of the stem to use.

**Lily Buds** are also known as golden needles. They are available dried from Chinese foodstores and should be soaked before use.

**Lotus Leaves** are usually sold dried and should be soaked in hot water before use. They are very large and often used as a wrapping for other ingredients when steaming.

**Mangetout** are tender pea pods with flat peas. They are sweet with a crisp texture. The whole pod is cooked and eaten.

**Mushrooms**, both fresh and dried, are widely used in Chinese cooking, very often for their texture rather than their flavour. Straw mushrooms are slippery. Dried mushrooms must be soaked in warm water for 25–30 minutes. The soaking liquid may be used as stock. Cut the hard stems of the mushrooms and use the caps.

**Noodles** may be made from a variety of ingredients, including rice, wheat and pulses, and most types are available both fresh and dried. Follow the packet instructions for cooking.

**Oyster Sauce** is a thick, soy-based sauce used as a flavouring in Cantonese cooking. It is available in bottles and will keep in the refrigerator for several months.

**Pak Choi** is an elongated dark green vegetable with smooth white stems. It is available from Chinese foodstores and some large supermarkets.

**Plum Sauce** has a sweet-and-sour fruity flavour.

**Rice** comes in many forms. White long-grain is the type most widely used in savoury dishes, while glutinous rice is used for desserts.

**Rice Vinegar** is available as red or white. Red rice vinegar is made from fermented rice and has a distinctive dark colour and depth of flavour. White rice vinegar is distilled from rice wine and has a strong flavour. It is available from Chinese supermarkets, but you can substitute cider vinegar, if necessary.

**Rice Wine** is usually made from glutinous rice and is available from Chinese foodstores. It is different from sake or Japanese rice wine and a better substitute, if it is unavailable, is dry sherry.

**Sesame Oil** is an aromatic oil made from toasted sesame seeds. It is not usually used for cooking, but for flavouring and is generally added to a dish shortly before serving.

**Sesame Seeds** add texture and a nutty flavour to dishes. Dry-frying them adds colour and accentuates the flavour.

**Shallots** are members of the onion family, but smaller and milder in taste.

**Soy Sauce** is an important Chinese seasoning and is made from fermented soy beans, yeast, salt and sugar. It may be light or dark. It is best used with other ingredients, such as wine or stock, for cooking, and mixed with other sauces, vinegar and strong flavourings, such as garlic and ginger, for dipping sauces.

**Spring Onions** are slender onions with small bulbs. Sometimes a recipe specifies separating the white and green parts – the white part is the main part of the onion, the green part is essentially the leaves.

**Spring Roll Skins** are thin wrappers made from wheat or rice flour and water. Wheat skins are usually sold frozen and must be thawed before use. Rice skins are dried and need gentle soaking before use. Both are available in a range of sizes from Chinese foodstores.

**Szechuan Peppercorns** are aromatic, hot red peppercorns. They are best used roasted and ground.

**Szechuan Preserved Vegetable** is a speciality from western China. It is the root of a variety of mustard green pickled in salt and chillies. It should be rinsed thoroughly before use. Other Chinese pickles include winter pickle and snow pickle.

**Tofu** is a soy product that is sold in blocks. Firm tofu (bean curd) is most suitable for stir-frying, but other types, including marinated and smoked, are available. It has a fairly bland flavour, but readily absorbs the flavours of other ingredients.

**Water Chestnuts** are the bulbs of an Asian water-plant and not related to the edible chestnut. They are sometimes available fresh from Chinese foodstores and easily obtained canned, whole or sliced.

**Wonton Wrappers** are readily available from Chinese foodstores. They are paper-thin squares of dough.

**Wood Ears** are a dried black fungus, sold in plastic bags in Chinese supermarkets. Soak them in a bowl of warm water for 20 minutes, drain and rinse in cold water before use.

# Equipment

*Traditional Chinese equipment, especially if you buy it from Chinese stores, is usually inexpensive. 'New improved' western versions may prove to be more expensive and less satisfactory.*

**Chinese Cleaver** is a very finely balanced tool with an extremely sharp blade. Good, strong, sharp kitchen knives are adequate, but it is worth learning how to use a cleaver. Heavy cleavers can be used for chopping through bones, such as spare ribs, while lighter ones are perfect for thinly slicing vegetables. The point can be used for precision work, such as deveining prawns.

**Chopsticks** are not difficult to use. Place one chopstick in the hollow between the thumb and index finger of your right hand if right-handed or left hand if left-handed. Keeping that chopstick completely still, hold the other between the tips of the index and middle finger, steady its upper half against the base of the index finger and use the tip of the thumb to keep it in place. To pick up food, move the upper chopstick with index and middle fingers. When eating rice and other difficult-to-hold foods, it is better to lift the bowl to the chin and 'shovel' the food into the mouth with the chopsticks, as the Chinese do. It is worth learning to use chopsticks as, after all, Chinese food is designed to be eaten this way.

A pair of long chopsticks is a wonderful, multi-purpose cooking tool. Chopsticks can be used for stirring, whipping and beating, lifting food in and out of a wok, fluffing up rice and separating noodles. They are available from most cookware shops, Chinese foodstores and restaurants.

**Steamers** may be as simple as a plate placed on a rack over boiling water in a covered saucepan. A wok with a well-fitting lid is ideal. Traditional Chinese steamers are made of bamboo, a material which allows excess steam to escape. They are designed to stand one on top of the other, so that several dishes can be steamed simultaneously. They come in a wide range of sizes and are available in Chinese supermarkets and good cookware shops.

**Strainer** made of metal with a long bamboo handle makes lifting foods from hot oil easier. A long-handled slotted spoon will do as well.

**Wok** is a round-based utensil, traditionally made of cast-iron. Its design means that it conducts heat more evenly than other types of cooking utensils, such as a frying pan. Because of its shape, the ingredients always return to the centre, where the heat is most intense, however vigorously you stir. The wok is also ideal for deep-frying – its conical shape requires far less oil than a flat-based deep-fryer. It has more depth, which means more heat, and more cooking surface, which, in turn, means a larger quantity of food can be cooked at the same time. Besides being ideal for stir-frying and deep-frying, the wok is also used for braising, steaming, boiling and poaching – in other words, the whole spectrum of Chinese cooking methods can be executed in a single utensil. For safety, however, you should always use a wok stand when deep-frying, steaming or braising.

All new woks, other than non-stick ones, must be seasoned before use. Wash thoroughly in hot water and detergent to remove the manufacturer's protective coating of oil. Dry the wok well and set it over a low heat. When the metal heats up, wipe the inside with a pad of kitchen paper that has been dipped in oil. Be careful not to burn your fingers. Repeat this process with fresh oiled paper until it remains clean. The wok is now seasoned. After use, it should be wiped out and rinsed in hot water without detergent. A wok brush may help remove any stubborn food. Dry the wok thoroughly. If you do not use the wok frequently, coat it with a little vegetable oil to prevent rusting. If the wok does rust, scour the rust off and then repeat the seasoning process.

**Wok Brush** is a bundle of stiff, split bamboo used for cleaning the wok. An ordinary kitchen brush is just as good.

**Wok Lid** is a dome-shaped cover, usually made of aluminium. Lids are sometimes supplied with the wok, but can also be bought separately. It is important that it fits snugly.

**Wok Scoop and Spatula** are often supplied with a wok. If they are not, it is worth investing in them, especially a scoop. This is a flat, slotted implement for adding ingredients and seasonings to a wok and for tossing the food around during stir-frying.

**Wok Stand** provides a secure base for the wok during deep-frying, braising and steaming. It is made of metal and may be a simple, open-sided frame or a solid metal ring with holes punched around the sides.

**Wok Trivet** is used as a stand when steaming on a plate. Trivets may be made of wood or metal.

# Cooking Techniques

*Chinese food generally takes longer to prepare than it does to cook, so it is important to start the preparation of each dish as far in advance as possible. Ensure that all of the vegetables are chopped and the sauces are blended before you start cooking.*

## Chopping

Cut the ingredients into small, uniform pieces to ensure that the food cooks evenly. Shredding vegetables thinly and slicing them diagonally ensures fast cooking, as it increases the area in contact with the hot oil.

## Stir-frying

This is the method of cooking most commonly associated with Chinese cuisine. The correct piece of equipment for this is a wok, as it gives the best results. However, any large frying pan or heavy saucepan will do.

Stir-frying in a wok is very healthy way to cook, as it uses very little oil and preserves the nutrients in the food. It is very important that the wok is pre-heated to very hot before you begin to cook. This can be tested by holding your hand flat about 7.5 cm/3 inches above the base of the interior, when you should be able to feel the heat radiating from it. The success in stir-frying lies in having the wok at just the right temperature and in ensuring correct timing when cooking the food.

Before you begin cooking, make sure that all the required ingredients have been prepared, so that they are ready to be added to the wok the instant the oil is the right heat. Cooking at too low a temperature or for too long will produce inferior results.

Add a small amount of oil to the hot wok and heat it, then add, in stages, the various ingredients to be cooked. Those requiring longer cooking go in first, while those that require only very little cooking go in last.

Using a wok scoop or long-handled metal or wooden spoon, constantly stir the ingredients for a very short time. This ensures that all the ingredients come into contact with the hot oil, so the natural juices of the food are sealed in, leaving it crisp and colourful. The technique also ensures that all the ingredients are evenly cooked. Stir-fry dishes look and taste best when served immediately.

## Deep-frying

Use a wok, deep-fryer or heavy-based saucepan. When deep-frying in a wok, use enough oil to give a depth of about 5 cm/2 inches. Heat it over a moderate heat until you can see a faint haze of smoke rising before gently lowering in the food to be fried. Make sure the oil is up to temperature before adding the food, so that the hot oil cooks the food quickly on the outside, forming a protective seal. If the oil is not hot enough, the food will act like a sponge and become soggy and greasy. Before frying the food, make sure that is thoroughly dry to prevent the oil from splattering. If the food has been marinated, let it drain well. If it is in batter, wait for it to stop dripping.

Cook the food in small batches to avoid overcrowding the wok, as this can reduce the temperature of the oil and lead to unevenly cooked food. Always remove the food from the oil with a long-handled bamboo strainer or slotted spoon and drain thoroughly on kitchen paper to absorb any excess oil. Once it has been strained, cooking oil can be used up to three times, but only for the same type of food. Always use a wok stand to ensure that the wok is steady when deep-frying.

## Steaming

This is a very popular method of cooking. There are two basic methods. In the first, food is arranged on a plate or in a bowl, which is then put inside a steamer on a perforated rack and placed over a large pan of boiling water. The plate or bowl can also be put inside a wok. The steam passes through the steamer and cooks the food. Larger items of food, such as dumplings, can be placed straight on to the rack or laid on cabbage leaves or soaked lotus leaves. The leaves not only prevent the food from falling through, but also add extra flavour.

In the second method, the bowl of ingredients is partially immersed in boiling water. The food is cooked partly by the boiling water and partly by the steam it produces.

## Braising

This is a similar technique to that used in the West and is generally used for cooking tougher cuts of meat and firm varieties of vegetables. The ingredients are stir-fried until lightly browned, then stock is added and brought to the boil. The heat is reduced to simmering until cooking is complete. Red braising uses the same method, but the food is braised in a reddish-brown liquid, such as soy sauce. This sauce can be re-used.

## Roasting

This method is used much less in China than it is in the West because most domestic kitchens do not have an oven. It is popular in restaurant kitchens, particularly in Canton and Peking. It usually involves hanging the meat or poultry on a hook in the oven or cooking it on a rotisserie.

# Basic Recipes

*Common to many recipes are standard preparations, such as stock, plain boiled rice and cornflour paste. Dipping sauces are also served with many dishes.*

## Chinese Stock

This basic stock is used not only for soup-making, but also for general use in Chinese cooking. It will keep for 4–5 days in the refrigerator. Alternatively, it can be frozen in small containers and thawed as required. These quantities make 2.5 litres/4½ pints.

| |
|---|
| 750 g/1 lb 10 oz chicken pieces |
| 750 g/1 lb 10 oz pork spare ribs |
| 3.75 litres/6 pints cold water |
| 3–4 pieces fresh ginger root, crushed |
| 3–4 spring onions, each tied into a knot |
| 3–4 tbsp Chinese rice wine or dry sherry |

Trim off any excess fat from the chicken and spare ribs, then chop them into large pieces. Put the chicken and ribs into a large pan with the water, ginger and spring onion knots, bring to the boil and skim off the scum. Reduce the heat and simmer, uncovered, for at least 2–3 hours. Strain the stock, discarding the chicken, pork, ginger and spring onions. Pour the liquid back into the pan and add the Chinese rice wine or sherry. Bring to the boil, then simmer for 2–3 minutes. Leave to cool, then store in the refrigerator.

## Plain Rice

Use long-grain or patna rice or, better still, try Thai fragrant rice. If using Thai fragrant rice, do not add salt during cooking. This amount serves 4.

| |
|---|
| 225 g/8 oz long-grain rice |
| about 200 ml/7 fl oz cold water |
| pinch of salt |
| ½ tsp oil (optional) |

Rinse the rice once. Place the rice in a saucepan and add just enough water so that there is no more than 1 cm/½ inch above the surface of the rice. Bring to the boil, add salt and oil, if using, and stir once to prevent the grains sticking to the base of the pan. Reduce the heat to very, very low, cover and cook for 15–20 minutes. Remove from the heat and let stand, covered, for about 10 minutes. Fluff up the rice with chopsticks or a fork before serving.

## Cornflour Paste

This is made by mixing 1 part cornflour with about 1½ parts cold water. Stir until smooth and use to thicken sauces.

# Dipping Sauces

Traditional sauces for Chinese food
include the following.

## Sweet & Sour Sauce

A tasty sweet-and-sour sauce which goes well with
many deep-fried foods. Store in a well-sealed
container in the refrigerator.

| |
|---|
| 2 tbsp ginger marmalade |
| 2 tbsp orange marmalade |
| 1/4 tsp salt |
| 1 tbsp white rice vinegar or cider vinegar |
| 1 tbsp hot water |

Combine all the ingredients in a small bowl, mixing
well.

## Salt & Pepper Sauce

This dry-fried salt and pepper mixture made with
Szechuan peppercorns is found throughout China as a
dip for deep-fried foods. The dry-frying method brings
out all the flavour of the peppercorns.

| |
|---|
| 4 tbsp Szechuan peppercorns |
| 1/3 cup coarse sea salt |

Preheat a wok or heavy-based frying pan (skillet) over
a medium heat. Add the peppercorns and salt and stir-
fry until the mixture begins to brown. Remove the
wok or pan from the heat and cool. Grind the mixture
in a grinder or in a mortar with a pestle.

## Spring Onion Sauce

Heated oil poured over the seasonings brings out their
full flavour. The sauce goes well with meat and
poultry dishes.

| |
|---|
| 3 tbsp finely chopped spring onions |
| 3 tbsp finely grated fresh ginger root |
| 2 tsp salt |
| 1 tsp light soy sauce |
| 3 tbsp peanut or sunflower oil |

Place the spring onions, ginger root, salt and soy sauce
in a small, heatproof bowl. Put the oil into a small pan
and cook over a moderate heat until it begins to
smoke. Remove the pan from the heat and pour the
oil over the seasonings. Let stand for at least 2–3
hours before using to allow the flavours to blend.

# Garnishes

Chinese food should always please the eye as well as
the palate. Dishes are often intricately garnished with
delicately cut vegetables, adding colour as well as a
finishing touch. It is traditional to garnish each dish
differently. Garnishes may be as simple or elaborate
as you wish. The simplest would just be sprigs of
fresh herbs, such as coriander, chervil or chives,
shreds of spring onion, chilli, lemon zest or radish, or
twists of lime or lemon. Some elaborate garnishes are
described below.

**Cucumber Fans** can be made by cutting a piece of
cucumber about 7.5 cm/3 inches long and dividing it
in half lengthways. Lay a piece of cucumber, cut side
down, and using a small, sharp knife, cut thin slices
along the length to within 1 cm/½ inch of the end.
Carefully turn alternate slices over, in half and tuck in.
Place in iced water until required.

**Carrot Flowers** are made from a peeled carrot.
Using a sharp knife, make about five or six tiny V-
shaped cuts along the length. then cut into slices: the
V-shapes will ensure that each slice looks like a flower.

**Fresh Chilli Flowers** are made from unpeeled,
trimmed chillies. Make four cuts lengthways from the
stem of the chilli to the tip to make four sections.
Remove and discard the seeds. Soak the chillies in cold
water; they will 'flower' in the water.

**Prawn Crackers** are compressed slivers of prawn
and flour paste, which expand into large, translucent
crisps when deep-fried.

**Radish Flowers** are made from trimmed radishes.
Using a sharp knife, make V-shaped cuts around the
top and remove the cut parts to expose the white of
the radish.

**Radish Roses** require trimmed radishes. Then,
holding the knife flat to the radish skin, make short,
vertical cuts around the sides, as if you were shaving
off the outer skin, but without detaching each 'petal'.
Plunge straight into iced water.

**Tomato Roses** are made by peeling off the skin of
the tomato in one long strip, using a sharp knife. Curl
the skin into a circle.

# Chinese Tea

*Tea grows in almost every part of China, but was not used as a beverage until the sixth century and was not commonly drunk for a further 200 years. It is undoubtedly the most popular beverage in the country today and, together with fuel, oil, rice, soy sauce and vinegar, is regarded as one of the seven essentials for any household.*

Tea is served throughout the day in China and is always offered to visitors. Not to offer tea is a mark of extreme discourtesy. In times when people were too poverty-stricken to afford tea, they would offer boiled water, calling it white tea, rather than be inhospitable to a visitor. However, tea is never drunk with food, except in a few places in the south. Even in tea houses, where people go for snacks and dim sum, tea is drunk before and after eating, but not with the food. This is because most food contains oil and this detracts from the flavour of the tea, spoiling its taste. Tea may be served before a meal and is a popular choice afterwards, as it is so refreshing.

There are hundreds of varieties of Chinese tea, the best coming from the south, where the climate is well suited to its cultivation. However, tea can be divided into two main categories: green, unfermented tea and black, fermented tea. To make green tea, the leaves are withered in the sun, during which about 60 per cent of the water content is lost. The leaves are then heat-treated to prevent fermentation, before being dried. This results in a very delicate-tasting, pale-coloured brew and is the most popular kind of tea in China. For black tea, the leaves are also withered after picking. They are then broken up to release enzymes and during the oxidation process, they turn brown. They are then dried, which turns them black.

The best green tea is said to be lung ching from Hanchow in the East of the country. Perhaps gunpowder tea is the best-known green tea in the West. It is so called because the leaves are tightly rolled into small balls and expand almost explosively when hot water is added. The best black tea is said to come from a mountainous region on the borders of Fukien. It is known as 'cliff' tea because of the precipitous heights at which it grows. One of the best-known varieties of this tea is called Ti Kuan Yin – Iron Goddess of Mercy. Chinese black teas are more popular than green ones in the West and varieties, such as Pouchong, also known as Congou and Keemum, are widely available.

Much of the tea exported by China is blended and known by a blend name rather than the name of the plantation. Most of it is large-leaf, requiring a longer brewing time than small- or broken-leaf teas. There are other types of Chinese tea available in the West, the best-known probably being jasmine tea. This may be either black or green leaves mixed with dried white jasmine flowers. It is very fragrant and slightly sweet. Chrysanthemum tea is similar, in that black or green tea leaves are mixed with dried white or yellow flower heads. However it is not so powerfully fragrant as jasmine tea. Smoked teas are fermented black teas that have been smoke-dried to produce a characteristic tarry flavour. Probably the best known is lapsang souchong. Finally, brick tea is something of a novelty, nowadays brought back from China by tourists as a souvenir. Before modern transportation, black teas were steamed and compressed into bricks to make transporting them easier. The required amount could then be broken off or grated. The tea usually incorporated a mixture of coarse leaves, stems and tea dust and was not of very high quality. The bricks are still produced and embossed with attractive symbols and designs.

Tea-making is regarded as an art in China. The choice of utensils and water is as important as the variety of leaves. Kettles are earthenware and teapots and cups are porcelain or earthenware. Tea-making utensils should always be washed separately to avoid contamination from greasy dishes. Spring water, melted snow, river water and rainwater – all pollution-free – are highly prized. Water must be freshly boiled, as re-boiled water loses its oxygen content and spoils the flavour of the tea. The teapot must be rinsed with boiling water to warm it thoroughly before the tea is added. Once made, the tea should be allowed to infuse for 3 minutes before being poured. It is always drunk very hot without milk or sugar.

# Alcoholic Drinks

Wine is an essential part of a formal meal. In fact, wine is never drunk on its own, but always as an accompaniment to food. Hardly surprisingly, rice wine is the most popular alcoholic drink in China. It is golden in colour and so is also known as yellow wine. The best is said to come from Shaoxing, its quality being attributed to the waters of the nearby lake and to a special type of yeast. The fact that it may be matured for as long as forty years probably also contributes to its fine flavour. Generally, however, it goes on sale when it has been matured for ten years. It is made from a mixture of rice, glutinous rice and millet. Another high-quality, slightly sweet rice wine, Chen Gang, comes from Fukien. Home-made glutinous rice wines are also popular.

Another popular drink is not really a wine at all. Made from sorghum, a kind of millet, Mao Tai is actually stronger than pure vodka. In the eighteenth century a salt merchant from north China was so mesmerized by the beauty of the village of Mao Tai and the surrounding countryside in South-West China that he decided to settle there. He started to make 'wine', using water from the river flowing through a nearby gorge. It rapidly became very popular throughout the whole of China and, following its introduction to the West at an international exposition in 1919, it achieved worldwide fame.

A number of other, highly potent spirits are produced in various regions of China. Some are considered to have medicinal properties and others are served as after-dinner liqueurs. Many Chinese people regard it as perfectly normal to drink spirits such as these throughout a meal, but this has little appeal to Western palates. In general, rice wine is served in regions south of the Yangtze river, where rice grows abundantly and the climate is warmer, while more powerful spirits are served in the north, where sorghum and millet grow and the climate is colder.

It may be something of a surprise to learn that the art of making wine with grapes has been known in China since the seventh century. However, it is only comparatively recently that the production of table wines has become of any importance. Cabernet and Muscat wines are produced in Shantung and both red and white wines are made in Manchuria. While drinkable, they are not yet of major interest, not even to the people of China.

If you are not going to serve rice wine throughout the meal, as the Chinese people do themselves, a minimum of one red and one white wine is essential for a formal occasion. Choose a light white wine to accompany appetizers and stir-fries and a full-bodied red wine for more robust dishes. If you are going to serve only one type of wine, a full-bodied red, such as Burgundy, is the better choice. If the occasion is a special one, you can extend the wine list to include sherry or even Champagne to begin with. Brandy, liqueurs or even whisky may be served at the end of the meal, if you are not making tea.

The Chinese never drink wine or other alcoholic drinks with the rice dish that is served at the end of a formal meal. This is because it is thought to be inappropriate, even sacrilegious to eat this valuable grain while drinking a beverage made from grain.

Drinking in China is a social activity and a solitary drinker is a very rare sight. The Chinese do not follow the western custom of individuals sipping their wine throughout the meal as desired, but drink with formal toasts. Given that a formal meal usually involves at least ten people and everyone needs to toast everyone else and return the toasts, copious quantities of wine may be consumed.

The toasting ritual begins with the host toasting the guest of honour and then both the host and guest drain their wine cups, turning them upside down afterwards. Everyone else also toast the host and guest. This process continues throughout the meal.

# Appetizers

A formal Chinese meal is likely to start with a selection of at least three different appetizers. These may range from robust and spicy to delicate and fragrant. As with all Chinese cuisine, harmony and balance are central, so the colour, aroma, texture and flavour of the dishes should complement and contrast. To be authentic, do not serve more than one dish of the same type.

The recipes in this chapter include many dishes that are popular in the West, such as Crispy Seaweed, Spring Rolls, Sesame Prawn Toasts and Barbecue Pork Ribs. Some may, perhaps, be less familiar. Try Rice Paper Parcels, Pork with Chilli and Garlic Sauce or Pot Sticker Dumplings, for example. They are so delicious that they will soon become family favourites, too.

# Crispy Wontons with Piquant Dipping Sauce

Mushroom-filled crispy wontons are served on skewers
with a chilli-flavoured dipping sauce.

| Serves 4 |
| --- |
| 1 tbsp vegetable oil |
| 1 tbsp chopped onion |
| 1 small garlic clove, chopped |
| $\frac{1}{2}$ tsp chopped fresh ginger root |
| 50 g/1$\frac{3}{4}$ oz chopped flat mushrooms |
| 16 wonton skins |
| vegetable oil, for deep-frying |
| salt |

| SAUCE |
| --- |
| 2 tbsp vegetable oil |
| 2 spring onions, thinly shredded |
| 1 red and 1 green chilli, seeded and thinly shredded |
| 3 tbsp light soy sauce |
| 1 tbsp vinegar |
| 1 tbsp dry sherry |
| pinch of sugar |

crisp. Remove with a slotted spoon
and drain on kitchen paper.

**4** To make the sauce, heat the oil in a
small saucepan until a small cube of
bread browns in a few seconds. Put
the spring onions and chillies in a
bowl and pour the hot oil slowly on
top. Then mix in the remaining
ingredients and serve with the crispy
wontons.

**1** Heat the oil in a preheated wok or
frying pan. Add the onion, garlic and
ginger root, and stir-fry for 2 minutes.
Stir in the mushrooms and fry for a
further 2 minutes. Season well with
salt and let cool.

**2** Place 1 teaspoon of the cooled
mushroom filling in the centre of
each wonton skin. Bring two opposite
corners together to cover the mixture
and pinch together to seal. Repeat
with the remaining corners.

**3** Thread the wontons on to
8 wooden skewers. Heat enough oil in
a large saucepan to deep-fry the
wontons in batches until golden and

# Crispy Seaweed

Popular in many Chinese restaurants, this dish is
served as a starter. This 'seaweed' is in fact
deep-fried spring greens.

| Serves 4 |
| --- |
| 225 g/8 oz spring greens |
| vegetable oil, for deep-frying |
| 1½ tsp caster sugar |
| 1 tsp salt |
| 25 g/1 oz flaked almonds |

**1** Wash the spring greens thoroughly. Trim off the excess tough stalks. Place on kitchen paper or a dry tea towel and let drain thoroughly.

**2** Using a sharp knife, shred the spring greens very finely then spread out the shreds on kitchen paper for about 30 minutes to dry.

**3** Heat the oil in a wok or deep-fat fryer. Remove the pan from the heat and add the spring greens in batches. Return the pan to the heat and deep-fry until the greens begin to float to the surface and become translucent and crinkled. Remove with a slotted spoon, and drain on kitchen paper. Keep each batch warm while you are deep-frying the next.

**4** Mix the sugar and salt together, sprinkle the mixture over the 'seaweed' and toss together thoroughly to mix well.

**5** Add the flaked almonds to the hot oil and fry until golden. Remove the almonds with a slotted spoon and drain on kitchen paper. Scatter on the crispy 'seaweed' and serve.

### COOK'S TIP

The greens must completely dry or they
will not crispen when fried.

# Spinach Meatballs

These are somewhat of a surprise. Balls of pork mixture
are coated in spinach and steamed to be served
with a sesame and soy sauce dip.

| Serves 4 |
| --- |
| 125 g/4¹/₂ oz pork |
| 1 small egg |
| 1-cm/¹/₂-inch piece fresh ginger root, chopped |
| 1 small onion, finely chopped |
| 1 tbsp boiling water |
| 25 g/1 oz canned bamboo shoots, drained and chopped |
| 2 slices smoked ham, chopped |
| 2 tsp cornflour |
| 450 g/1 lb fresh spinach |
| 2 tsp sesame seeds |
| SAUCE |
| 150 ml/¹/₄ pint vegetable stock |
| ¹/₂ tsp cornflour |
| 1 tsp cold water |
| 1 tsp light soy sauce |
| ¹/₂ tsp sesame oil |
| 1 tbsp chopped chives |

**1** Mince the pork very finely in a food processor or meat mincer. Beat the egg in a bowl and stir into the pork.

**2** Put the ginger, onion and bamboo shoots in a separate bowl, add the boiling water and let stand for 5 minutes. Drain and add to the pork, together with the ham and cornflour. Mix well and roll into 12 balls with your hands.

**3** Wash the spinach and remove the stalks. Blanch in boiling water for 10 seconds, drain, rinse in cold water and drain again. Slice the spinach into thin strips, then mix with the sesame seeds. Spread out the mixture in a shallow baking tin and roll the meatballs in it to coat on all sides.

**4** Place the meatballs on a heatproof plate in the base of a steamer, cover and steam for about 8–10 minutes, until cooked through.

**5** Meanwhile, heat the sauce ingredients in a saucepan. Transfer the cooked meatballs to a warm plate and serve with the sauce.

# Spring Rolls

Thin slices of vegetables are wrapped in pastry and deep-fried until crisp. Spring roll wrappers are available from Chinese foodstores and some supermarkets.

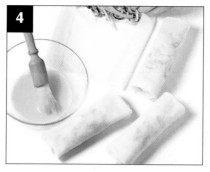

| Makes 12 |
| --- |
| 5 Chinese dried mushrooms (or open-cup mushrooms) |
| 1 large carrot |
| 50 g/1¾ oz canned bamboo shoots, drained |
| 2 spring onions |
| 50 g/1¾ oz Chinese leaves |
| 2 tbsp vegetable oil |
| 225 g/8 oz beansprouts |
| 1 tbsp soy sauce |
| 12 spring roll wrappers |
| 1 egg, beaten |
| vegetable oil for deep-frying |
| salt |

**1** Place the dried mushrooms in a small bowl and cover with warm water. Soak for 20–25 minutes. Drain the mushrooms and squeeze out the excess water. Remove the tough centres and slice the mushrooms fairly thinly.

**2** Cut the carrot and bamboo shoots into very thin julienne strips. Chop the spring onions and shred the Chinese leaves.

**3** Heat the oil in a preheated wok or frying pan. Add the mushrooms, carrot and bamboo shoots, and stir-fry for 2 minutes. Add the spring onions, Chinese leaves, beansprouts and soy sauce. Season with salt and stir-fry for 2 minutes. Set aside to cool.

**4** Divide the mixture into 12 equal portions and place one portion on the edge of each spring roll wrapper. Fold

in the sides and roll each one up, brushing the join with a little beaten egg to seal.

**5** Heat the oil for deep-frying in a wok or large saucepan. Add the spring rolls, in batches, and deep-fry for 4–5 minutes, or until golden and crispy.

Take care that the oil is not too hot or the spring rolls will brown on the outside before cooking on the inside. Remove and drain on kitchen paper. Keep each batch of spring rolls warm while the others are being cooked. Serve at once.

# Pork Pancake Rolls

This is another classic Dim Sum dish which is adaptable to almost any filling of your choice. Here the traditional mixture of pork and cabbage is used.

| Serves 4 |
| --- |
| 4 tsp vegetable oil |
| 1–2 garlic cloves, crushed |
| 225 g/8 oz minced pork |
| 225/8 oz Chinese cabbage, thinly shredded |
| 4$^{1}/_{2}$ tsp light soy sauce |
| $^{1}/_{2}$ tsp sesame oil |
| 8 spring roll skins, 25 cm/10 inches square, thawed if frozen |
| oil, for deep-frying |
| chilli sauce, to serve |

**COOK'S VARIATION**

You could substitute minced chicken or prawns for the pork.

**COOK'S TIP**

Allow the pancake rolls to stand for a little while after rolling to allow them to seal firmly.

**1** Heat the vegetable oil in a preheated wok and fry the garlic for 30 seconds. Add the pork and stir-fry for 2–3 minutes, until sealed.

**2** Add the cabbage, soy sauce and sesame oil and stir-fry for 2–3 minutes. Set aside to cool.

**3** Spread out the spring roll skins on a work surface and spoon 2 tbsp of the pork mixture along one edge of each. Roll the skin over once and fold in the sides. Roll again to make a sausage shape, brushing the edges with a little water to seal.

**4** Heat the oil for deep-frying in a wok until it is almost smoking. Reduce the heat slightly and fry the pancake rolls for 3–4 minutes, until golden brown. Remove from the oil with a slotted spoon and drain. Transfer to a warm serving plate and serve with chilli sauce.

# Lettuce-Wrapped Minced Meat

Serve the minced meat and lettuce leaves
on separate dishes: the guests then
wrap their own parcels.

| Serves 4 |
| --- |
| 225 g/8 oz minced pork or chicken |
| 1 tbsp finely chopped Chinese mushrooms |
| 1 tbsp finely chopped water chestnuts |
| pinch of sugar |
| 1 tsp light soy sauce |
| 1 tsp Chinese rice wine or dry sherry |
| 1 tsp cornflour |
| 2–3 tbsp vegetable oil |
| 1/2 tsp finely chopped ginger root |
| 1 tsp finely chopped spring onions |
| 1 tbsp finely chopped Szechuan preserved vegetables (optional) |
| 1 tbsp oyster sauce |
| a few drops of sesame oil |
| salt and pepper |
| 8 crisp lettuce leaves, to serve |

**1** Mix the minced meat with the mushrooms, water chestnuts, sugar, soy sauce, wine, cornflour, and salt and pepper.

**2** Heat the oil in a preheated wok or frying pan and add the ginger and spring onions followed by the meat. Stir-fry for 1 minute.

**3** Add the Szechuan preserved vegetables and continue stirring for 1 more minute. Add the oyster sauce and sesame oil, blend well and cook for 1 more minute. Transfer to a warm serving dish.

**4** To serve, place about 2–3 tablespoons of the mixture on a lettuce leaf, tuck in the sides and roll it up tightly to form a small parcel. Eat with your fingers.

### COOK'S VARIATION

You can use Chinese leaves instead of lettuce for the wrappers.

# Steamed Cabbage Rolls

These small cabbage parcels are quick and easy to prepare and cook and are ideal for a speedy starter.

| Serves 4 |
|---|
| 8 cabbage leaves, trimmed |
| 225 g/8 oz minced chicken |
| 175 g/6 oz minced prawns |
| 1 tsp cornflour |
| 1/2 tsp chilli powder |
| 1 egg, lightly beaten |
| 1 tbsp vegetable oil |
| 1 leek, sliced |
| 1 garlic clove, thinly sliced |
| sliced fresh red chilli, to garnish |

**1** Bring a large pan of water to the boil. Blanch the cabbage leaves for 2 minutes. Drain, rinse under cold water and drain again. Spread the leaves out on work surface.

**2** Mix the chicken, prawns, cornflour, chilli powder and egg together in a bowl. Place 2 tbsp of the mixture towards one end of each cabbage leaf.

**3** Fold the sides of the cabbage around the filling and roll up to form a firm parcel.

**4** Place the parcels, seam side down, on a heatproof plate and cook in a steamer for 10 minutes, or until cooked through.

**5** Meanwhile, heat the oil in a preheated wok and sauté the leek and garlic for 1–2 minutes.

**6** Transfer the cabbage parcels to warm serving plates. Serve them with the leek and garlic sauté and garnish with fresh red chilli slices.

**COOK'S TIP**

Use Chinese cabbage or Savoy for this recipe, choosing leaves of a similar size for the parcels.

1

2

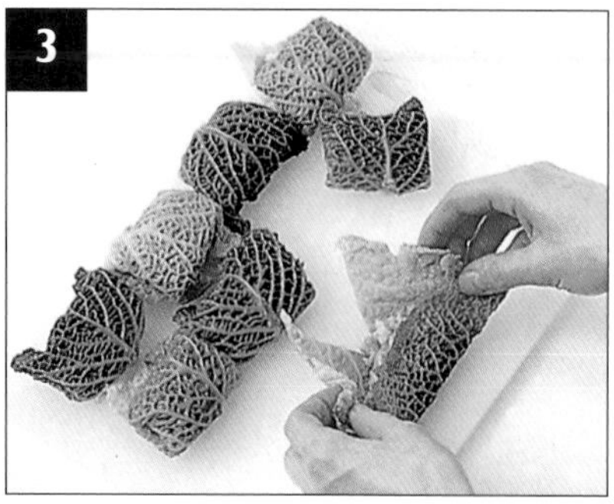
3

# Rice Paper Parcels

These special rice paper wrappers are available in Chinese supermarkets and health-food shops. Do not use the rice paper sold for making cakes.

| Serves 4 |
| --- |
| 1 egg white, lightly beaten |
| 2 tsp cornflour |
| 2 tsp Chinese rice wine or dry sherry |
| 1 tsp caster sugar |
| 2 tsp hoi-sin sauce |
| 225 g/8 oz peeled, cooked prawns |
| 4 spring onions, thinly sliced |
| 25 g/1 oz water chestnuts, chopped |
| 8 Chinese rice paper wrappers |
| vegetable oil, for deep-frying |
| hoi-sin sauce, for serving |

### COOK'S VARIATION

For a spicier flavour, serve the parcels with a hot chilli sauce instead of hoi-sin sauce.

### COOK'S TIP

Use this filling inside steamed dumplings (see page 34) if the rice papers are unavailable.

1 Mix together the egg white, cornflour, Chinese rice wine or sherry, sugar and hoisin sauce. Add the prawns, spring onions and water chestnuts, mixing well.

2 Soften the rice papers by dipping in water. Spoon a little of the prawn mixture into the centre of each paper and wrap the paper around the filling to make a secure parcel.

3 Heat the oil in a wok until almost smoking. Reduce the heat slightly and deep-fry the parcels for 4–5 minutes, until crisp. Remove from the oil with a slotted spoon and drain on absorbent kitchen paper. Transfer to a warm serving dish, spoon a little hoisin sauce on top and serve immediately.

# Deep-Fried Prawns

Use raw tiger prawns in their shells.
They are 7–10 cm (3–4 inches) long, and you should
get 18–20 prawns per 450 g (1 lb).

| Serves 4 |
| --- |
| 250–300 g/9–10¹/₂ oz raw prawns in their shells, thawed if frozen |
| 1 tbsp light soy sauce |
| 1 tsp Chinese rice wine or dry sherry |
| 2 tsp cornflour |
| vegetable oil, for deep-frying |
| 2–3 spring onions, to garnish |

### SPICY SALT & PEPPER

| |
| --- |
| 1 tbsp salt |
| 1 tsp ground Szechuan peppercorns |
| 1 tsp Chinese five-spice powder |

**1** Pull the legs off the prawns, but leave the shells intact. Dry on kitchen paper.

**2** Place the prawns in a bowl with the soy sauce, wine and cornflour. Turn to coat thoroughly and marinate for about 25–30 minutes.

**3** To make the spicy salt and pepper, mix the salt, pepper and five-spice powder together. Place in a frying pan and dry-fry, stirring constantly, for about 3–4 minutes over a low heat. Remove from the heat and set aside to cool.

**4** Heat the oil in a preheated wok until smoking. Deep-fry the prawns in batches until golden brown. Remove with a slotted spoon and drain on kitchen paper.

**5** Place the spring onions in a bowl, pour on 1 tablespoon of the hot oil and leave for 30 seconds. Transfer the prawns to a serving dish, garnish with the spring onions, and serve immediately with the spicy salt and pepper as a condiment.

# Sesame Prawn Toasts

These small toasts are easy to prepare and are one of the most
popular Chinese appetizers in the West. Make sure you
serve plenty of them as they are very tasty.

| Serves 4 |
| --- |
| 225 g/8 oz cooked, peeled prawns |
| 1 spring onion |
| $^1/_4$ tsp salt |
| 1 tsp light soy sauce |
| 1 tbsp cornflour |
| 1 egg white, beaten |
| 3 thin slices white bread, crusts removed |
| 4 tbsp sesame seeds |
| vegetable oil, for deep-frying |

**COOK'S TIP**

This is even better if you can obtain
raw prawns, as the cooked ones
sometimes tend to become detached
from the toasts.

**COOK'S TIP**

Fry the triangles in two batches,
keeping them warm, to prevent them
from sticking together and overcooking.

**1** Put the prawns and spring onion in
a food processor and process until
finely minced or chop very finely by
hand. Stir in the salt, soy sauce,
cornflour and egg white.

**2** Spread the prawn mixture on to
one side of each slice of bread.

**3** Spread the sesame seeds on top of
the prawn mixture on each slice of
bread, pressing firmly.

**4** Cut each slice into four equal
triangles or strips.

**5** Heat the oil for deep-frying in a
wok until almost smoking. Carefully
place the triangles in the oil, coated
side down, and cook for 2–3 minutes,
until golden brown. Remove with a
slotted spoon and drain on kitchen
paper. Serve hot.

# Deep-Fried Spare Ribs

The spare ribs should be chopped
into small bite-size pieces
before or after cooking.

| Serves 4 |
| --- |
| 8–10 finger spare ribs |
| 1 tsp Chinese five-spice powder or |
| 1 tbsp mild curry powder |
| 1 tbsp Chinese rice wine or |
| dry sherry |
| 1 egg |
| 2 tbsp flour |
| vegetable oil for deep-frying |
| 1 tsp finely shredded |
| spring onions |
| 1 tsp finely shredded fresh green or |
| red hot chillies, seeded |
| salt and pepper |
| Spicy Salt and Pepper |
| (see page 30), to serve |

**5** Pour 1 tablespoon of the hot oil
over the spring onions and chillies
and leave for 30–40 seconds. Transfer
the ribs to a serving dish and garnish
with the spring onions and chillies.
Serve with the spicy salt and pepper.

**COOK'S TIP**

You could add 1 tablespoon brown
sugar and 1 teaspoon chilli sauce to
the marinade in step 1 for a richer and
spicier flavour.

**1** Chop the ribs into 3–4 small pieces.
Place the ribs in a bowl with the
Chinese five-spice or curry powder,
rice wine or sherry, and salt and
pepper. Turn to coat them thoroughly
and marinate for 1–2 hours.

**2** Beat the egg and flour together in a
bowl to make a smooth batter. Dip the
marinated ribs in the batter, one by
one, to coat well.

**3** Heat the oil in a preheated wok
until smoking. Add the ribs and deep-
fry for 4–5 minutes, then remove
with a slotted spoon and drain on
kitchen paper.

**4** Reheat the oil over a high heat, add
the ribs and deep-fry once more for
another minute. Remove with a
slotted spoon and drain again on
kitchen paper.

# Pork with Chilli & Garlic Sauce

Any leftovers from this dish can be used for
a number of other dishes, but it may
be so popular that nothing is left.

| Serves 4 |
| --- |
| 450 g/1 lb boneless leg of pork, not skinned |
| fresh parsley, to garnish |
| **SAUCE** |
| 1 tsp finely chopped garlic |
| 1 tsp finely chopped spring onions |
| 2 tbsp light soy sauce |
| 1 tsp red chilli oil |
| 1/2 tsp sesame oil |

**1** Tie the pork together in one piece with kitchen string and place it in a large saucepan. Add enough cold water to cover and bring to a rolling boil over a medium heat.

**2** Lower the heat, skim off the scum that rises to the surface, cover and simmer gently for 25–30 minutes.

**3** Remove the pan from the heat. Leave the meat in the liquid covered, for at least 1–2 hours. Lift out the meat with 2 slotted spoons and set aside, skin side up, for 2–3 hours or until completely cold.

**4** To serve, cut off and discard the skin, but leave a very thin layer of fat on top, rather like a ham joint. Cut the meat in small thin slices across the grain and arrange decoratively on a serving plate. Mix together the sauce ingredients and pour a little of the sauce evenly over the pork. Garnish with parsley and serve with the remaining sauce.

# Pork Dim Sum

These small steamed parcels are classically served
as an appetizer and are very adaptable
to your favourite fillings.

| Serves 4 |
| --- |
| 400 g/14 oz lean minced pork |
| 2 spring onions, chopped |
| 50 g/1³/₄ oz canned bamboo shoots, drained and chopped |
| 1 tbsp light soy sauce |
| 1 tbsp Chinese rice wine or dry sherry |
| 2 tsp sesame oil |
| 2 tsp caster sugar |
| 1 egg white, lightly beaten |
| 4¹/₂ tsp cornflour |
| 24 wonton wrappers |

**1** Mix together the minced pork, onions, bamboo shoots, soy sauce, Chinese rice wine or sherry, sesame oil, sugar and egg white in a bowl until well incorporated.

**2** Stir in the cornflour, mixing well.

**3** Place a portion of the mixture in the centre of each wonton wrapper and lightly brush the edges of the wrappers with water.

**4** Bring the wrappers together in the centre, pinching together to 'gather' at the top.

**5** Line a steamer with a clean damp tea towel and arrange the wontons in a single layer inside. Cover and steam for 5–7 minutes, until cooked through. Serve immediately in the steamer.

### COOK'S VARIATION

You can use almost any of your favourite fillings, such as prawns, minced chicken or crabmeat, instead of pork.

### COOK'S TIP

You can use additional flavourings, such as chilli and ginger. Dim sum is traditionally served with a small bowl of soy sauce for dipping.

# Barbecue Spare Ribs

This is a simplified version of the half saddle of pork ribs
seen hanging in the windows of Cantonese restaurants.
Use the specially small, thin ribs known as finger ribs.

| Serves 4 |
| --- |
| 450 g/1 lb finger spare ribs |
| 1 tbsp sugar |
| 1 tbsp light soy sauce |
| 1 tbsp dark soy sauce |
| 3 tbsp hoi-sin sauce |
| 1 tbsp Chinese rice wine or dry sherry |
| 4–5 tbsp water or Chinese Stock (see page 16) |
| fresh coriander leaves, to garnish |
| mild chilli sauce, to serve |

**1** Trim off any excess fat from the ribs and cut them into separate pieces. Place them in an ovenproof dish. Mix the sugar, light and dark soy sauces, hoi-sin sauce and Chinese rice wine or sherry together in a bowl and pour the mixture on to the ribs, turning to coat thoroughly. Marinate for about 2–3 hours.

**2** Add the water or stock to the ribs and spread them out in the dish. Roast in a preheated oven at 220°C/425°F/Gas 7, for 15 minutes.

**3** Turn the ribs over, lower the heat to 190°C/375°F/Gas 5 and cook for a further 30–35 minutes.

**4** To serve, chop each rib into 3–4 small, bite-size pieces with a large knife or Chinese cleaver and arrange on a serving dish. Pour the sauce from the baking dish over them and garnish with fresh coriander leaves. Serve immediately with mild chilli sauce for dipping.

# Barbecue Pork (Char Siu)

Also called honey-roasted pork, these are the strips of
reddish meat sometimes seen hanging in the
windows of Cantonese restaurants.

| Serves 4 |
| --- |
| 450 g/1 lb pork fillet |
| 150 ml/¼ pint |
| boiling water |
| 1 tbsp clear honey, dissolved in |
| a little hot water |
| shredded lettuce, to serve |

| MARINADE |
| --- |
| 1 tbsp sugar |
| 1 tbsp crushed yellow bean sauce |
| 1 tbsp light soy sauce |
| 1 tbsp hoi-sin sauce |
| 1 tbsp oyster sauce |
| ½ tsp chilli sauce |
| 1 tbsp brandy or rum |
| 1 tsp sesame oil |

**1** Cut the pork into strips about
2.5 cm/1 inch thick and 18–20 cm/
7–8 inches long and place in a large
shallow dish. Thoroughly combine
the marinade ingredients in a bowl
and pour the mixture over the pork,
turning it until well coated. Cover,
and marinate for at least 3–4 hours,
turning occasionally.

**2** Remove the pork strips from the
dish with a slotted spoon, reserving
the marinade. Arrange the pork strips
on a rack over a baking tin. Place the
tin in a preheated oven at
220°C/425°F/Gas 7, and pour in the
boiling water. Roast for about
10–15 minutes.

**3** Lower the oven temperature to
180°C/350°F/Gas 4. Baste the pork
strips with the reserved marinade and

turn them over. Roast for a further
10 minutes.

**4** Remove the pork from the oven,
brush with the honey syrup, and
then lightly brown under a preheated
grill for 3–4 minutes, turning once
or twice.

**5** To serve, allow the pork to cool
slightly before cutting it. Cut across
the grain into thin slices and arrange
on a bed of shredded lettuce. Make a
sauce by boiling the marinade and the
drippings in the roasting tin for a few
minutes, strain and pour over the
pork. Serve immediately.

# Pot Sticker Dumplings

These dumplings obtain their name from the fact that
they will stick to the pot when steamed if they
were not fried crisply enough initially.

| Serves 4 |
| --- |
| **DUMPLINGS** |
| 175 g/6 oz plain flour |
| pinch of salt |
| 3 tbsp vegetable oil |
| 6–8 tbsp boiling water |
| oil, for deep-frying |
| sliced spring onion and chives, to garnish |
| **FILLING** |
| 150 g/5$^{1}/_{2}$ oz lean chicken, very finely chopped |
| 25 g/1 oz canned bamboo shoots, drained and chopped |
| 2 spring onions, finely chopped |
| $^{1}/_{2}$ small red pepper, seeded and finely chopped |
| $^{1}/_{2}$ tsp Chinese curry powder |
| 1 tbsp light soy sauce |
| 1 tsp caster sugar |
| 1 tsp sesame oil |

**1** First make the dumplings. Mix together the flour and salt in a bowl. Make a well in the centre, add the oil and water and mix well to form a soft dough. Knead the dough on a lightly floured surface, wrap in clingfilm and let stand for 30 minutes.

**2** Meanwhile, mix the filling ingredients together in a bowl.

**3** Divide the dough into 12 equal pieces and roll each into a 12.5-cm/5-inch round.

**4** Spoon a portion of the filling on to one half of each round and fold the dough over the filling to form a semi-circle. Twist the edges firmly together to seal, pressing together well.

**5** Heat a little oil into a heavy-based frying pan and cook the dumplings, in batches, until browned and slightly crisp, adding more oil as necessary. Drain the dumplings thoroughly, set them aside and keep warm until they have all been cooked.

**6** Return the dumplings to the pan and add 125 ml/4 fl oz/$^{1}/_{2}$ cup water. Cover and steam for 5 minutes, or until the dumplings are cooked. Remove with a slotted spoon and serve immediately, garnished with spring onion and chives.

# Steamed Duck Buns

The dough used in this recipe may be wrapped around a
multitude of fillings, such as chicken, pork or prawns,
or sweet fillings as an alternative.

| Serves 4 |
| --- |
| **DOUGH** |
| 300 g/10½ oz plain flour |
| 15 g/½ oz dried yeast |
| 1 tsp caster sugar |
| 2 tbsp warm water |
| 175 ml/6 fl oz warm milk |
| **FILLING** |
| 300 g/10½ oz duck breasts |
| 1 tbsp light brown sugar |
| 1 tbsp light soy sauce |
| 2 tbsp clear honey |
| 1 tbsp hoi-sin sauce |
| 1 tbsp vegetable oil |
| 1 leek, finely chopped |
| 1 garlic clove, crushed |
| 1 tbsp grated fresh ginger root |

**1** Place the duck breast in a glass
bowl. Mix together the sugar, soy
sauce, honey and hoi-sin sauce. Pour
the mixture over the duck and
marinate for 20 minutes.

**2** Remove the duck from the
marinade and roast on a rack over
a roasting tin in a preheated oven at
200°C/400°F/Gas 6 for 35–40 minutes.
Cool, remove the meat from the
bones and dice.

**3** Heat the oil and stir-fry the leek,
garlic and ginger for 2–3 minutes,
until tender. Mix with the duck meat.

**4** To make the dough, sift the flour
into a mixing bowl. Mix together the
yeast, sugar and water and leave in a
warm place for about 15 minutes.

Pour the yeast mixture into the flour,
with the milk, mixing to form a firm
dough. Knead the dough for 5 minutes
and roll into a sausage shape 2.5 cm/
1 inch in diameter. Cut into 16 equal
pieces, cover and let stand for 20–25
minutes.

**5** Flatten each dough piece into a
10-cm/4-inch round. Place 1 tbsp of
filling in the centre of each round and
draw up the sides, twisting at the top.

**6** Place the dumplings on a damp tea
towel in a steamer, cover and steam
for 20 minutes. Serve hot.

# Chinese Omelette

This is a fairly filling omelette, as it contains chicken
and prawns. It is cooked as
a whole and sliced for serving

| Serves 4 |
| --- |
| 8 eggs |
| 225 g/8 oz shredded cooked chicken |
| 12 large cooked prawns, peeled and deveined |
| 2 tbsp chopped chives |
| 2 tsp light soy sauce |
| dash of chilli sauce |
| 2 tbsp vegetable oil |

**COOK'S VARIATION**

Substitute 150 g/5 oz cooked or
canned crabmeat for the prawns,
if wished.

**COOK'S TIP**

Add peas or other vegetables
to the omelette and serve as a main
course for 2 people.

**1** Lightly beat the eggs in a large
mixing bowl. Add the chicken and
prawns, mixing well.

**2** Stir in the chives, soy sauce and
chilli sauce, mixing well.

**3** Heat the oil in a large frying pan
over a medium heat and add the egg
mixture, tilting the pan to coat the
base. Gently stir the omelette with a
fork while it is cooking.

**4** When the omelette is set, slide it
out of the pan and cut into squares or
slices to serve.

**5** Transfer to a warm serving plate
and serve immediately.

# Salads & Pickles

Western-style salads rarely appear in China, but combinations of lightly cooked and raw dressed vegetables, served either warm or cold, are popular. The best and freshest vegetables are always used and ingredients are matched so that crunchy and melt-in-the-mouth textures and sweet and spicy flavours simultaneously delight the palate. Try Sweet & Sour Tofu Salad or Hot & Sour

Duck Salad, for example.

Dressings often feature citrus juice, particularly lime, as well as soy and fish sauces. Nuts

and seeds provide a garnish, as well as 'crunch factor', and honey adds a touch of sweetness and an attractive glaze.

Pickling fresh vegetables in the summer for eating in the winter is a long-standing tradition in China. They are used in soups and stir-fries, as a condiment and served as appetizers. Pickled vegetables are frequently spiced with chillies or a sweet-and-sour combination of vinegar and honey.

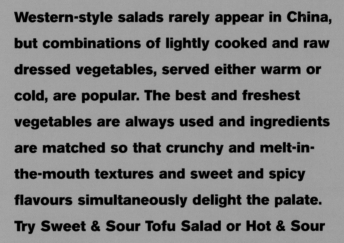

# Sweet & Sour Tofu Salad

Tofu mixed with crisp stir-fried vegetables, then
tossed in a piquant sweet-and-sour dressing
makes an ideal light meal or starter.

| Serves 4-6 |
| --- |
| 2 tbsp vegetable oil |
| 1 tbsp sesame oil |
| 1 garlic clove, crushed |
| 450 g/1 lb tofu, cubed |
| 1 onion, sliced |
| 1 carrot, cut into julienne strips |
| 1 celery stick, sliced |
| 2 small red peppers, seeded and sliced |
| 225 g/8 oz mangetout, trimmed and halved |
| 115 g/4 oz broccoli, trimmed and divided into florets |
| 115 g/4 oz thin French beans, halved |
| 2 tbsp oyster sauce |
| 1 tbsp tamarind concentrate |
| 1 tbsp fish sauce |
| 1 tbsp tomato purée |
| 1 tbsp light soy sauce |
| 1 tbsp chilli sauce |
| 2 tbsp sugar |
| 1 tbsp white vinegar |
| pinch of ground star anise |
| 1 tsp cornflour |
| 300 ml/½ pint water |

**1** Heat the vegetable oil in a preheated wok or large, heavy-based frying pan. Add the crushed garlic and stir-fry for a few seconds.

**2** Add the tofu, in batches, and stir-fry over a low heat, until golden on all sides. Remove with a slotted spoon and keep warm.

**3** Add the onion, carrot, celery, red pepper, mangetout, broccoli and green beans to the pan and stir-fry for about 2–3 minutes, or until tender-crisp.

**4** Add the oyster sauce, tamarind concentrate, fish sauce, tomato purée, soy sauce, chilli sauce, sugar, vinegar and star anise, mixing well to blend. Stir-fry for a further 2 minutes.

**5** Mix the cornflour with the water to make a smooth paste and add to the wok or frying pan, together with the fried tofu. Stir-fry gently until the sauce boils and thickens slightly.

**6** Serve the salad immediately, on warm plates.

# Sweet & Sour Cucumber

Chunks of cucumber are marinated in vinegar
and sweetened with honey to make
a sweet-and-sour appetizer.

| Serves 4 |
| --- |
| 1 cucumber |
| 1 tsp salt |
| 2 tsp honey |
| 2 tbsp rice vinegar |
| 3 tbsp chopped fresh coriander |
| 2 tsp sesame oil |
| $1/4$ tsp crushed red peppercorns |
| strips of red and yellow pepper, to garnish |

**1** Peel thin strips off the cucumber along the length. This gives a pretty striped effect. Cut the cucumber in quarters lengthways and then into 2.5-cm/1-inch long pieces. Place them in a colander.

**2** Sprinkle the salt over the cucumber and set aside for 30 minutes to allow the salt to draw out excess water. Wash the cucumber thoroughly under cold running water to remove the salt, drain and pat dry with kitchen paper.

**3** Place the cucumber in a bowl. Combine the honey with the vinegar and pour the mixture over the cucumber. Mix together and marinate for 15 minutes.

**4** Stir in the coriander and sesame oil, and place in a serving bowl.

**5** Sprinkle the crushed red peppercorns on top of the salad. Serve garnished with strips of red and yellow pepper.

# Chinese Hot Salad

Stir-fried vegetables with a little touch of chilli.
To serve cold, add French dressing as the
vegetables cool, toss well and serve.

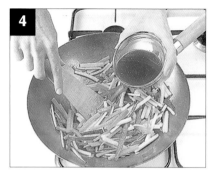

| Serves 4 |
| --- |
| 1 tbsp dark soy sauce |
| 1½–2 tsp sweet chilli sauce |
| 2 tbsp dry sherry |
| 1 tbsp brown sugar |
| 1 tbsp wine vinegar |
| 2 tbsp sunflower oil |
| 1 garlic clove, crushed |
| 4 spring onions, sliced thinly diagonally |
| 225 g/8 oz courgettes, cut into julienne strips about 4 cm/1½ inches long |
| 225 g/8 oz carrots, cut into julienne strips about 4 cm/1½ inches long |
| 1 red or green pepper, cored, seeded and sliced thinly |
| 400 g/14 oz can beansprouts, well drained |
| 125 g/4½ oz French or fine beans, cut into 5-cm/2-inch lengths |
| 1 tbsp sesame oil |
| salt and pepper |
| 1–2 tsp sesame seeds, to garnish |

**1** Blend the soy sauce, chilli sauce, sherry, sugar, vinegar, and salt and pepper together.

**2** Heat the 2 tablespoons of sunflower oil in a preheated wok, swirling it around until it is really hot.

**3** Add the garlic and spring onions to the wok and stir-fry for 1–2 minutes.

**4** Add the courgettes, carrots and pepper and stir-fry for 1–2 minutes, then add the soy sauce mixture to the vegetables and bring to the boil.

**5** Add the beansprouts and French beans and stir-fry for about 1–2 minutes, making sure all the vegetables are coated with the sauce.

**6** Drizzle the sesame oil over the vegetables. Stir–fry for 30 seconds and sprinkle with sesame seeds.

**7** Transfer to a serving dish and serve immediately or cool and serve with French dressing.

# Oriental Salad

This colourful crisp salad has a fresh
orange dressing and is topped
with crunchy vermicelli.

| Serves 4–6 |
| --- |
| 25 g/1 oz dried vermicelli |
| ¹/₂ head Chinese leaves |
| 115 g/4 oz beansprouts |
| 6 radishes |
| 115 g/4 oz mangetout |
| 1 large carrot |
| 115 g/4 oz sprouting beans |
| **DRESSING** |
| juice of 1 orange |
| 1 tbsp sesame seeds, toasted |
| 1 tsp honey |
| 1 tsp sesame oil |
| 1 tbsp hazelnut oil |

**1** Break the vermicelli into small
strands. Heat a wok or frying pan and
dry-fry the vermicelli until lightly
golden. Remove from the pan and set
aside.

**2** Shred the Chinese leaves and wash
with the beansprouts. Drain
thoroughly and place in a large bowl.
Slice the radishes. Trim the
mangetout and cut each into 3. Cut
the carrot into thin matchsticks. Add
the sprouting beans and prepared
vegetables to the bowl.

**3** Place all the dressing ingredients in
a screw-top jar and shake until well-
blended. Pour the dressing over the
salad and toss.

**4** Transfer the salad to a serving bowl
and sprinkle over the reserved
vermicelli before serving.

# Pickled Vegetables

Pickled vegetables can be marinated
for as little as 30 minutes
or for several days.

| Serves 4 |
| --- |
| **PICKLED CUCUMBER** |
| 1 cucumber, about<br>30 cm/12 inches long |
| 1 tsp salt |
| 2 tsp caster sugar |
| 1 tsp rice vinegar |
| 1 tsp red chilli oil |
| a few drops of sesame oil |
| **MIXED PICKLED VEGETABLES** |
| 350 g/12 oz Chinese leaves,<br>cut into bite-size pieces |
| 50 g/1³/₄ oz French beans,<br>topped and tailed |
| 115 g/4 oz carrots, diced |
| 3 fresh red chillies, seeded<br>and finely chopped |
| 2 tsp Szechuan peppercorns |
| 2 tbsp coarse salt |
| 2 tbsp rice wine |

**1** To make Pickled Cucumber, halve the cucumber, unpeeled, lengthways. Scrape off and discard the seeds and cut the flesh across into thick chunks.

**2** Sprinkle the cucumber with the salt and mix thoroughly. Set aside for at least 20–30 minutes, longer if possible, then pour the accumulated juice away.

**3** Mix the cucumber with the sugar, vinegar and chilli oil.

**4** Transfer the pickled cucumber to a serving dish and lightly sprinkle with the sesame oil just before serving.

**5** To make Mixed Pickled Vegetables, place the Chinese leaves, beans and carrots in a glass bowl, together with the chillies, Szechuan peppercorns, salt and rice wine. Stir the mixture

well, cover and leave to marinate in the refrigerator for about 4 days, stirring from time to time. Serve the mixed pickled vegetables cold, as a salad.

# Hot & Sour Duck Salad

This is a lovely tangy salad, drizzled with a lime juice
and fish sauce dressing. It makes a splendid starter
or light main course dish.

| Serves 4 |
| --- |
| 2 heads crisp salad lettuce, washed and separated into leaves |
| 2 shallots, thinly sliced |
| 4 spring onions, chopped |
| 1 celery stick, cut into julienne strips |
| 5-cm/2-inch piece cucumber, cut into julienne strips |
| 115 g/4 oz beansprouts |
| 200 g/7 oz can water chestnuts, drained and sliced |
| 4 duck breast fillets, roasted and sliced |
| orange slices, to serve |

### DRESSING

| |
| --- |
| 3 tbsp fish sauce |
| 1½ tbsp lime juice |
| 2 garlic cloves, crushed |
| 1 fresh red chilli, seeded and very finely chopped |
| 1 fresh green chilli, seeded and very finely chopped |
| 1 tsp palm sugar or demerara sugar |

**1** Mix the lettuce leaves with the shallots, spring onions, celery, cucumber, beansprouts and water chestnuts. Place the mixture on a large serving platter.

**2** Arrange the duck breast slices on top of the salad in an attractive overlapping pattern.

**3** To make the dressing, put the fish sauce, lime juice, garlic, chillies and sugar into a small pan. Heat gently,

stirring constantly. Taste and adjust the piquancy if liked by adding more lime juice, or add more fish sauce to reduce the sharpness.

**4** Drizzle the warm salad dressing over the duck salad and serve.

# Cucumber & Beansprout Salad

This is a very light dish and is ideal
on its own for a summer meal
or as a starter.

| Serves 4 |
| --- |
| 350 g/12 oz beansprouts |
| 1 small cucumber |
| 1 green pepper, seeded and cut into matchsticks |
| 1 carrot, cut into matchsticks |
| 2 tomatoes, finely chopped |
| 1 celery stick, cut into matchsticks |
| 1 garlic clove, crushed |
| dash of chilli sauce |
| 2 tbsp light soy sauce |
| 1 tsp wine vinegar |
| 2 tsp sesame oil |
| 16 chives |

### COOK'S TIP

Mung beansprouts are the most commonly available, but you could also try soya, aduki, alfalfa, lentil or chick pea sprouts.

### COOK'S TIP

The vegetables may be prepared in advance, but do not assemble the dish until just before serving, otherwise the beansprouts will discolour.

**1** Blanch the beansprouts in boiling water for 1 minute. Drain and rinse under cold water. Drain well again.

**2** Halve the cucumber lengthways. Scoop out the seeds with a teaspoon and discard. Cut the flesh into matchsticks and mix with the beansprouts, pepper, carrot, tomatoes and celery.

**3** Mix together the garlic, chilli sauce, soy sauce, vinegar and sesame oil. Pour the dressing over the vegetables, tossing well to coat and spoon on to serving plates. Garnish with chives and serve.

# Broccoli, Pepper & Almond Salad

This is a colourful, crunchy salad with a delicious dressing.
It is better left overnight if possible
for the flavours to mingle.

| Serves 4 |
| --- |
| 450 g/1 lb small broccoli florets |
| 50 g/1³/₄ oz baby corn cobs, halved, lengthways |
| 1 red pepper, seeded and cut into thin strips |
| 50 g/2 oz blanched almonds |
| **DRESSING** |
| 1 tbsp sesame seeds |
| 1 tbsp peanut oil |
| 2 garlic cloves, crushed |
| 2 tbsp light soy sauce |
| 1 tbsp clear honey |
| 2 tsp lemon juice |
| pepper |
| lemon zest, to garnish |

**1** Blanch the broccoli and baby corn cobs in boiling water for 5 minutes. Drain well, rinse under cold running water and drain thoroughly again.

**2** Transfer the broccoli and baby corn cobs to a large mixing bowl and add the pepper and almonds.

**3** To make the dressing, heat a wok or small heavy-based frying pan and add the sesame seeds. Dry-fry, stirring constantly, for about 1 minute, or until the sesame seeds are lightly browned and are giving off a delicious aroma.

**4** Mix the peanut oil, garlic, soy sauce, honey and lemon juice together and season with pepper to taste. Add the sesame seeds and mix together well.

**5** Pour the dressing over the salad, cover and set aside in the refrigerator fora minimum of 4 hours and preferably overnight.

**6** Garnish the salad with lemon zest and serve.

### COOK'S TIP

Take care when browning the sesame seeds, as they will quickly burn. Dry-fry over a low heat and stir constantly.

# Soups

In China, soup is not usually served as a
separate course, but is one of several dishes
forming the main part of the meal. Chinese
soups are usually clear broths flavoured with
finely sliced vegetables, spices and herbs.
They sometimes contain meat, poultry, fish
or seafood and many include noodles,
wontons and dumplings. Some of the
recipes in this chapter are substantial

enough to provide
a light lunch – try
Shrimp Dumpling
Soup.

Their basis is a
good quality stock,
together with the

freshest vegetables. It is always better to
use home-made stock (see page 16), as
stock and bouillon cubes tend to be rather
salty and lack depth of flavour.

Most Chinese soups are a balance of two
flavours – crab and ginger, for example. The
solid ingredients, meat, vegetables or
seafood, are cooked until crisply tender so
that they retain their texture and colour,
making the soup visually appealing.

# Mixed Vegetable Soup

Select three or four vegetables for this soup: the Chinese like
to blend different colours, flavours and textures
to create harmony as well as contrast.

| Serves 4 |
|---|
| about 25–60 g/1–2 oz each of 3 or 4 of the following: |
| mushrooms, carrots, asparagus, mangetout, |
| bamboo shoots, baby corn cobs, |
| cucumber, tomatoes, |
| spinach, lettuce, |
| Chinese leaves, |
| tofu |
| 600 ml/1 pint |
| Chinese Stock (see page 16) |
| 1 tbsp light soy sauce |
| a few drops of sesame oil (optional) |
| salt and pepper |
| finely chopped spring onions, to garnish |

**1** Cut your selection of vegetables
into roughly uniform shapes and sizes
(slices, shreds or cubes).

**2** Bring the stock to a rolling boil in a
wok and add the vegetables, bearing
in mind that some require a longer
cooking time than others: add carrots
and baby corn cobs first, cook for
2 minutes, then add asparagus,
mushrooms, Chinese leaves and tofu
and cook for another minute.

**3** Add the spinach, lettuce,
watercress, cucumber and tomato. Stir
and bring back to the boil.

**4** Add the soy sauce and sesame oil,
and adjust the seasoning. Serve
immediately, garnished with
spring onions.

# Vegetarian Hot & Sour Soup

This is a popular Chinese soup, which is unusual in
that it is thickened. The 'hot' flavour is achieved
by the addition of plenty of black pepper.

| Serves 4 |
| --- |
| 4 Chinese dried mushrooms (or open-cup mushrooms) |
| 115 g/4 oz firm tofu |
| 50 g/1¾ oz canned bamboo shoots, drained |
| 600 ml/1 pint vegetable stock or water |
| 50 g/1¾ oz peas |
| 1 tbsp dark soy sauce |
| 2 tbsp white wine vinegar |
| 2 tbsp cornflour |
| salt and pepper |
| sesame oil, to serve |

**1** Place the dried mushrooms in a
bowl and cover with warm water. Set
aside to soak for 20–25 minutes.

**2** Drain the mushrooms and squeeze
out the excess water, reserving the
soaking water. Remove the stalks and
tough centres and cut the mushroom
caps into thin shreds. Shred the tofu
and bamboo shoots.

**3** Bring the stock or water to the boil
in a large saucepan. Add the
mushrooms, tofu, bamboo shoots and
peas. Bring back to the boil, lower the
heat and simmer for
2 minutes.

**4** Mix together the soy sauce, vinegar
and cornflour with 2 tablespoons of
the reserved mushroom soaking
liquid to make a smooth paste. Stir
the into the soup, together with the
remaining mushroom soaking liquid.
Bring to the boil and season with salt

and plenty of pepper. Simmer for 2
minutes.

**5** Ladle the soup into individual
warm bowls with a few drops of
sesame oil in each and serve.

# Chinese Cabbage Soup

This is a piquant soup, which is slightly sweet-and-sour in flavour.
Cabbage is cooked in a vegetable broth with sugar, vinegar and chilli
and served as a hearty meal or appetizer.

### Serves 4

450 g/1 lb Chinese cabbage

600 ml/1 pint
vegetable stock

1 tbsp rice wine vinegar

1 tbsp light soy sauce

1 tbsp caster sugar

1 tbsp Chinese rice wine or
dry sherry

1 fresh red chilli, thinly sliced

1 tbsp cornflour

2 tbsp water

**1** Trim the cabbage and shred the leaves. Heat the stock in a large saucepan, add the cabbage and cook for 10–15 minutes.

**2** Mix the vinegar, soy sauce, sugar and Chinese rice wine or sherry together and add to the broth, together with the chilli. Bring to the boil and cook for 2–3 minutes.

**3** Blend the cornflour with the water to form a smooth paste. Gradually stir the cornflour mixture into the soup, stirring constantly until the broth thickens. Cook for a further 4–5 minutes. Lade the soup into warm bowls and serve immediately.

### COOK'S TIP

Cook a little rice and spoon into the base of the soup dishes. Ladle the soup over the rice and serve immediately.

# Wonton Soup

Filled wontons are served in a clear soup. The recipe for the wonton skins makes 24 but the soup requires only 12 – freeze the rest for another time.

| Serves 4 |
| --- |
| **WONTON SKINS** |
| 1 egg |
| 6 tbsp water |
| 225 g/8 oz plain flour |
| **FILLING** |
| 115 g/4 oz frozen chopped spinach, thawed |
| 15 g/$^{1}/_{2}$ oz/1 tbsp pine nuts, toasted and chopped |
| 25g/1 oz minced Quorn |
| salt |
| **SOUP** |
| 600 ml/1 pint vegetable stock |
| 1 tbsp dry sherry |
| 1 tbsp light soy sauce |
| 2 spring onions, chopped |

**1** Beat the egg lightly in a bowl and mix with the water. Stir in the flour to form a stiff dough. Knead lightly, then cover with a damp cloth and set aside to rest for 30 minutes.

**2** Roll the dough out into a large sheet about 5 mm/¼ inch thick. Cut out 24 × 7-cm/3-inch squares. Dust each one with flour. Only 12 squares are required so freeze the rest.

**3** To make the filling, squeeze out the excess water from the spinach. Mix the spinach with the pine nuts and Quorn. Season with salt.

**4** Divide the mixture into 12 and place one portion in the centre of each square. Seal by pressing the opposite corners of each square together.

**5** To make the soup, bring the vegetable stock, sherry and soy sauce to the boil in a large saucepan. Add the wontons and boil rapidly for 2–3 minutes.

**6** Add the spring onions to the soup, ladle into warm bowls and serve immediately

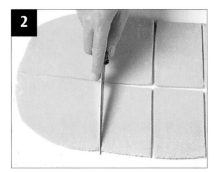

# Spinach & Tofu Soup

This is a very colourful and delicious soup. If spinach is not in season,
watercress or lettuce can be used instead.

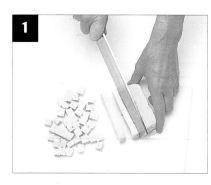

| Serves 4 |
| --- |
| 1 cake tofu |
| 115 g/4 oz spinach leaves without stems |
| 700 ml/1¼ pints Chinese Stock (see page 16) or water |
| 1 tbsp light soy sauce |
| salt and pepper |

**1** Cut the tofu into small pieces about
5 mm/¼ inch thick. Wash the spinach
leaves and cut them into small pieces
or shreds, discarding any discoloured
leaves and tough stalks. (If possible,
use fresh young spinach leaves, which
have not yet developed tough ribs.
Otherwise, it is important to cut out
all the ribs and stems for this soup.)

**2** In a wok or large pan, bring the
stock to a rolling boil. Add the tofu
and soy sauce, bring back to the boil
and simmer for about 2 minutes over
a medium heat.

**3** Add the spinach and simmer for
1 more minute.

**4** Skim the surface of the soup to
make it clear, adjust the seasoning
and serve immediately.

## COOK'S TIP

For a stronger flavour, you could use
smoked or marinated tofu.

# Beef & Vegetable Noodle Soup

Thin strips of beef are marinated in soy sauce and garlic to form
the basis of this delicious soup. Served with noodles,
it is both filling and delicious.

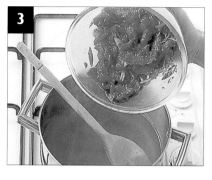

| Serves 4 |
| --- |
| 225 g/8 oz lean beef, cut into thin strips |
| 1 garlic clove, crushed |
| 2 spring onions, chopped |
| 3 tbsp soy sauce |
| 1 tsp sesame oil |
| 225 g/8 oz egg noodles |
| 850 ml/1½ pints beef stock |
| 13 baby corn cobs, sliced |
| ½ leek, shredded |
| 125 g/4½ oz broccoli florets |
| pinch of chilli powder |

### COOK'S VARIATION

If wished, add 1 tablespoon
grated fresh ginger root to the marinade
in step 1 for a spicier flavour.

### COOK'S TIP

Vary the vegetables used, or use those
to hand. If desired, use a few drops of
chilli sauce in place of chilli powder, but
remember it is very hot.

**1** Put the beef in a shallow glass bowl
with the garlic and spring onions. Add
the soy sauce and sesame oil, cover
and marinate for 30 minutes.

**2** Cook the noodles in boiling water
for 3–4 minutes, drain and reserve.

**3** Bring the beef stock to the boil in a
large saucepan and add the beef,
together with the marinade, the baby
corn cobs, leek and broccoli. Cover
and simmer for 7–10 minutes, until
the beef and vegetables are cooked
through and tender.

**4** Stir in the noodles and chilli
powder and cook for a further
2–3 minutes. Serve immediately.

# Noodles in Soup

Noodles in soup (tang mein) are more popular than
fried noodles (chow mein) in China. You can use different
ingredients for the dressing, if preferred.

| Serves 4 |
|---|
| 225 g/8 oz cooked chicken fillet, pork fillet, or other cooked meat |
| 3–4 Chinese dried mushrooms, soaked in warm water for 30 minutes |
| 115 g/4 oz canned sliced bamboo shoots, rinsed and drained |
| 115 g/4 oz spinach leaves, lettuce hearts, or Chinese leaves, shredded |
| 2 spring onions, shredded finely |
| 225 g/8 oz egg noodles |
| about 600 ml/1 pint Chinese Stock (see page 16) |
| 2 tbsp light soy sauce |
| 2 tbsp vegetable oil |
| 1 tsp salt |
| 1/2 tsp sugar |
| 2 tsp Chinese rice wine or dry sherry |
| a few drops of sesame oil |
| 1 tsp red chilli oil (optional) |

**1** Cut the meat into thin shreds. Squeeze dry the soaked mushrooms and discard the hard stalks.

**2** Thinly shred the mushrooms, bamboo shoots, spinach leaves and spring onions.

**3** Cook the noodles in boiling water according to the instructions on the packet, then drain and rinse under cold water. Place in a bowl. Bring the stock to a boil, add about 1 tablespoon soy sauce and pour it over the noodles. Keep warm.

**4** Heat the oil in a preheated wok, add the meat, vegetables and about half the spring onions. Stir-fry for about 2–3 minutes. Add the salt, sugar, Chinese rice wine or sherry, sesame oil and chilli oil, if using.

**5** Pour the mixture in the wok over the noodles, garnish with the remaining spring onions and serve immediately.

# Mushroom & Cucumber Noodle Soup

A light, refreshing clear soup of mushrooms, cucumber and small pieces of rice noodles, flavoured with soy sauce and a touch of garlic.

| Serves 4 |
| --- |
| 115 g/4 oz flat or open-cup mushrooms |
| $^1/_2$ cucumber |
| 2 spring onions |
| 1 garlic clove |
| 2 tbsp vegetable oil |
| 25 g/1 oz/$^1/_4$ cup Chinese rice noodles |
| $^3/_4$ tsp salt |
| 1 tbsp soy sauce |

**1** Wash the mushrooms and slice thinly. Do not remove the peel as this adds more flavour. Halve the cucumber lengthways. Scoop out and discard the seeds, using a teaspoon, and slice the cucumber thinly.

**2** Chop the spring onions finely and cut the garlic clove into thin strips.

**3** Heat the oil in a preheated wok or large saucepan. Add the spring onions and garlic, and stir-fry for 30 seconds. Add the mushrooms and stir-fry for 2–3 minutes.

**4** Stir in 600 ml/1 pint water. Break the noodles into short lengths and add them to the soup. Bring to the boil.

**5** Add the cucumber slices, salt and soy sauce, and simmer for 2–3 minutes.

**6** Serve the soup in warm bowls, distributing the noodles and vegetables evenly among them.

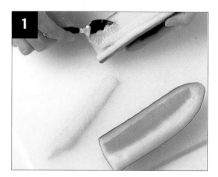

# Fish Soup with Wontons

This soup is topped with small wontons
filled with prawns, making it both
very tasty and satisfying.

| Serves 4 |
| --- |
| 125 g/4¹/₂ oz large, cooked, peeled prawns |
| 1 tsp chopped chives |
| 1 small garlic clove, finely chopped |
| 1 tbsp vegetable oil |
| 12 wonton wrappers |
| 1 small egg, beaten |
| 850 ml/1¹/₂ pints fish stock |
| 175 g/6 oz white fish fillet, diced |
| dash of chilli sauce |
| sliced fresh red chilli and chives, to garnish |

**5** Add the chilli sauce and the
wontons and cook for a further
5 minutes. Ladle the soup into warm
individual serving bowls, garnish
with red chilli slices and chives and
serve immediately.

**COOK'S VARIATION**

Replace the prawns
with cooked crabmeat for an
alternative flavour.

**1** Roughly chop a quarter of the
prawns and mix together with the
chives and garlic.

**2** Heat the oil in a preheated wok or
heavy-based frying pan and stir-fry
the mixture for 1–2 minutes. Set
aside to cool completely.

**3** Spread out the wonton wrappers
on a work surface and spoon a little of
the filling into the centre of each.
Brush the edges with beaten egg and
fold in half, pressing out the air and
sealing the edges well. Pinch into a
round shape. Let stand while you are
preparing the soup.

**4** Pour the fish stock into a large
saucepan and bring to the boil. Add
the white fish fillet and the remaining
prawns. Cook over a medium heat for
5 minutes.

# Seafood & Tofu Soup

Use prawn, squid or scallops, or a
combination of all three
for this delicious soup.

| Serves 4 |
|---|
| 225 g/8 oz seafood, such as peeled prawns, squid, scallops, thawed if frozen |
| $^1/_2$ egg white, beaten lightly |
| 1 tbsp Cornflour Paste (see page 16) |
| 1 cake tofu |
| 700 ml/1$^1/_4$ pints Chinese Stock (see page 16) |
| 1 tbsp light soy sauce |
| salt and pepper |
| fresh coriander leaves, to garnish (optional) |

**1** Small prawns can be left whole; larger ones should be cut into smaller pieces. Cut the squid and scallops into small pieces.

**2** If raw, mix the prawns and scallops with the egg white and cornflour paste to prevent them from becoming tough when they are cooked.

**3** Cut the tofu into about 24 small cubes.

**4** Bring the stock to a rolling boil. Add the tofu and soy sauce, bring back to the boil and simmer for 1 minute.

**5** Stir in the seafood, raw pieces first, cooked ones last. Bring back to boil and simmer for just 1 minute. Adjust the seasoning and serve garnished with coriander leaves, if wished.

# Shrimp Dumpling Soup

These dumplings filled with shrimp and pork
may be made slightly larger and served
as dim sum on their own.

| Serves 4 |
| --- |
| **FOR THE DOUGH** |
| 150 g/5¹/₂ oz plain flour |
| 50 ml/2 fl oz boiling water |
| 5 tsp cold water |
| 1¹/₂ tsp vegetable oil |
| **FOR THE FILLING** |
| 125 g/4¹/₂ oz minced pork |
| 125 g/4¹/₂ oz cooked peeled shrimp, chopped |
| 50 g/1³/₄ oz canned water chestnuts, drained and chopped |
| 1 celery stick, chopped |
| 1 tsp cornflour |
| 1 tbsp sesame oil |
| 1 tbsp light soy sauce |
| **FOR THE SOUP** |
| 850 ml/1¹/₂ pints fish stock |
| 50 g/1³/₄ oz transparent noodles |
| 1 tbsp Chinese rice wine or dry sherry |
| chopped chives, to garnish |

**1** First make the dumplings. Mix together the flour, boiling water, cold water and oil in a bowl to make a pliable dough. Knead on a lightly floured surface for 5 minutes and cut into 16 equal-size pieces.

**2** Roll the dough into rounds approximately 7.5 cm/3 inches in diameter.

**3** Mix the filling ingredients together and spoon a little of the mixture into the centre of each round. Bring the dough together along the centre of the filling to form small, long dumplings. Press the edges together to seal and twist the dough along the seam.

**4** Pour the fish stock into a large saucepan and bring to the boil. Add the noodles, dumplings and Chinese rice wine or dry sherry, bring back to the boil and simmer over a medium heat for 4–5 minutes, until the noodles and dumplings are cooked.

**5** Ladle the soup into warm individual bowls, garnish with chopped chives and serve immediately.

# Crab & Ginger Soup

Two classic ingredients in Chinese cooking
are blended together in this
recipe for a special soup.

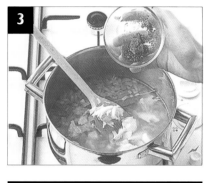

| Serves 4 |
| --- |
| 1 carrot, chopped |
| 1 leek, chopped |
| 1 bay leaf |
| 850 ml/1½ pints stock |
| 2 medium-size cooked crabs |
| 2.5-cm/1-inch piece fresh ginger root, grated |
| ½ tsp ground star anise |
| 5 ml/1 tsp light soy sauce |
| salt and pepper |

### COOK'S TIP

Loosen the crab by banging the back
underside with your fist, then force the
body away from the shell with your
thumbs.

### COOK'S TIP

If freshly cooked crabs are unavailable,
use drained canned crabmeat or thawed
frozen crabmeat instead.

**1** Put the carrot, leek, bay leaf and
fish stock in a large saucepan and
bring to the boil. Reduce the heat,
cover and cook for 10 minutes.

**2** Meanwhile, remove all the meat
from the cooked crabs. Break off the
claws, break the joints and remove all
the meat. You may require a fork or
skewer for this. Add the crabmeat to
the fish stock.

**3** Add the ginger, soy sauce and star
anise to the fish stock and bring to
the boil. Simmer for 10 minutes and
adjust the seasoning to taste.

**4** Spoon into warm individual
serving bowls and garnish with crab
claws. Serve immediately.

# Three-Flavour Soup

Ideally, use raw prawns in this soup. If that
is not possible, add ready-cooked
ones at the very last stage.

| Serves 4 |
| --- |
| 115 g/4 oz boneless skinless chicken breast |
| 115 g/4 oz raw peeled prawns |
| salt |
| $1/2$ egg white, beaten lightly |
| 2 tsp Cornflour Paste (see page 16) |
| 115 g/4 oz honey-roast ham |
| 700 ml/$1^1/4$ pints Chinese Stock (see page 16) or water |
| finely chopped spring onions, to garnish |

**1** Thinly slice the chicken into small shreds. If the prawns are large, cut each in half lengthways, otherwise leave whole.

**2** Place the chicken and prawns in a bowl and mix with a pinch of salt, the egg white and cornflour paste until thoroughly coated.

**3** Cut the ham into small thin slices approximately the same size as the chicken pieces.

**4** Bring the stock or water to a rolling boil, add the chicken, the raw prawns and the ham. Bring the soup back to the boil and simmer for 1 minute.

**5** Adjust the seasoning and ladle the soup into warm individual bowls. Garnish with the spring onions and serve immediately.

# Curried Chicken & Sweetcorn Soup

Tender cooked chicken strips and baby corn cobs are the main flavours
in this delicious clear soup, with just a hint of ginger.

| Serves 4 |
| --- |
| 175 g/6 oz can sweetcorn, drained |
| 850 ml/1 1/2 pints chicken stock |
| 350 g/12 oz cooked, lean chicken, cut into strips |
| 16 baby corn cobs |
| 1 tsp Chinese curry powder |
| 1-cm/1/2-inch piece fresh ginger root, grated |
| 3 tbsp light soy sauce |
| 2 tbsp chopped chives |

**1** Put the canned sweetcorn in a food processor with 150 ml/1/4 pint of the chicken stock and process until smooth. Rub through a strainer, pressing with the back of a spoon to remove any husks.

**2** Pour the remaining stock into a large saucepan and add the chicken strips. Stir in the sweetcorn purée.

**3** Add the baby corn cobs and bring the soup to the boil. Boil for 10 minutes, then add the curry powder, ginger and soy sauce. Cook for a further 10–15 minutes and stir in the chives. Serve immediately in warm bowls.

### COOK'S TIP

Prepare the soup up to 24 hours in advance without adding the chicken, then cool, cover and store in the refrigerator. Add the chicken just before serving and heat through.

# Prawn Soup

A mixture of textures and flavours makes this an interesting
and colourful soup. The egg may be made into
a flat omelette and added as thin strips.

| Serves 4 |
| --- |
| 2 tbsp sunflower oil |
| 2 spring onions, thinly sliced diagonally |
| 1 carrot, coarsely grated |
| 115 g/4 oz large closed-cup mushrooms, sliced thinly |
| 1 litre/1³/₄ pints fish or vegetable stock |
| ¹/₂ tsp Chinese five-spice powder |
| 1 tbsp light soy sauce |
| 115 g/4 oz large peeled and deveined cooked prawns, or peeled and deveined cooked tiger prawns, thawed if frozen |
| ¹/₂ bunch of watercress, trimmed and roughly chopped |
| 1 egg, beaten well |
| salt and pepper |
| 4 large prawns in shells, to garnish (optional) |

**1** Heat the oil in a preheated wok. Add the spring onions and stir-fry for a minute, then add the carrots and mushrooms and continue to stir-fry for about 2 minutes.

**2** Add the stock and bring to the boil, then season to taste with salt and pepper, five-spice powder and soy sauce. Lower the heat and simmer for 5 minutes.

**3** If the prawns are really large, cut them in half before adding them to the wok, then continue to simmer for 3–4 minutes.

**4** Add the roughly chopped watercress to the wok and mix well, then slowly pour in the beaten egg in a circular movement so that it cooks in threads in the soup.

**5** Adjust the seasoning to taste and ladle the soup into warm individual soup bowls. Top each serving with a whole prawn and serve immediately.

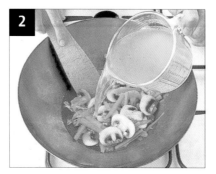

# Peking Duck Soup

This is a hearty and robustly flavoured soup,
containing pieces of duck and vegetables
cooked in a rich stock.

| Serves 4 |
| --- |

850 ml/1¹/₂ pints
chicken or duck stock

1 tbsp Chinese rice wine or
dry sherry

1 tbsp light soy sauce

225 g/8 oz Chinese leaves,
shredded

125 g/4¹/₂ oz lean duck
breast meat, finely diced

2 garlic cloves, crushed

pinch of ground star anise

1 tbsp sesame seeds

1 tsp sesame oil

1 tbsp chopped fresh parsley

**1** Bring the stock to the boil in a large
saucepan. Add the sherry or rice wine,
soy sauce, Chinese leaves and duck.
Reduce the heat and simmer for 15
minutes.

**2** Stir in the garlic and star anise and
cook for a further 10–15 minutes,
until the duck is tender.

**3** Meanwhile, dry-fry the sesame
seeds in a hot, wok or heavy-based
frying pan, stirring constantly.
Remove from the pan and stir into
the soup, together with the sesame oil
and parsley. Ladle into warm
individual soup bowls and
serve immediately.

### COOK'S TIP

If Chinese leaves are unavailable, use
green cabbage.

# Clear Chicken & Egg Soup

This tasty chicken soup has the addition of poached eggs,
making it both delicious and filling. Use fresh, home-made
chicken stock for a better flavour.

| Serves 4 |
| --- |
| 1 tsp salt |
| 1 tbsp rice wine vinegar |
| 4 eggs |
| 850 ml/1 $^1/_2$ pints chicken stock |
| 1 leek, sliced |
| 125 g/4$^1/_2$ oz broccoli florets |
| 125 g/4$^1/_2$ oz shredded cooked chicken |
| 2 open-cap mushrooms, sliced |
| 1 tbsp Chinese rice wine or dry sherry |
| dash of chilli sauce |
| chilli powder, to garnish |

**1** Bring a large saucepan of water to the boil and add the salt and vinegar. Reduce the heat so that it is just simmering and carefully break the eggs into the water, one at a time. Poach for 1 minute and remove with a slotted spoon.

**2** Bring the chicken stock to the boil in a separate pan and add the leek, broccoli, chicken, mushrooms and sherry and season with chilli sauce to taste. Cook for 10–15 minutes.

**3** Add the poached eggs to the soup and cook for a further 2 minutes. Ladle the soup into warm individual soup bowls, dividing the eggs among them. Dust with a little chilli powder and serve immediately.

### COOK'S VARIATION

For a vegetarian version, use vegetable stock and 115 g/4 oz shredded firm tofu instead of the chicken.

### COOK'S TIP

Use 4 dried Chinese mushrooms, rehydrated according to the packet instructions, in place of the open-cap mushrooms.

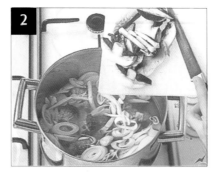

# Chicken Soup with Almonds

This soup can also be made using turkey
or pheasant breasts. Pheasant gives
a stronger, gamey flavour.

| Serves 4 |
| --- |
| 1 large or 2 small boneless skinless chicken breasts |
| 1 tbsp sunflower oil |
| 4 spring onions, thinly sliced diagonally |
| 1 carrot, cut into julienne strips |
| 700 ml/1¼ pints chicken stock |
| finely grated rind of ½ lemon |
| 40 g/1½ oz ground almonds |
| 1 tbsp light soy sauce |
| 1 tbsp lemon juice |
| 25 g/1 oz flaked almonds, toasted |
| salt and pepper |

**1** Using a very sharp knife, cut
each chicken breast into 4 strips
lengthways, then slice the strips very
thinly across the grain to produce fine
shreds of chicken.

**2** Heat the oil in a preheated wok.
Add the chicken and stir-fry for
3–4 minutes, until sealed and almost
completely cooked through. Then add
the carrot and continue to stir-fry for
2–3 minutes. Add the spring onions
and stir-fry for a further
2 minutes.

**3** Add the stock to the wok and bring
to the boil. Add the lemon rind,
ground almonds, soy sauce and lemon
juice and season to taste with salt and
pepper. Bring back to the boil, lower
the heat and simmer, uncovered, for
5 minutes, stirring occasionally.

**4** Add most of the toasted flaked
almonds and continue to cook for a
further 1–2 minutes. Check and adjust
the seasoning.

**5** Ladle the soup into warm
individual soup bowls, sprinkle with
the remaining almonds to garnish and
serve immediately.

# Lamb & Rice Soup

This is a very filling soup, as it contains
rice and tender pieces of lamb.
Serve before a light main course.

  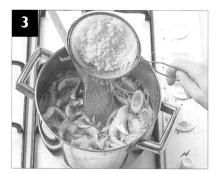

| Serves 4 |
| --- |
| 50 g/1³/₄ oz rice |
| 850 ml/1¹/₂ pints lamb stock |
| 150 g/5¹/₂ oz lean lamb, cut into strips |
| 1 leek, sliced |
| 1 garlic clove, thinly sliced |
| 2 tsp light soy sauce |
| 1 tsp rice wine vinegar |
| 1 medium open-cap mushroom, sliced |

**1** Cook the rice in boiling salted water for 10–15 minutes. Drain and rinse under cold running water.

**2** Meanwhile, bring the lamb stock to the boil in a large saucepan. Add the lamb strips, leek, garlic, soy sauce and vinegar. Reduce the heat, cover and simmer for 10 minutes, until the lamb is cooked through.

**3** Add the mushroom slices and the rice and cook for a further 2–3 minutes, until the mushroom is cooked.

**4** Ladle into warm individual bowls and serve immediately.

### COOK'S TIP

Use a few dried Chinese mushrooms, rehydrated according to the packet instructions and chopped, instead of the open-cap mushroom. Add with the lamb.

# Pork & Szechuan Vegetable Soup

Sold in cans, Szechuan preserved vegetable is pickled
mustard root, which is quite hot and salty,
so rinse in water before use.

| Serves 4 |
| --- |
| 225 g/8 oz pork fillet |
| 2 tsp Cornflour Paste (see page 16) |
| 115 g/4 oz Szechuan preserved vegetable |
| 700 ml/1¼ pints Chinese Stock (see page 16) or water |
| salt and pepper |
| a few drops of sesame oil (optional) |
| 2–3 spring onions, sliced, to garnish |

**1** Cut the pork across the grain into thin shreds and place in a bowl. Add the cornflour paste and mix thoroughly.

**2** Wash and rinse the Szechuan preserved vegetable, then cut into thin shreds approximately the same size as the pork.

**3** Bring the stock or water to a rolling boil, add the pork and stir to separate the shreds. Bring back to the boil.

**4** Add the Szechuan preserved vegetable and bring back to the boil once more. Adjust the seasoning and sprinkle with sesame oil, if using. Ladle into warm individual soup bowls, garnish with spring onions and serve immediately.

# Fish & Seafood

China's extensive coastline and the many rivers and inland lakes ensure an abundance of fresh fish and seafood. They are prepared in a variety of ways, often marinated with herbs and spices, and cooked in combination with fresh vegetables. Steaming is a favourite technique for cooking whole fish, while seafood is frequently stir-fried. Whole fish and fillets are also braised or poached.

Shellfish may be fried at a high temperature in a flavoured oil, which penetrates the shells to create a delicious sauce.

Black bean sauce, fresh chillies, ginger, pineapple and other fruits, soy sauce, lemon grass, cashew nuts and rice wine are typical ingredients used to flavour many fish dishes.

The recipes in this chapter reflect the different regional approaches to preparing fish. Try Fish in Szechuan Hot Sauce for a spicy way of serving freshwater fish, which abound in western China, or Fried Squid Flowers, a Cantonese seafood speciality.

# Trout with Pineapple

Pineapple is widely used in Chinese cooking.
The tartness of fresh pineapple complements
fish particularly well.

| Serves 4 |
| --- |
| 4 trout fillets, skinned |
| 2 tbsp vegetable oil |
| 2 garlic cloves, cut into slivers |
| 4 slices fresh pineapple, peeled and diced |
| 1 celery stick, sliced |
| 1 tbsp light soy sauce |
| 50 ml/2 fl oz fresh or unsweetened pineapple juice |
| 150 ml/¼ pint fish stock |
| 1 tsp cornflour |
| 2 tsp water |
| shredded celery leaves and fresh red chilli strips, to garnish |

**1** Using a sharp knife, cut the trout fillets into strips.

**2** Heat 1 tablespoon of the oil in a preheated wok until almost smoking and cook the fish for 2 minutes, stirring well. Remove from the wok and set aside.

**3** Add the remaining oil, reduce the heat and stir-fry the garlic, pineapple and celery for 1–2 minutes.

**4** Add the soy sauce, pineapple juice and stock to the wok. Bring to the boil and cook for 2–3 minutes to reduce the sauce.

**5** Blend the cornflour with the water to form a paste and stir it into the wok. Bring the sauce to the boil and cook, stirring constantly, until the sauce thickens and clears.

**6** Return the fish to the wok, and cook, stirring gently, until heated through.

**7** Transfer to a warm serving dish, garnish with shredded celery leaves and red chilli strips and serve.

### COOK'S TIP

Use canned pineapple instead of fresh, choosing slices in unsweetened, natural juice in preference to a syrup.

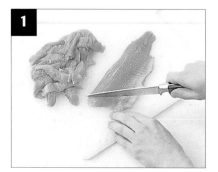

# Fish with Black Bean Sauce

Any firm steaks such as salmon
or turbot can be cooked
by the same method.

| Serves 4–6 |
| --- |
| 1 sea bass or trout, weighing about 675g/1½ lb, cleaned |
| 1 tsp salt |
| 1 tbsp sesame oil |
| 2–3 spring onions, cut in half lengthways |
| 1 tbsp light soy sauce |
| 1 tbsp Chinese rice wine or dry sherry |
| 1 tbsp finely shredded ginger root |
| 1 tbsp oil |
| 2 tbsp crushed black bean sauce |
| 2 spring onions, shredded finely |

**TO GARNISH**

| |
| --- |
| fresh coriander leaves (optional) |
| lemon slices |

**1** Using a sharp knife, score both sides of the fish with diagonal cuts at 2.5-cm/1-inch intervals. Rub both the inside and outside of the fish with the salt and sesame oil.

**2** Place the spring onions on a heatproof platter and put the fish on top. Blend the soy sauce and wine with the ginger shreds and pour the mixture evenly all over the fish.

**3** Place the fish on the platter in a bamboo steamer or inside a wok on a rack. Cover tightly and steam vigorously for 12–15 minutes, adding more water if necessary, until the fish is tender and cooked through.

**4** Heat the oil in a preheated wok or saucepan until hot, then stir in the black bean sauce. Remove the fish from the steamer and transfer to a serving dish. Pour the hot black bean sauce over the whole length of the fish and place the shredded spring onions on top. Serve garnished with coriander leaves, if using, and lemon slices.

# Crispy Fish with Chillies

This is a hot dish, not for the faint hearted.
It may be made without the chilli
flavourings if preferred.

| Serves 4 |
| --- |
| 450 g/1 lb white fish fillets |

### FOR THE BATTER

| |
| --- |
| 50 g/1¾ oz plain flour |
| 1 egg, separated |
| 1 tbsp peanut oil |
| 4 tbsp milk |
| vegetable oil, for deep-frying |

### FOR THE SAUCE

| |
| --- |
| 1 fresh red chilli, chopped |
| 2 garlic cloves, crushed |
| pinch of chilli powder |
| 3 tbsp tomato purée |
| 1 tbsp rice wine vinegar |
| 2 tbsp dark soy sauce |
| 2 tbsp Chinese rice wine |
| 2 tbsp water |
| pinch of caster sugar |

**3** Pour off all but 1 tbsp of oil from the wok and return it to the heat. Add the chilli, garlic, chilli powder, tomato purée, vinegar, soy sauce, wine, water and sugar and cook, stirring, for 3–4 minutes.

**4** Return the fish to the wok and stir gently to coat it thoroughly in the sauce. Cook for 2–3 minutes, until completely heated through. Transfer the fish and sauce to a warm serving dish and serve immediately.

**1** Cut the fish into 2.5-cm/1-inch cubes and set aside. Sift the flour into a mixing bowl and make a well in the centre. Add the egg yolk and oil to the bowl and gradually stir in the milk, incorporating the flour to form a smooth batter. Let stand for 20 minutes.

**2** Beat the egg white until it forms peaks and fold it into the batter. Heat the oil in a preheated wok. Dip the fish into the batter and fry it, in batches, for 8–10 minutes, until cooked through and golden. Remove the fish from the wok with a slotted spoon and keep warm while you cook the remaining batches.

# Braised Fish Fillets

Any white fish is ideal for this dish.
Lemon sole is particularly delicious
cooked in this way.

| Serves 4 |
| --- |
| 3–4 small Chinese dried mushrooms |
| 300–350 g/10$^1$/$_2$–12 oz fish fillets |
| 1 tsp salt |
| $^1$/$_2$ egg white, lightly beaten |
| 1 tsp Cornflour Paste (see page 16) |
| 600 ml/1 pint vegetable oil |
| 1 tsp finely chopped fresh ginger root |
| 2 spring onions, finely chopped |
| 1 garlic clove, finely chopped |
| $^1$/$_2$ small green pepper, seeded and cut into small cubes |
| $^1$/$_2$ small carrot, thinly sliced |
| 50 g/1$^3$/$_4$ oz canned sliced bamboo shoots, rinsed and drained |
| $^1$/$_2$ tsp sugar |
| 1 tbsp light soy sauce |
| 1 tsp Chinese rice wine or dry sherry |
| 1 tbsp chilli bean sauce |
| 2–3 tbsp Chinese Stock (see page 16) or water |
| a few drops of sesame oil |

**1** Soak the dried mushrooms in warm water for 30 minutes, then drain on kitchen paper, reserving the soaking water for stock. Squeeze the mushrooms to extract all the moisture, cut off and discard any hard stems and slice the caps thinly.

**2** Cut the fish into bite-size pieces, then place in a shallow dish and mix with a pinch of salt, the egg white and cornflour paste, turning the fish to coat well.

**3** Heat the oil and deep-fry the fish pieces for about 1 minute. Remove with a slotted spoon and drain on kitchen paper.

**4** Pour off the oil, leaving about 1 tablespoon in the wok. Add the ginger, spring onions and garlic to flavour the oil for a few seconds, then add the vegetables and stir-fry for about 1 minute.

**5** Add the sugar, soy sauce, wine or sherry, chilli bean sauce, stock or water, and remaining salt, and bring to the boil. Add the fish pieces, stir to coat well with the sauce, and braise for another minute. Sprinkle with sesame oil and serve immediately.

# Mullet with Ginger

Ginger is used widely in Chinese cooking for its strong, pungent flavour.
Always use fresh ginger where possible, but ground ginger may be
used as an alternative when fresh is not available.

| Serves 4 |
| --- |
| 1 whole mullet, cleaned and scaled |
| 2 spring onions, finely chopped |
| 1 tsp grated fresh ginger root |
| 125 ml/4 fl oz/$\frac{1}{2}$ cup garlic wine vinegar |
| 125 ml/4 fl oz light soy sauce |
| 3 tsp caster sugar |
| dash of chilli sauce |
| 125 ml/4 fl oz fish stock |
| 1 green pepper, seeded and thinly sliced |
| 1 large tomato, peeled, seeded and cut into thin strips |
| salt and pepper |
| sliced tomato, to garnish |

**1** Wash the fish inside and out and pat dry with kitchen paper.

**2** Make three diagonal slits in the flesh on each side of the fish. Season the fish with salt and pepper inside and out.

**3** Place the fish on a heatproof plate and scatter the spring onions and ginger over the top. Cover and steam for 10 minutes, or until the fish is cooked through.

**4** Meanwhile, place the vinegar, soy sauce, sugar, chilli sauce, fish stock, pepper and tomato in a saucepan and bring to the boil. Cook over a high heat to reduce and thicken the sauce.

**5** Transfer the fish to a serving dish, pour the sauce over it, garnish with tomato slices and serve immediately.

### COOK'S TIP

Use fillets of fish for this recipe if wished and reduce the cooking time for the fish to 5–7 minutes.

# Fish in Szechuan Hot Sauce

This is a classic Szechuan recipe. When served
in a restaurant, the fish head and tail
are removed before cooking.

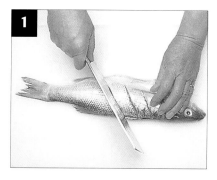

### Serves 4

1 carp, bream, sea bass, trout,
grouper or grey mullet,
about 750 g/1 lb 10 oz, gutted

1 tbsp light soy sauce

1 tbsp Chinese rice wine
or dry sherry

vegetable oil, for deep-frying

flat-leaf parsley or coriander
sprigs, to garnish

### SAUCE

2 garlic cloves, finely chopped

2–3 spring onions,
finely chopped

1 tsp finely chopped ginger root

2 tbsp chilli bean sauce

1 tbsp tomato purée

2 tsp sugar

1 tbsp rice vinegar

125 ml/4 fl oz Chinese
Stock (see page 16)
or water

1 tbsp Cornflour
Paste (see page 16)

$^1/_2$ tsp sesame oil

**1** Wash the fish and dry well on
kitchen paper. Score both sides of the
fish to the bone with a sharp knife,
making diagonal cuts at intervals of
about 2.5 cm/1 inch. Rub the fish with
the soy sauce and wine on both sides,
then marinate in the refrigerator for
10–15 minutes.

**2** Heat the oil in a preheated wok
until smoking. Deep-fry the fish in
the hot oil for about 3–4 minutes on
both sides, or until golden brown.

**3** Pour off the oil, leaving about
1 tablespoon in the wok. Push the fish
to one side of the wok and add the
garlic, the white parts of the spring
onions, ginger, chilli bean sauce, tomato
purée, sugar, vinegar and stock. Bring to
the boil and braise the fish in the sauce
for 4–5 minutes, turning it over once,
until it is tender and cooked through.

**4** Add the green parts of the spring
onions and stir in the cornflour paste.
Sprinkle with sesame oil and serve,
garnished with parsley or coriander.

# Steamed Snapper with Fruit & Ginger Stuffing

Red mullet may be used in place of the whole snapper, although they are a little more difficult to stuff because their size. Use one mullet per person.

### Serves 4

1.4 kg/3 lb whole snapper,
cleaned and scaled

175 g/6 oz spinach

orange slices and shredded
spring onion,
to garnish

### FOR THE STUFFING

50 g/1¾ oz cooked
long-grain rice

1 tsp grated fresh
ginger root

2 spring onions,
finely chopped

2 tsp light soy sauce

1 tsp sesame oil

½ tsp ground star anise

1 orange,
segmented and chopped

**1** Wash the fish inside and out and pat dry with kitchen paper. Blanch the spinach for 40 seconds, then drain well. Arrange the spinach on a heatproof plate and place the fish on top.

**2** Thoroughly mix all the stuffing ingredients together.

**3** Spoon the stuffing into the body cavity of the fish, pressing it in well with a spoon.

**4** Cover the plate and cook in a steamer for 10 minutes, or until the fish is cooked through. Garnish with orange slices and shredded spring onion and serve.

# Spiced Scallops

Scallops are available both fresh and frozen.
Make sure they are completely
thawed before cooking.

| Serves 4 |
|---|
| 12 large scallops with coral attached, thawed if frozen, or 350 g/12 oz small scallops without coral, thawed |
| 4 tbsp sunflower oil |
| 4–6 spring onions, thinly sliced diagonally |
| 1 garlic clove, crushed |
| 2.5-cm/1-inch piece fresh ginger root, finely chopped |
| 225 g/8 oz mangetout |
| 115 g/4 oz button or closed-cup mushrooms, sliced |
| 2 tbsp Chinese rice wine or dry sherry |
| 2 tbsp light soy sauce |
| 1 tbsp clear honey |
| $1/4$ tsp ground allspice |
| 1 tbsp sesame seeds, toasted |
| salt and pepper |

**1** Wash and dry the scallops, discarding any black pieces. Detach the corals, if using. Slice each scallop into 3–4 pieces and halve the corals if they are large.

**2** Heat 2 tablespoons of oil in a preheated wok. Add the spring onions, garlic and ginger, and stir-fry for a minute or so. Add the mangetout and continue to stir-fry for 2–3 minutes. Remove from the wok with a slotted spoon and transfer to a bowl.

**3** Add the remaining oil to the wok. When it is really hot, add the scallops and corals, and stir-fry for 2–3 minutes. Add the mushrooms and continue to cook for a further 1–2 minutes.

**4** Add the wine or sherry, soy sauce, honey and allspice, with salt and pepper to taste. Mix thoroughly, then return the vegetable mixture to the wok.

**5** Season well and toss together over a high heat for a minute or so, until piping hot. Serve immediately, sprinkled with sesame seeds.

# Stir-Fried Prawns & Vegetables

This colourful and delicious dish is cooked with vegetables.
Vary them according to seasonal availability.

| Serves 4 |
| --- |
| 50 g/1¾ oz mangetout |
| ½ small carrot, thinly sliced lengthways |
| 50 g/1¾ oz baby corn cobs |
| 50 g/1¾ oz straw mushrooms |
| 175–225 g/6–8 oz raw tiger prawns, peeled and deveined |
| 1 tsp salt |
| ½ egg white, beaten lightly |
| 1 tsp Cornflour Paste (see page 16) |
| about 300 ml/½ pint vegetable oil |
| 1 spring onion, cut into short sections |
| 4 slices fresh ginger root, finely chopped |
| ½ tsp sugar |
| 1 tbsp light soy sauce |
| 1 tsp Chinese rice wine or dry sherry |
| a few drops of sesame oil |

1 tablespoon in the wok. Add the mangetout, carrot, baby corn, mushrooms, spring onion and ginger root. Stir-fry for about 1 minute.

**5** Return the prawns to the wok and add the sugar, soy sauce and Chinese rice wine or dry sherry. Blend well. Sprinkle with the sesame oil, transfer to a warm serving dish and serve immediately.

**1** Top and tail the mangetout. Cut the carrot into slices the same size as the mangetout. Halve the baby corn cobs and straw mushrooms.

**2** Mix the prawns with a pinch of salt, the egg white and cornflour paste.

**3** Heat the oil in a preheated wok. Add the prawns, stirring to separate them. Stir-fry and remove from the wok with a slotted spoon as soon as their colour changes.

**4** Pour off the oil, leaving about

# Seafood Combination

Use any combination of fish and shellfish
in this delicious dish of coated fish
served in a wine sauce.

| Serves 4 |
| --- |
| 2 tbsp dry white wine |
| 1 egg white, lightly beaten |
| 1/2 tsp Chinese five-spice powder |
| 1 tsp cornflour |
| 300 g/10 1/2 oz raw prawns, peeled and deveined |
| 125 g/4 1/2 oz prepared squid, cut into rings |
| 125 g/4 1/2 oz white fish fillets, cut into strips |
| vegetable oil, for deep-frying |
| 1 green pepper, seeded and cut into thin strips |
| 1 carrot, cut into thin strips |
| 4 baby corn cobs, halved lengthways |

**1** Mix together the wine, egg white, Chinese five-spice powder and cornflour in a large bowl.

**2** Add the prawns, squid and fish fillets to the mixture and stir to evenly coat. Remove the prawns with a slotted spoon, reserving any remaining cornflour mixture.

**3** Heat the oil in a preheated wok and deep-fry the prawns, squid and fish for 2–3 minutes. Remove the seafood from the wok with a slotted spoon and set aside.

**4** Pour off all but 1 tablespoon of the oil from the wok and return to the heat. Add the pepper, carrot and corn cobs to the wok and stir-fry for 4–5 minutes.

**5** Return the seafood to the wok with any reserved cornflour mixture and toss well to heat through thoroughly.

**6** Transfer to a warm serving dish and serve immediately.

### COOK'S TIP

Using a sharp knife, open up the squid rings and score a lattice pattern on the flesh to make them look more attractive.

# Szechuan Prawns

This spicy dish would make an excellent
light main course. Serve with rice or
noodles and a leafy green salad.

### Serves 4

225–300 g/8–10½ oz raw
tiger prawns

pinch of salt

½ egg white, lightly beaten

1 tsp Cornflour
Paste (see page 16)

600 ml/1 pint
vegetable oil

fresh coriander
leaves, to garnish

### SAUCE

1 tsp finely chopped fresh ginger root

2 spring onions,
finely chopped

1 garlic clove, finely chopped

3–4 small dried red chillies,
seeded and chopped

1 tbsp light soy sauce

1 tsp Chinese rice wine or dry sherry

1 tbsp tomato purée

1 tbsp oyster sauce

2–3 tbsp Chinese Stock
(see page 16) or water

a few drops of sesame oil

**1** Peel and devein the prawns, then
mix with the salt, egg white and
cornflour paste until coated all over.

**2** Heat the oil in a preheated wok
until it is smoking, then deep-fry the
prawns for about 1 minute. Remove
with a slotted spoon and drain on
kitchen paper.

**3** Pour off the oil, leaving about
1 tablespoon in the wok. Add all the
ingredients for the sauce, bring to the

boil and stir until smooth and
thoroughly blended.

**4** Add the prawns to the sauce,
stirring to blend. Garnish with
coriander leaves and serve.

### COOK'S TIP

If raw prawns are not available,
omit steps 1 and 2 and add the cooked
prawns before the sauce
in step 3.

# Sizzled Chilli Prawns

Large prawns are marinated in a chilli mixture
then stir-fried with cashews. Serve with
fluffy rice and braised vegetables.

| Serves 4 |
| --- |
| 5 tbsp soy sauce |
| 5 tbsp Chinese rice wine or dry sherry |
| 3 dried red chillies, seeded and chopped |
| 2 garlic cloves, crushed |
| 2 tsp grated fresh ginger root |
| 5 tbsp water |
| 500 g/1 lb 2 oz peeled cooked tiger prawns, deveined |
| 1 large bunch spring onions, chopped |
| 75 g/2³/₄ oz salted cashew nuts |
| 3 tbsp vegetable oil |
| 2 tsp cornflour |
| boiled rice and braised vegetables, to serve |

**1** Mix the soy sauce with the Chinese rice wine or sherry, chillies, garlic, ginger and water in a large bowl.

**2** Add the prawns, spring onions and cashew nuts and mix thoroughly so that they are well coated. Cover tightly and marinate in the refrigerator for at least 2 hours, stirring occasionally.

**3** Heat the oil in a preheated wok or large, heavy-based frying pan. Remove the prawns, spring onions and cashews from the marinade with a slotted spoon and add to the wok or pan, reserving the marinade. Stir-fry over a high heat for 1–2 minutes.

**4** Mix the marinade and cornflour. Add to the pan and cook for 30 seconds, until the marinade forms a slightly thickened shiny glaze over the prawn mixture.

**5** Transfer the chilli prawns to a warm serving dish and serve immediately, with plenty of boiled rice and a selection of braised vegetables.

# Prawn Stir-Fry with Lemon Grass

A very quick and tasty stir-fry using prawns, cucumber and oyster mushrooms, flavoured with lemon grass.

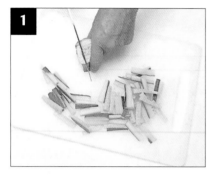

| Serves 4 |
| :---: |
| ½ cucumber |
| 2 tsp cornflour |
| 2 tbsp water |
| 1 tbsp dark soy sauce |
| ½ tsp fish sauce |
| 2 tbsp sunflower oil |
| 6 spring onions, halved lengthways and cut into 4-cm/1½-inch lengths |
| 1 stalk lemon grass, thinly sliced |
| 1 garlic clove, chopped |
| 1 tsp chopped fresh red chilli |
| 115 g/4 oz oyster mushrooms, torn into pieces |
| 1 tsp chopped fresh ginger root |
| 350 g/12 oz cooked peeled prawns, deveined |
| 2 tbsp Chinese rice wine or dry sherry |
| boiled rice, to serve |

**5** Stir the cornflour and soy sauce mixture and Chinese rice wine or dry sherry into the wok or pan and heat through, stirring constantly, until the sauce has thickened and is piping hot.

**6** Transfer to a warm serving dish and serve immediately with boiled rice.

**1** Cut the cucumber into thin strips measuring about 5 mm x 4 cm/ ¼ x 1¾ inches.

**2** In a small bowl, mix together the cornflour, water, soy sauce and fish sauce until smooth and set aside.

**3** Heat the oil in a preheated wok or large frying pan. Add the spring onions, cucumber, lemon grass, garlic, chilli, mushrooms and ginger and stir-fry for 2 minutes.

**4** Add the prawns and stir-fry for a further minute.

# Shrimp Fu Yong

The classic ingredients of this popular dish are eggs,
carrots and shrimp. Add extra ingredients such as
peas or crabmeat if wished.

| Serves 4 |
| --- |
| 2 tbsp vegetable oil |
| 1 carrot, grated |
| 5 eggs, beaten |
| 225 g/8 oz raw shrimp, peeled and deveined |
| 1 tbsp light soy sauce |
| pinch of Chinese five-spice powder |
| 2 spring onions, chopped |
| 2 tsp sesame seeds |
| 1 tsp sesame oil |

**1** Heat the oil in a preheated wok. Add the carrot and stir-fry for 1–2 minutes. Push the carrot to one side of the wok and add the eggs. Cook, stirring gently, for 1–2 minutes.

**2** Stir in the shrimp, soy sauce and five-spice powder and stir-fry for 2–3 minutes, until the shrimp change colour and the fu yong is almost dry.

**3** Turn out on to a warm serving plate, sprinkle with spring onions, sesame seeds and sesame oil and serve immediately.

**COOK'S TIP**

If only cooked prawns are available, add just before the end of cooking, but make sure they are fully incorporated into the fu yong.

# Cantonese Prawns

This prawn dish is very simple
and is ideal for supper or lunch
when time is short.

| Serves 4 |
| --- |
| 5 tbsp vegetable oil |
| 4 garlic cloves, crushed |
| 675 g/1¹/₂ lb raw prawns, peeled and deveined |
| 5-cm/2-inch piece fresh ginger root, chopped |
| 175 g/6 oz lean pork, diced |
| 1 leek, sliced |
| 3 eggs, beaten |
| shredded leek and red pepper matchsticks, to garnish |

| SAUCE |
| --- |
| 2 tbsp Chinese rice wine or dry sherry |
| 2 tbsp light soy sauce |
| 2 tsp caster sugar |
| 150 ml/¹/₄ pint fish stock |
| 4¹/₂ tsp cornflour |
| 3 tbsp water |

**1** Heat 2 tablespoons of the oil in a preheated wok and stir-fry the garlic for 30 seconds. Stir in the prawns and stir-fry for 5 minutes, until they change colour. Remove the prawns from the wok with a slotted spoon and keep warm.

**2** Add the remaining oil to the wok and stir-fry the ginger, pork and leek for 4–5 minutes, until the pork is lightly browned and sealed.

**3** Add the rice wine, sherry, soy sauce, sugar and fish stock to the wok. Blend the cornflour with the water to form a smooth paste and stir it into the wok. Cook, stirring, until the sauce thickens and clears.

**4** Return the prawns to the wok and add the beaten eggs. Cook for 5–6 minutes, gently stirring occasionally, until the egg sets. Transfer to a serving dish, garnish with shredded leek and pepper matchsticks and serve immediately.

### COOK'S TIP

Do not stir too vigorously after adding the eggs in step 4, or they will beak up into small hard pieces. They should be lightly scrambled.

# Sweet & Sour Prawns

A favourite with everyone, this superb dish tastes
as wonderful as it looks and takes
only minutes to prepare.

### Serves 4

300–350 g/10$^1$/$_2$–12 oz unpeeled raw
king or tiger prawns
vegetable oil for deep-frying
fresh coriander leaves,
to garnish

### SAUCE

1 tbsp vegetable oil

2 tsp finely chopped
spring onions

1 tsp finely chopped fresh ginger root

1 tbsp light soy sauce

2 tbsp sugar

3 tbsp rice vinegar

1 tsp Chinese rice wine or
dry sherry

125 ml/4 fl oz Chinese Stock
(see page 16) or water

1 tbsp Cornflour
Paste (see page 16)

a few drops of sesame oil

coriander leaves,
to garnish

**1** Remove the heads and legs from
the prawns, but leave the body shells
intact

**2** Heat the oil in a preheated wok.
Deep-fry the prawns in hot oil for
about 45–50 seconds, or until they
become bright orange. Remove with a
slotted spoon and drain on kitchen
paper.

**3** To make the sauce, heat the oil in a
preheated wok and add the spring
onions, ginger, soy sauce, sugar, rice
vinegar, Chinese rice wine wine or

sherry and stock or water. Bring the
mixture to the boil.

**4** Add the prawns to the sauce, blend
well, then thicken the sauce with the
cornflour paste. Stir until the sauce is

smooth and then add the sesame oil.

**5** Serve hot, garnished with coriander
leaves.

# Baked Crab with Ginger

The crab is interchangeable with lobster. In Chinese restaurants,
only live crabs and lobsters are used, but ready-cooked
ones can be used at home.

| Serves 4 |
| --- |
| 1 large or 2 medium crabs, weighing about 675 g/1½ lb in total |
| 2 tbsp Chinese rice wine or dry sherry |
| 1 egg, lightly beaten |
| 1 tbsp cornflour |
| 3–4 tbsp vegetable oil |
| 1 tbsp finely chopped fresh ginger root |
| 3–4 spring onions, cut into sections |
| 2 tbsp light soy sauce |
| 1 tsp sugar |
| about 75 ml/5 tbsp Chinese Stock (see page 16) or water |
| ½ tsp sesame oil |
| coriander leaves, to garnish |

**1** Cut the crab in half from the under-belly. Break off the claws and crack them with the back of the cleaver or a large kitchen knife.

**2** Discard the legs and crack the shell, breaking it into several pieces. Discard the feathery gills and the stomach sac. Place in a bowl with the wine, egg and cornflour and marinate for 10–15 minutes.

**3** Heat the oil in a large preheated wok and stir-fry the crab with the ginger and spring onions for 2–3 minutes.

**4** Add the soy sauce, sugar and stock or water, blend well and bring to the boil. Cover and cook for 3–4 minutes, then remove the lid from the wok. Sprinkle with sesame oil and transfer to a warm serving dish. Garnish with fresh coriander leaves and serve immediately.

## COOK'S TIP

Provide finger bowls for your guests as the only way to tackle this dish is with the hands.

# Squid in Oyster Sauce & Vegetables

Squid is a delicious fish, which contrary to popular belief, is not rubbery.
If prepared and cooked correctly, it is a quick-cooking,
attractive and tasty ingredient.

| Serves 4 |
| --- |
| 450 g/1 lb prepared squid |
| 150 ml/¼ pint vegetable oil |
| 1-cm/½-inch piece fresh ginger root, grated |
| 50 g/1¾ oz mangetout |
| 5 tbsp hot fish stock |
| red pepper triangles, to garnish |

| SAUCE |
| --- |
| 1 tbsp oyster sauce |
| 1 tbsp light soy sauce |
| pinch of caster sugar |
| 1 garlic clove, crushed |

**1** First prepare the squid by cutting down the centre of the bodies lengthways. Flatten the squid out, inside uppermost, and score a lattice design with a sharp knife, deep into the flesh.

**2** Prepare the sauce by combining the oyster sauce, soy sauce, sugar and crushed garlic.

**3** Heat the oil in a preheated wok until almost smoking. Lower the heat slightly and cook the squid until they curl. Remove with a slotted spoon and drain on kitchen paper.

**4** Pour off all but 2 tablespoons of the oil and return the wok to the heat. Add the ginger and mangetout and stir-fry for 1 minute. Return the squid to the wok and pour in the sauce and stock. Simmer the mixture

for 3 minutes, until thickened and heated through.

**5** Transfer to a warm serving dish, garnish with pepper triangles and serve immediately.

### COOK'S TIP

Take care not to overcook the squid, otherwise it will become rubbery and unappetizing.

# Fried Squid Flowers

The addition of green pepper and black bean sauce
to the squid makes a colourful and delicious dish
from the Cantonese school.

| Serves 4 |
| --- |
| 350–400 g/12–14 oz prepared and cleaned squid |
| 1 green pepper, seeded |
| 3–4 tbsp vegetable oil |
| 1 garlic clove, finely chopped |
| 1/4 tsp finely chopped fresh ginger root |
| 2 tsp finely chopped spring onions |
| 1/2 tsp salt |
| 2 tbsp crushed black bean sauce |
| 1 tsp Chinese rice wine or dry sherry |
| a few drops of sesame oil |

**1** Open up the squid and score the inside of the flesh deeply in a criss-cross pattern with a cleaver or sharp knife.

**2** Cut the squid into pieces about the size of an oblong postage stamp. Blanch in a bowl of boiling water for a few seconds. Drain and dry well on kitchen paper.

**3** Cut the pepper into small triangular pieces. Heat the oil in a preheated wok and stir-fry the pepper for about 1 minute. Add the garlic, ginger, spring onions, salt and squid. Continue stirring for 1 minute.

**4** Finally add the black bean sauce and wine, and blend well. Transfer to a warm serving dish, sprinkle with sesame oil and serve immediately.

# Fish & Ginger Stir-fry

This delicious and spicy recipe is a really
quick fish dish, ideal for midweek family meals
or light lunches at weekends.

| Serves 4 |
|---|
| 4 tbsp cornflour |
| $^1/_2$ tsp ground ginger |
| 675 g/1$^1/_2$ lb firm white fish fillets, skinned and cubed |
| 3 tbsp peanut oil |
| 2.5-cm/1-inch fresh ginger root, grated |
| 1 leek, thinly sliced |
| 1 tbsp white wine vinegar |
| 2 tbsp Chinese rice wine or dry sherry |
| 3 tbsp dark soy sauce |
| 1 tsp caster sugar |
| 2 tbsp lemon juice |

**1** Mix the cornflour and ginger in a bowl. Add the cubes of fish in batches, turning to coat evenly.

**2** Heat the oil in a preheated wok. Add the ginger and leek and stir-fry for 1 minute.

**3** Add the coated fish and cook for a further 5 minutes, until browned, stirring to prevent the fish from sticking together.

**4** Add the remaining ingredients and cook over a low heat for 3–4 minutes, until the fish is cooked through. Transfer to a serving dish and serve.

### COOK'S TIP

Use any firm white fish which will hold its shape, such as cod, haddock or monkfish.

# Poultry Dishes

Chinese cooks fully appreciate the
versatility of poultry. Chicken is probably
second only to pork in its popularity and
duck is usually served on special occasions.
Chicken lends itself perfectly to fast-cooking
methods, such as stir-frying. The meat can
easily be shredded, sliced or diced and its
delicate flavour blends with other ingredients,
from ginger and chillies to lemon and honey.

Recipes in this
chapter include
many Western
favourites, such as
Lemon Chicken.
Duck, with its
strong flavour

and richer, fattier meat, is usually prepared
with piquant or fruity sauces as a
counterbalance. It is sometimes cooked
with its skin on, which becomes deliciously
crisp. Although Aromatic & Crispy Duck is a
universally favourite dish, do not overlook
the other superb duck recipes in this
chapter, including Duck with Mangoes.

# Chinese Chicken Salad

This is a refreshing dish suitable for a summer meal or light lunch.
Its delicate combination of flavours provides
an interesting alternative to western-style salads.

| Serves 4 |
| --- |
| 225 g/8 oz skinless, boneless chicken breast |
| 2 tsp light soy sauce |
| 1 tsp sesame oil |
| 1 tsp sesame seeds |
| 2 tbsp vegetable oil |
| 125 g/4$^{1}/_{2}$ oz beansprouts |
| 1 red pepper, seeded and thinly sliced |
| 1 carrot, cut into matchsticks |
| 3 baby corn cobs, sliced |
| snipped chives and carrot matchsticks, to garnish |

### SAUCE

| |
| --- |
| 2 tsp rice wine vinegar |
| 1 tbsp light soy sauce |
| dash of chilli oil |

**1** Place the chicken in a shallow glass dish. Mix together the soy sauce and sesame oil in a small bowl and pour the mixture over the chicken. Sprinkle with sesame seeds and let stand for 20 minutes.

**2** Remove the chicken from the marinade and cut the meat into thin slices. Heat the vegetable oil in a preheated wok and stir-fry the chicken for 4–5 minutes, until cooked through. Remove with a slotted spoon and cool.

**3** Add the beansprouts, pepper, carrot and baby corn cobs to the wok and stir-fry for 2–3 minutes. Remove from the wok with a slotted spoon and cool.

**4** Mix the sauce ingredients together. Arrange the chicken and vegetables together on a serving plate. Spoon the sauce over the salad, garnish with chives and carrot matchsticks and serve immediately.

### COOK'S VARIATION

Add 150 g/5 oz mangetout instead of the pepper, if wished.

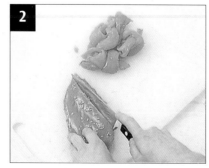

# Chicken with Beansprouts

This is the basic Chicken Chop Suey to be found
in almost every Chinese restaurant
all over the world.

| Serves 4 |
| --- |
| 115 g/4 oz boneless skinless chicken breasts |
| 1 tsp salt |
| ¼ egg white, beaten lightly |
| 2 tsp Cornflour Paste (see page 16) |
| about 300 ml/½ pint vegetable oil |
| 1 small onion, thinly sliced |
| 1 small green pepper, seeded and cut into thin matchsticks |
| 1 small carrot, cut into thin matchsticks |
| 115 g/4 oz fresh beansprouts |
| ½ tsp sugar |
| 1 tbsp light soy sauce |
| 1 tsp Chinese rice wine or dry sherry |
| 2–3 tbsp Chinese Stock (see page 16) |
| a few drops of sesame oil |
| chilli sauce, to serve |

**1** Thinly shred the chicken and mix
with a pinch of the salt, the egg white
and cornflour paste in that order.

**2** Heat the oil in a preheated wok.
Add the chicken and stir-fry for about
1 minute, until no longer pink,
stirring to separate the shreds.
Remove with a slotted spoon and
drain on kitchen paper.

**3** Carefully pour off the excess oil
from the wok, leaving about
2 tablespoons. Add the onion, green
pepper and carrot and stir-fry

for about 2 minutes, until tender, but
still crisp. Then add the beansprouts
and stir-fry for a few seconds, until
just tender.

**4** Add the chicken with the remaining
salt, sugar, soy sauce and Chinese rice
wine or sherry. Blend well and add the
stock or water. Sprinkle with the
sesame oil and serve at once.

# Kung Po Chicken with Cashew Nuts

Beware – this is quite a fiery dish, so if
you prefer a milder flavour, reduce the
number of dried chillies.

| Serves 4 |
|---|
| 225–300 g/8–10$\frac{1}{2}$ oz boneless skinless chicken breasts |
| $\frac{1}{4}$ tsp salt |
| $\frac{1}{3}$ egg white |
| 1 tsp Cornflour Paste (see page 16) |
| 1 green pepper, seeded |
| 4 tbsp vegetable oil |
| 1 spring onion, cut into short sections |
| a few small slices of fresh ginger root |
| 4–5 small dried red chillies, soaked, seeded and shredded |
| 2 tbsp crushed yellow bean sauce |
| 1 tsp Chinese rice wine or dry sherry |
| 115 g/4 oz roasted cashew nuts |
| a few drops of sesame oil |
| boiled rice, to serve |

1 minute, then add the chicken,
together with the yellow bean sauce
and rice wine or sherry. Blend well
and stir-fry for another minute.
Finally, stir in the cashew nuts and
sesame oil. Serve hot.

### COOK'S VARIATION

Peanuts, walnuts or almonds can be
used instead of the cashew nuts
if wished.

**1** Cut the chicken into small cubes
about the size of sugar lumps. Place in
a small bowl and mix with a pinch of
salt, the egg white and the cornflour
paste, in that order.

**2** Cut the green pepper into cubes or
triangles about the same size as the
chicken pieces.

**3** Heat the oil in a preheated wok,
add the chicken cubes and stir-fry for
about 1 minute, or until the colour
changes. Remove with a slotted spoon
and keep warm.

**4** Add the spring onion, ginger,
chillies and green pepper. Stir-fry for

# Chicken with Yellow Bean Sauce

Ready-made yellow bean sauce is available from supermarkets
and Chinese foodstores. It is made from yellow soya beans
and is quite salty in flavour.

| Serves 4 |
| --- |
| 450 g/1 lb skinless, boneless chicken breasts |
| 1 egg white, beaten |
| 1 tbsp cornflour |
| 1 tbsp wine vinegar |
| 1 tbsp light soy sauce |
| 1 tsp caster sugar |
| 3 tbsp vegetable oil |
| 1 garlic clove, crushed |
| 1-cm/$\frac{1}{2}$-inch piece fresh ginger root, grated |
| 1 green pepper, seeded and diced |
| 2 large mushrooms, sliced |
| 3 tbsp yellow bean sauce |
| red or green pepper strips, to garnish |

Stir in the vinegar and soy sauce mixture and return the chicken to the wok. Cook, stirring, for 1–2 minutes. Transfer to a warm serving dish, garnish with pepper strips and serve immediately.

**VARIATION**

Although darker in colour, black bean sauce would work equally well in this recipe.

**1** Cut the chicken into 2.5-cm/1-inch cubes. Mix the egg white and cornflour and dip the chicken pieces into the mixture to coat. Set aside for 20 minutes.

**2** Mix the vinegar, soy sauce and sugar in a bowl. Remove the chicken from the egg white mixture with a slotted spoon. Heat the oil in a preheated wok and stir-fry the chicken for 3–4 minutes, until golden brown. Remove the chicken from the wok and set aside.

**3** Add the garlic, ginger, pepper and mushrooms to the wok and stir-fry for 1–2 minutes.

**4** Add the yellow bean sauce and cook, stirring constantly, for 1 minute.

# Peanut Sesame Chicken

A quick-to-make chicken and vegetable dish, sesame seeds and peanuts
give it crunch and the fruit juice glaze gives
a lovely shiny coating to the sauce.

| Serves 4 |
| --- |
| 2 tbsp vegetable oil |
| 2 tbsp sesame oil |
| 450 g/1 lb boneless skinless chicken breasts, sliced into strips |
| 225 g/8 oz broccoli, divided into small florets |
| 225 g/8 oz baby or dwarf corn cobs, halved if large |
| 1 small red pepper, seeded and sliced |
| 2 tbsp soy sauce |
| 250 ml/9 fl oz orange juice |
| 2 tsp cornflour |
| 2 tbsp toasted sesame seeds |
| 50 g/1¾ oz roasted, shelled, unsalted peanuts |
| rice or noodles, to serve |

**1** Heat the oils in a preheated wok or large, heavy-based frying pan, add the chicken strips and stir-fry for about 4–5 minutes, until browned.

**2** Add the broccoli, corn cobs and red pepper and stir-fry for a further 1–2 minutes.

**3** Meanwhile, mix together the soy sauce, orange juice and cornflour. Stir into the chicken and vegetable mixture and cook, stirring constantly, until the sauce has thickened slightly and a glaze has developed.

**4** Stir in the sesame seeds and peanuts, mixing well. Heat for a further 3–4 minutes. Serve at once, with rice or noodles.

# Braised Chicken

This is a delicious way to cook a whole chicken.
It has a wonderful glaze,
which is served as a sauce.

| Serves 4 |
| --- |
| 1.5 kg/3 lb 5 oz chicken |
| 3 tbsp vegetable oil |
| 1 tbsp peanut oil |
| 2 tbsp dark brown sugar |
| 5 tbsp dark soy sauce |
| 150 ml/$\frac{1}{4}$ pint water |
| 2 garlic cloves, crushed |
| 1 small onion, chopped |
| 1 fresh red chilli, chopped |
| celery leaves and snipped chives, to garnish |

**1** Clean the chicken inside and out with damp kitchen paper.

**2** Put the oil in a large wok, add the sugar and heat gently until the sugar caramelizes. Stir in the soy sauce until thoroughly mixed.

**3** Add the chicken and turn it in the mixture to coat all over.

**4** Add the water, garlic, onion and chilli. Cover and simmer, turning the chicken from time to time, for approximately 1 hour, until it is tender and cooked through.

**5** Remove the chicken from the wok and set aside to rest. Increase the heat and reduce the sauce in the wok until it has thickened. Cut the chicken into individual portions and arrange on a arm serving plate.

**6** Garnish with celery leaves and chives and serve with the sauce.

### COOK'S TIP

You could prepare this recipe with chicken portions, reducing the cooking time to 25–30 minutes.

### COOK'S TIP

When caramelizing the sugar, do not have the heat too high, otherwise it may burn.

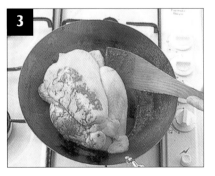
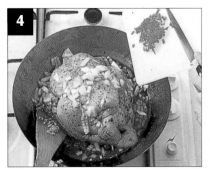

# Chicken with Pepper

Golden brown, deep-fried strips of chicken are
perfectly complemented by the tender-crisp
green pepper and the hint of chilli.

| Serves 4 |
|---|
| 300 g/10¹/₂ oz boneless skinless chicken breasts |
| 1 tsp salt |
| ¹/₂ egg white |
| 2 tsp Cornflour Paste (see page 16) |
| 1 green pepper, seeded |
| 300 ml/¹/₂ pint vegetable oil |
| 1 spring onion, finely shredded |
| a few strips of ginger root, finely shredded |
| 1–2 fresh red chillies, seeded and finely shredded |
| ¹/₂ tsp sugar |
| 1 tbsp Chinese rice wine or dry sherry |
| a few drops of sesame oil |

**1** Cut the chicken breasts into strips, then mix in a bowl with a pinch of the salt, the egg white and cornflour paste, in that order.

**2** Cut the pepper into thin shreds the same size and length as the chicken strips.

**3** Heat the oil in a preheated wok, and deep-fry the chicken strips, in batches, for about 1 minute, or until no longer pink. Remove the chicken strips with a slotted spoon, set aside and keep warm.

**4** Pour off the excess oil from the wok, leaving about 1 tablespoon. Add the spring onion, ginger, chillies and pepper. Stir-fry for about 1 minute, then return the chicken to the wok. Add the remaining salt, the sugar and wine or sherry. Stir-fry for another minute, sprinkle with sesame oil, transfer to a warm dish and serve immediately.

### COOK'S VARIATION

To make chicken with celery, substitute 4–6 thinly sliced celery sticks for the pepper, following the same method.

# Spicy Peanut Chicken

This quick dish has many variations, but is a classic combination
of ingredients, with peanuts, chicken and chillies
blending to give a wonderfully flavoured dish.

| Serves 4 |
| --- |
| 300 g/10½ oz skinless, boneless chicken breasts |
| 2 tbsp peanut oil |
| 125 g/4½ oz shelled peanuts |
| 1 fresh red chilli, sliced |
| 1 green pepper, seeded and cut into strips |
| fried rice, to serve |

| SAUCE |
| --- |
| 150 ml/¼ pint chicken stock |
| 1 tbsp Chinese rice wine or dry sherry |
| 1 tbsp light soy sauce |
| 1½ tsp light brown sugar |
| 2 garlic cloves, crushed |
| 1 tsp grated fresh ginger root |
| 1 tsp wine vinegar |
| 1 tsp sesame oil |

**1** Cut the chicken into 2.5-cm/1-inch cubes and set aside. Heat the peanut oil in a preheated wok and stir-fry the peanuts for 1 minute. Remove with a slotted spoon and set aside. Add the chicken and cook for 1–2 minutes. Stir in the chilli and green pepper and cook for 1 minute. Remove the ingredients from the wok with a slotted spoon and set aside.

**2** Blend half the peanuts in a food processor or crush with a rolling pin until almost smooth. Return the peanuts to the wok and add the chicken stock, Chinese rice wine or sherry, soy sauce, sugar, garlic, ginger and vinegar.

**3** Heat the sauce without boiling and stir in the chicken, chilli and pepper. Sprinkle the sesame oil into the wok, stir the mixture and cook for 1 minute. Transfer to serving plates and serve hot with fried rice.

**COOK'S TIP**

If necessary, blend the peanuts with a little of the stock to form a softer paste.

# Chicken Fu Yong

Most people associate fu yong with an omelette,
however, a fu yong dish should use egg whites
only to create a very delicate texture.

| Serves 4 |
| --- |
| 175 g/6 oz boneless skinless chicken breasts |
| 1 tsp Chinese rice wine or dry sherry |
| 1 tbsp cornflour |
| 3 eggs, beaten |
| $^1/_2$ tsp finely chopped spring onions |
| 3 tbsp vegetable oil |
| 115 g/4 oz peas |
| 1 tsp light soy sauce |
| salt and pepper |
| few drops of sesame oil |

**1** Cut the chicken across the grain
into very small, paper-thin slices,
using a cleaver. Place the slices in a
shallow dish, add ½ teaspoon salt,
pepper, the rice wine or sherry and
cornflour, and turn in the mixture
until they are well coated.

**2** Beat the eggs in a small bowl with a
pinch of salt and add the spring
onions.

**3** Heat the oil in a preheated wok,
add chicken slices and stir-fry for
about 1 minute, making sure that the
slices are kept separated. Pour the
beaten eggs over the chicken, and
lightly scramble until set. Do not stir
too vigorously, or the mixture will
break up in the oil. Stir the oil from
the bottom of the wok so that the fu
yong rises to the surface.

**4** Add the peas, soy sauce and salt to
taste and blend well. Sprinkle with
sesame oil and serve immediately.

# Chilli Chicken

This is quite a hot dish, using fresh chillies.
If you prefer a milder dish, halve the
number of chillies used.

| Serves 4 |
|---|
| 350 g/12 oz skinless, boneless chicken |
| $^1/_2$ tsp salt |
| 1 egg white, lightly beaten |
| 2 tbsp cornflour |
| 4 tbsp vegetable oil |
| 2 garlic cloves, crushed |
| 1-cm/$^1/_2$-inch piece fresh ginger root, grated |
| 1 red pepper, seeded and diced |
| 1 green pepper, seeded and diced |
| 2 fresh red chillies, chopped |
| 2 tbsp light soy sauce |
| 1 tbsp Chinese rice wine or dry sherry |
| 1 tbsp wine vinegar |

**1** Cut the chicken into cubes and place in a mixing bowl. Add the salt, egg white, cornflour and 1 tbsp of the oil. Turn the chicken in the mixture to coat.

**2** Heat the remaining oil in a preheated wok. Add the garlic and ginger and stir-fry for 30 seconds.

**3** Add the chicken pieces to the wok and stir-fry for 2–3 minutes, until golden brown.

**4** Stir in the peppers, soy sauce, Chinese rice wine or sherry and wine vinegar and cook for a further 2–3 minutes, until the chicken is cooked through. Transfer to a warm serving dish and serve immediately.

### COOK'S VARIATION

This recipe also works well with lean tender steak, cut into thin strips.

### COOK'S TIP

When preparing the chillies, wear rubber gloves to prevent the juices burning and irritating your hands.

# Szechuan Chilli Chicken

In China, the chicken pieces are chopped through
the bone for this dish, but if you do not possess
a cleaver, use boneless chicken meat.

| Serves 4 |
|---|
| 450 g/1 lb chicken thighs |
| 1/4 tsp pepper |
| 1 tbsp sugar |
| 2 tsp light soy sauce |
| 1 tsp dark soy sauce |
| 1 tbsp Chinese rice wine or dry sherry |
| 2 tsp cornflour |
| 2–3 tbsp vegetable oil |
| 1–2 garlic cloves, crushed |
| 2 spring onions, cut into short sections, with the green and white parts separated |
| 4–6 small dried red chillies, soaked and seeded |
| 2 tbsp yellow bean sauce |
| about 150 ml/1/4 pint Chinese Stock (see page 16) or water |

**1** Cut or chop the chicken thighs into
bite-size pieces and place in a shallow
dish. Mix together the pepper, sugar,
soy sauce, Chinese rice wine or sherry
and cornflour. Pour the mixture over
the chicken, turning to coat, and
marinate for 25–30 minutes.

**2** Heat the oil in a preheated wok,
add the chicken pieces and stir-fry for
about 1–2 minutes, until lightly
brown. Remove the chicken pieces
with a slotted spoon, set aside and
keep warm.

**3** Add the garlic, the white parts of
the spring onions, the chillies and
yellow bean sauce to the wok. Stir-fry
for about 30 seconds, blending well.

**4** Return the chicken pieces to the
wok and stir-fry for approximately
1–2 minutes. Add the stock or water,
bring to the boil, lower the heat and
cover. Braise over a medium heat for

5–6 minutes, stirring once or twice.
Transfer to a warm serving dish,
garnish with the green parts of the
spring onions and serve immediately.

# Chicken Chop Suey

Both well known and popular, chop suey dishes are easy
to make and delicious. They are based on beansprouts and
soy sauce with a meat or vegetable flavouring.

| Serves 4 |
| --- |
| 4 tbsp light soy sauce |
| 2 tsp light brown sugar |
| 500 g/1 lb 2 oz skinless, boneless chicken, cut into strips |
| 3 tbsp vegetable oil |
| 2 onions, quartered |
| 2 garlic cloves, crushed |
| 350 g/12 oz beansprouts |
| 3 tsp sesame oil |
| 1 tbsp cornflour |
| 3 tbsp water |
| 425 ml/³/₄ pint Chinese Stock (see page 16) or chicken stock |
| shredded leek, to garnish |

**1** Mix the soy sauce and sugar
together. Place the chicken in a
shallow glass dish and spoon the soy
mixture over it, turning to coat. Let
stand for 20 minutes.

**2** Heat the vegetable oil in a
preheated wok. Add the chicken and
stir-fry for 2–3 minutes, until golden
brown all over.

**3** Add the onion quarters and the
garlic and stir-fry for a further
2 minutes.

**4** Add the beansprouts and cook for a
further 4–5 minutes. Stir in the
sesame oil.

**5** Blend the cornflour with the water
to form a smooth paste. Pour the
stock into the wok, together with the
cornflour paste and bring to the boil,
stirring until the sauce is thickened
and clear.

**6** Transfer to a warm serving dish,
garnish with shredded leek and serve.

**VARIATION**

This recipe may be made with beef,
pork or mixed vegetables, changing the
flavour of the stock accordingly.

# Chicken with Mushrooms

Chinese dried mushrooms should be used for this dish –
otherwise use fresh shiitake mushrooms
rather than fresh white mushrooms.

| Serves 4 |
| --- |
| 300–350 g/10½–12 oz boneless skinless chicken breasts |
| ½ tsp sugar |
| 1 tbsp light soy sauce |
| 1 tsp Chinese rice wine or dry sherry |
| 2 tsp cornflour |
| 4–6 Chinese dried mushrooms, soaked in warm water for 30 minutes |
| 1 tbsp finely shredded fresh ginger root |
| salt and pepper |
| a few drops of sesame oil |
| fresh coriander or flat leaf parsley leaves, to garnish |

**1** Cut the chicken into bite-size pieces and place in a bowl. Mix together the sugar, soy sauce, Chinese rice wine or sherry and cornflour. Pour the mixture over the chicken, turning to coat thoroughly. Marinate for 25–30 minutes.

**2** Drain the mushrooms and pat dry with absorbent kitchen paper. Slice the mushrooms into thin shreds, discarding any hard pieces of stem.

**3** Place the chicken pieces, well spread out, on a heatproof dish that will fit inside a bamboo steamer. Arrange the mushroom and ginger shreds on top of the chicken and sprinkle with salt, pepper and sesame oil to taste.

**4** Place the dish on the rack inside a hot steamer or on a rack in a wok filled with hot water and steam over high heat for 20 minutes. Serve immediately, garnished with coriander or parsley leaves.

### COOK'S TIP

If using fresh shiitake mushrooms, be careful not to overcook them, as they will then become tough.

# Crispy Chicken

In this recipe the chicken is brushed in a syrup and
deep-fried until golden. It is a little time consuming,
but well worth the effort.

| Serves 4 |
|---|
| 1.5 kg/3 lb 5 oz oven-ready chicken |
| 2 tbsp clear honey |
| 2 tsp Chinese five-spice powder |
| 2 tbsp wine vinegar |
| 850 ml/1$^1/_2$ pints vegetable oil, for frying |
| chilli sauce, to serve |

**1** Wash the chicken inside and out and pat dry with kitchen paper. Bring a large saucepan of water to the boil and remove from the heat. Place the chicken in the water, cover and set aside for 20 minutes. Remove the chicken from the water and pat thoroughly dry with kitchen paper. Chill in the refrigerator overnight.

**2** Mix the honey, Chinese five-spice powder and vinegar together. Brush some of the mixture over the chicken and return the chicken to the refrigerator for 20 minutes. Repeat this process until all the glaze has been used. Return the chicken to the refrigerator for at least 2 hours after the final coating.

**3** Using a cleaver or a very sharp knife, open the chicken out by splitting it through the centre through the breast and then cut each half into four pieces.

**4** Heat the oil for deep-frying in a wok until almost smoking. Reduce the heat and fry each piece of chicken for 5–7 minutes, until golden and cooked through. Remove from the oil and drain on absorbent kitchen paper. Serve hot with a little chilli sauce.

### COOK'S TIP

If it is easier, buy chicken portions and use instead of a whole chicken.

# Chicken with Celery & Cashew Nuts

Yellow bean sauce, widely available in bottles, gives
this quick and easy dish a really authentic taste.
Pecan nuts can be used in place of cashews.

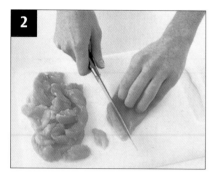

| Serves 4 |
|---|
| 500 g/1 lb 2 oz boneless skinless chicken breasts |
| 2 tbsp sunflower or vegetable oil |
| 115 g/4 oz unsalted cashew nuts |
| 4–6 spring onions, thinly sliced diagonally |
| 5–6 celery sticks, thinly sliced diagonally |
| 175 g/6 oz jar yellow bean sauce |
| salt and pepper |
| celery leaves, to garnish (optional) |
| boiled rice, to serve |

**1** Cut the chicken into thin slices across the grain using a Chinese cleaver or very sharp knife.

**2** Heat the oil in a preheated wok. Add the cashew nuts and stir-fry until they begin to brown, then add the chicken and stir-fry until well sealed and almost cooked through.

**3** Add the spring onions and celery and continue to stir-fry for 2–3 minutes.

**4** Add the yellow bean sauce, season lightly with salt and pepper and toss until the chicken and vegetables are thoroughly coated with the sauce and piping hot.

**5** Transfer to a warm serving dish, garnish with the celery leaves, if wished, and serve immediately with boiled rice.

# Stir-Fried Duck with Broccoli & Peppers

This is an attractive dish using different coloured peppers and broccoli to make it both tasty and appealing to the eye.

| Serves 4 |
| --- |
| 1 egg white |
| 2 tbsp cornflour |
| 450 g/1 lb skinless, boneless duck meat |
| vegetable oil, for deep-frying |
| 1 red pepper, seeded and diced |
| 1 yellow pepper, seeded and diced |
| 125 g/4½ oz small broccoli florets |
| 1 garlic clove, crushed |
| 2 tbsp light soy sauce |
| 2 tsp Chinese rice wine or dry sherry |
| 1 tsp light brown sugar |
| 125 ml/4 fl oz Chinese Stock (see page 16) or chicken stock |
| 2 tsp sesame seeds |

**1** Beat the egg white and cornflour together in a mixing bowl. Cut the duck into 2.5-cm/1-inch cubes and stir into the egg white mixture. Let stand for 30 minutes.

**2** Heat the oil for deep-frying in a wok until almost smoking. Remove the duck from the egg white mixture and fry in the oil for 4–5 minutes, until crisp. Remove the duck from the oil with a slotted spoon and drain on kitchen paper.

**3** Add the peppers and broccoli to the wok and fry for 2–3 minutes. Remove with a slotted spoon and drain on kitchen paper.

**4** Pour all but 2 tablespoons of oil from the wok and return it to the heat. Add the garlic and stir-fry for 30 seconds. Stir in the soy sauce, rice wine or sherry, sugar and stock and bring to the boil. Stir in the duck and vegetables and cook for 1–2 minutes. Spoon the duck and vegetables on to a warm serving plate and sprinkle with sesame seeds. Serve immediately.

# Aromatic & Crispy Duck

The pancakes traditionally served with this dish take
ages to make. Buy ready-made ones from Chinese foodstores,
or use crisp lettuce instead.

| Serves 4 |
| --- |
| 2 large duck quarters |
| 1 tsp salt |
| 3–4 pieces star anise |
| 1 tsp Szechuan red peppercorns |
| 1 tsp cloves |
| 2 cinnamon sticks, broken into pieces |
| 2–3 spring onions, cut into short sections |
| 4–5 small slices fresh ginger root |
| 3–4 tbsp Chinese rice wine or dry sherry |
| vegetable oil, for deep-frying |

### TO SERVE

| |
| --- |
| 12 ready-made pancakes or 12 crisp lettuce leaves |
| hoi-sin or plum sauce |
| $^1/_4$ cucumber, thinly shredded |
| 3–4 spring onions, thinly shredded |

**1** Rub the duck pieces with the salt and arrange the star anise, peppercorns, cloves and cinnamon on top. Sprinkle with the spring onions, ginger and wine or sherry. Marinate for at least 3–4 hours.

**2** Arrange the duck pieces (with the marinade spices) on a plate that will fit inside a bamboo steamer. Pour some hot water into a wok, place the bamboo steamer in the wok, sitting on a trivet. Put in the duck and cover with the bamboo lid. Steam the duck pieces (with the marinade) over high heat for at least 2–3 hours, until tender and cooked through. Top up the hot water from time to time as required.

**3** Remove the duck and set aside to cool for at least 4–5 hours – this is very important, for unless the duck is cold and dry, it will not be crispy.

**4** Pour off the water and wipe the wok dry. Pour in the oil and heat until smoking. Deep-fry the duck pieces, skin-side down, for 4–5 minutes, or until crisp and brown. Remove and drain on kitchen paper.

**5** Scrape the meat off the bones on to a dish. Put the pancakes or lettuce, hoisin or plum sauce, cucumber and spring onions on serving dishes. To serve, place 1 teaspoon of hoi-sin or plum sauce on the centre of a pancake (or lettuce leaf), add a few pieces of cucumber and spring onion, with a portion of the duck meat. Wrap up to form a small parcel and eat with your fingers.

# Duck In Spicy Sauce

Chinese five-spice powder gives a lovely flavour
to this sliced duck, and the chilli
adds a little subtle heat.

| Serves 4 |
| --- |
| 1 tbsp vegetable oil |
| 1 tsp grated fresh ginger root |
| 1 garlic clove, crushed |
| 1 fresh red chilli, chopped |
| 350 g/12 oz skinless, boneless duck meat, cut into strips |
| 125 g/4$^1/_2$ oz cauliflower florets |
| 50 g/1$^3/_4$ oz mangetout |
| 50 g/1$^3/_4$ oz baby corn cobs, halved lengthways |
| 300 ml/$^1/_2$ pint chicken stock |
| 1 tsp Chinese five-spice powder |
| 2 tsp Chinese rice wine or dry sherry |
| 1 tsp cornflour |
| 2 tsp water |
| 1 tsp sesame oil |

**1** Heat the vegetable oil in a preheated wok. Add the ginger, garlic, chilli and duck and stir-fry for 2–3 minutes. Remove with a slotted spoon and set aside.

**2** Add the vegetables to the wok and stir-fry for 2–3 minutes. Pour off any excess oil from the wok.

**3** Return the duck to the wok and pour in the stock. Sprinkle the Chinese five-spice powder over the top, stir in the Chinese rice wine or sherry and cook over a low heat for 15 minutes, until the duck is tender.

**4** Blend the cornflour with the water to form a smooth paste and stir it into the wok, together with the sesame oil.

Bring to the boil, stirring until the sauce has thickened and cleared. Transfer the duck in spicy sauce to a warm serving dish and serve immediately.

### COOK'S TIP

Omit the chilli for a milder dish, or seed the chilli before adding it to remove some of the heat.

# Honey & Soy Glazed Duck

This honey and soy glaze gives a wonderful sheen
and flavour to the duck skin. It is so simple,
yet utterly delicious.

### Serves 4

1 tsp dark soy sauce

2 tbsp clear honey

1 tsp garlic vinegar

2 garlic cloves, crushed

1 tsp ground star anise

2 tsp cornflour

2 tsp water

2 large boneless duck breasts,
about 225g/8 oz each

### TO GARNISH

celery leaves

cucumber matchsticks

snipped chives

**1** Mix together the soy sauce, honey,
vinegar, garlic and star anise.

**2** Blend the cornflour with the water
to form a smooth paste and stir it into
the honey and soy sauce mixture.

**3** Place the duck breasts in a shallow
ovenproof dish and brush the soy
marinade over them, turning to coat
them completely. Cover and marinate
in the refrigerator for at least 2 hours
or overnight if possible.

**4** Cook the duck in a preheated oven
at 220°C/425°F/Gas Mark 7 for about
20–25 minutes, basting frequently
with the glaze.

**5** Remove the duck from the oven
and cook under a preheated grill for
3–4 minutes to caramelize the top of
the duck.

**6** Transfer the duck to a chopping
board and cut into thin slices.

**7** Arrange the duck slices on a warm
serving plate, garnish with celery
leaves, cucumber matchsticks and
snipped chives and serve.

### COOK'S TIP

The duck breasts are cooked through if
the juices run clear when a knife is
inserted into the thickest part of the
flesh.

# Duck With Mangoes

Use fresh mangoes in this recipe for a terrific flavour
and colour. If unavailable, use canned mangoes
and rinse them before using.

| Serves 4 |
| --- |
| 2 medium-size ripe mangoes |
| 300 ml/½ pint chicken stock |
| 2 large skinless duck breasts, about 225 g/8 oz each |
| 2 garlic cloves, crushed |
| 1 tsp grated fresh ginger root |
| 3 tbsp vegetable oil |
| 1 tsp wine vinegar |
| 1 tsp light soy sauce |
| 1 leek, sliced |
| freshly chopped parsley, to garnish |

**1** Peel the mangoes and cut the flesh from each side of the stone. Cut the flesh into strips.

**2** Put half the mango pieces and the stock in a food processor and process until smooth. Alternatively, press half the fruit through a fine strainer and mix with the stock.

**3** Rub the duck with the garlic and ginger. Heat the oil in a preheated wok and cook the duck breasts, turning, until sealed. Reserve the oil in the wok and remove the duck. Place on a rack over a roasting tin and cook in a preheated oven at 220°C/425°F/Gas 7 for 20 minutes, until cooked through.

**4** Meanwhile, place the mango and stock mixture in a saucepan and add the vinegar and soy sauce. Bring to the boil and cook over a high heat until reduced by half.

**5** Heat the oil reserved in the wok. Add the leek and remaining mango and stir-fry for 1 minute. Remove from the wok with a slotted spoon, arrange on the base of a serving dish and keep warm.

**6** Slice the cooked duck breasts and arrange the slices on top of the leek and mango mixture.

**7** Pour the sauce on top and serve immediately.

# Meat Dishes

The most popular meat throughout China is pork, as it is both economical and versatile. All cuts are tender and suitable for all cooking techniques, including stir-frying, braising and steaming. A spit-roasted pig is an essential feature of a festive occasion, such as a wedding. For everyday meals, the richness of the meat is balanced by spicy or fruity marinades and sauces and crisp vegetables.

Lamb is popular in northern China, but is rarely eaten elsewhere. Most lamb recipes are light and simple.

Beef is eaten in all regions of China, but as it is much less versatile and economic than pork, it is not so popular. Only certain cuts, such as fillet and sirloin, lend themselves to fast-cooking techniques. Other cuts of beef are usually braised.

Two meat dishes, one of which is usually pork, are served at family meals. For a formal dinner, at least two meat dishes would form part of the appetizers, as well.

# Lamb Meatballs in Soy Sauce

These small meatballs are made with minced lamb
and spiced with chilli, garlic, parsley and Chinese
curry powder for a delicious flavour.

| Serves 4 |
| --- |
| 450 g/1 lb minced lamb |
| 3 garlic cloves, crushed |
| 2 spring onions, finely chopped |
| $^1/_2$ tsp chilli powder |
| 1 tsp Chinese curry powder |
| 1 tbsp chopped fresh parsley |
| 25 g/1 oz fresh white breadcrumbs |
| 1 egg, beaten |
| 3 tbsp vegetable oil |
| 125 g/4$^1/_2$ oz Chinese cabbage, shredded |
| 1 leek, sliced |
| 1 tbsp cornflour |
| 2 tbsp water |
| 300 ml/$^1/_2$ pint lamb stock |
| 1 tbsp dark soy sauce |
| shredded leek, to garnish |

**1** Mix the lamb, garlic, spring onions, chilli powder, Chinese curry powder, chopped parsley and breadcrumbs together in a bowl. Work the egg into the mixture, bringing it together until firm. Roll into 16 small balls of even size between the palms of your hands.

**2** Heat the oil in a preheated wok. Add the cabbage and leek and stir-fry for 1 minute. Remove from the wok with a slotted spoon and set aside.

**3** Add the meatballs to the wok and fry, turning gently but frequently, for 3–4 minutes, until browned all over and almost cooked through.

**4** Mix the cornflour and water to a smooth paste. Pour the stock and soy sauce into the wok and cook for 2–3 minutes. Stir in the cornflour paste. Bring to the boil, stirring until thick and clear.

**5** Return the cabbage and leek to the wok and cook for 1 minute, until heated through. Transfer the cabbage and leek to a warm serving dish, top with the meatballs and garnish with the shredded leek. Serve immediately.

# Hot Lamb

This really is quite a spicy dish, using 2 chillies in the rich sauce.
Halve the number of chillies to reduce the heat or
seed the chillies before using if desired.

| Serves 4 |
| :---: |
| 450 g/1 lb lean boneless lamb, cut into 2.5-cm/1-inch cubes |
| 2 tbsp hoi-sin sauce |
| 1 tbsp dark soy sauce |
| 1 garlic clove, crushed |
| 2 tsp grated fresh ginger root |
| 2 tbsp vegetable oil |
| 2 onions, sliced |
| 1 fennel bulb, sliced |
| 4 tbsp water |
| SAUCE |
| 1 large fresh red chilli, cut into thin strips |
| 1 fresh green chilli, cut into thin strips |
| 2 tbsp rice wine vinegar |
| 2 tsp light brown sugar |
| 2 tbsp peanut oil |
| 1 tsp sesame oil |

**1** Place the lamb in a shallow glass dish. Mix together the hoi-sin sauce, soy sauce, garlic and ginger in a bowl. Pour the mixture over the lamb, turning it to coat well. Marinate for 20 minutes.

**2** Heat the vegetable oil in a preheated wok until nearly smoking. Lower the heat slightly, add the lamb and stir-fry for 1–2 minutes. Add the onions and fennel and cook for a further 2 minutes, until they begin to brown. Stir in the water, cover and cook for 2–3 minutes.

**3** Meanwhile, make the sauce. Put the chillies, vinegar, sugar, peanut oil and sesame oil in a saucepan and cook over a low heat for 3–4 minutes, stirring occasionally.

**4** Transfer the lamb and onions to a warm serving dish, top with the sauce and serve immediately.

**VARIATION**

Use beef, pork or duck instead of the lamb and vary the vegetables, using leeks or celery instead of the onion and fennel.

# Stir-fried Lamb with Sesame Seeds

This is a very simple, but delicious dish, in which lean pieces of lamb
are cooked in sugar and soy sauce and sprinkled with sesame seeds,
then served on a bed of leeks and carrot.

| Serves 4 |
| --- |
| 2 tbsp peanut oil |
| 450 g/1 lb boneless lean lamb, cut into strips |
| 2 leeks, sliced |
| 1 carrot, cut into matchsticks |
| 2 garlic cloves, crushed |
| 75 ml/3 fl oz lamb or vegetable stock |
| 2 tsp light brown sugar |
| 1 tbsp dark soy sauce |
| $4^1/_2$ tsp sesame seeds |

**1** Heat the peanut oil in a large
preheated wok.

**2** Add the lamb and stir-fry for
2–3 minutes. Remove the lamb from
the wok with a slotted spoon, set
aside and keep warm.

**3** Add the leek, carrot and garlic and
stir-fry in the remaining oil for
1–2 minutes. Remove the vegetables
from the wok and carefully drain off
any remaining oil.

**4** Place the stock, sugar and soy sauce
in the wok and add the lamb. Cook,
stirring constantly, for 2–3 minutes,
or until the lamb is thoroughly coated
with the sauce.

**5** Sprinkle the sesame seeds over the
top, turning the lamb to coat.

**6** Spoon the leek and carrot mixture
on to a warm serving plate and top
with the sesame-coated lamb. Serve
immediately.

### COOK'S TIP

To bring out the full flavour and
fragrance of the sesame seeds, dry-fry
or toast them briefly before sprinkling
them over the lamb.

### COOK'S TIP

Be careful not to burn the sugar in the
wok when heating and coating the
meat, otherwise the flavour of the dish
will be spoiled.

# Five-Spiced Lamb

Chinese five-spice powder is a blend of cinnamon, fennel,
star anise, ginger and cloves. It gives an authentic
Chinese flavour to many dishes.

| Serves 4 |
| --- |
| 675 g/1½ lb lean boneless lamb (leg or fillet) |
| 2 tsp Chinese five-spice powder |
| 3 tbsp sunflower oil |
| 1 red pepper, seeded and thinly sliced |
| 1 green pepper, seeded and thinly sliced |
| 1 yellow or orange pepper, seeded and thinly sliced |
| 4–6 spring onions, thinly sliced diagonally |
| 175 g/6 oz French or fine beans, cut into 4-cm/1½-inch lengths |
| 2 tbsp soy sauce |
| 4 tbsp Chinese rice wine or dry sherry |
| salt and pepper |
| Chinese noodles, to serve |
| **TO GARNISH** |
| strips of red and yellow pepper |
| fresh coriander leaves |

**1** Cut the lamb into narrow strips, about 4 cm/1½ inches long, across the grain. Place in a bowl, add the five-spice powder and ¼ teaspoon salt, mix well, cover and marinate in a cool place for at least an hour or up to 24 hours.

**2** Heat half the oil in a preheated wok until it is almost smoking. Lower the heat slightly, add the lamb and stir-fry briskly for 3–4 minutes, until almost cooked. Remove from the wok with a slotted spoon and keep warm.

**3** Add the remaining oil to the wok and when hot, add the peppers and spring onions. Stir-fry for 2–3 minutes, then add the beans and stir-fry for 1–2 minutes.

**4** Add the soy sauce and rice wine or sherry to the wok. Return the lamb to the wok, together with any juices. Cook, stirring, for 1–2 minutes until the lamb is hot and thoroughly coated in the sauce. Season to taste.

**5** Serve with noodles, garnished with strips of red and green pepper and fresh coriander.

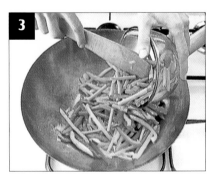

# Lamb in Garlic Sauce

This dish contains Szechuan pepper
which is quite hot and may be replaced
with black pepper if preferred.

| Serves 4 |
| --- |
| 450 g/1 lb lamb fillet or loin |
| 2 tbsp dark soy sauce |
| 2 tsp sesame oil |
| 2 tbsp Chinese rice wine or dry sherry |
| 1/2 tsp Szechuan pepper |
| 4 tbsp vegetable oil |
| 4 garlic cloves, crushed |
| 50 g/1 3/4 oz canned water chestnuts, drained and quartered |
| 1 green pepper, seeded and sliced |
| 1 tbsp wine vinegar |
| 1 tbsp sesame oil |

**1** Cut the lamb into 2.5-cm/1-inch pieces and place in a shallow dish.

**2** Mix together 1 tablespoon of the soy sauce, the sesame oil, Chinese rice wine or sherry and Szechuan pepper in a bowl.

**3** Pour the mixture over the lamb, turning to coat, and marinate for 30 minutes.

**4** Heat the vegetable oil in a large preheated wok.

**5** Remove the lamb from the marinade and add to the wok, together with the garlic. Stir-fry for 2–3 minutes, then remove the lamb from the wok with a slotted spoon and set aside.

**6** Add the water chestnuts and pepper and stir-fry for 1 minute. Add

the remaining soy sauce and the wine vinegar.

**7** Return the lamb to the wok and add the sesame oil. Cook for 1–2 minutes. Transfer to a warm serving dish and serve immediately.

**COOK'S TIP**

Sesame oil is used as a flavouring, rather than oil for frying, as it burns readily, hence it is added at the end of cooking.

# Oyster Sauce Beef

This is a standard meat and vegetables recipe,
which can be adapted for most kinds of meat
and whatever vegetables are in season.

| Serves 4 |
| --- |
| 350 g/12 oz steak |
| 1 tsp sugar |
| 1 tbsp light soy sauce |
| 1 tsp Chinese rice wine or dry sherry |
| 1 tsp Cornflour Paste (see page 16) |
| $^1/_2$ small carrot |
| 50 g/1$^3/_4$ oz mangetout |
| 50 g/1$^3/_4$ oz canned bamboo shoots, drained |
| 50 g/1$^3/_4$ oz canned straw mushrooms |
| about 300 ml/$^1/_2$ pint vegetable oil |
| 1 spring onion, cut into short sections |
| 2–3 small slices fresh ginger root |
| $^1/_2$ tsp salt |
| 2 tbsp oyster sauce |
| 2–3 tbsp Chinese Stock (see page 16) or water |

**1** Cut the steak into small, thin slices. Place in a shallow dish with the sugar, soy sauce, wine and cornflour paste and marinate for 25–30 minutes.

**2** Slice the carrots, mangetout, bamboo shoots and straw mushrooms so that as far as possible the vegetable pieces are of uniform size and thickness.

**3** Heat the oil in a preheated wok and add the beef slices. Stir-fry for about 1 minute, then remove with a slotted spoon and keep warm.

**4** Carefully pour off the excess oil, leaving about 1 tablespoon in the wok. Add the carrot, mangetout, bamboo shoots, straw mushrooms, spring onion and ginger and stir-fry for about 2 minutes.

**5** Return the steak to the wok and add the salt, oyster sauce and stock or water. Blend well and cook, stirring constantly, until heated through.

**6** Transfer to a warmed serving dish and serve immediately.

# Beef & Pak Choi

A colourful selection of vegetables is stir-fried
with tender strips of steak to make this tasty,
nutritious and quick dish.

| Serves 4 |
| --- |
| 1 large head of pak choi, about 250–275 g/9–9¹/₂ oz, torn into large pieces |
| 2 tbsp vegetable oil |
| 2 garlic cloves, crushed |
| 450 g/1 lb rump or fillet steak, cut into thin strips |
| 150 g/5¹/₂ oz mangetout, trimmed |
| 150 g/5¹/₂ oz baby corn cobs |
| 6 spring onions, chopped |
| 2 red peppers, seeded and thinly sliced |
| 2 tbsp oyster sauce |
| 1 tbsp fish sauce |
| 1 tbsp sugar |
| boiled rice or noodles, to serve |

**1** Steam the pak choi leaves over boiling water until they are just tender. Remove from the steamer and keep warm.

**2** Heat the oil in a preheated wok or a large, heavy-based frying pan. Add the garlic and strips of steak and stir-fry for 1–2 minutes, until just browned all over.

**3** Add the mangetout, baby corn cobs, spring onions, pepper, oyster sauce, fish sauce and sugar, mixing thoroughly. Stir-fry for a further 2–3 minutes until the vegetables are just tender, but still remain crisp and firm to the bite.

**4** Arrange the pak choi leaves on the base of a warm serving dish and spoon the beef and vegetable mixture into the centre. Serve the stir-fry immediately, with plain boiled rice or noodles.

## VARIATION

Chinese flat cabbage or Chinese flowering cabbage could be used instead of pak choi.

# Spicy Beef & Broccoli Stir-Fry

This is a great combination of ingredients in terms
of colour and flavour, and is so simple
and quick to prepare.

| Serves 4 |
| --- |
| 225 g/8 oz lean steak, trimmed |
| 2 garlic cloves, crushed |
| dash of chilli oil |
| 1-cm/$^1/_2$-inch piece fresh ginger root, grated |
| $^1/_2$ tsp Chinese five-spice powder |
| 2 tbsp dark soy sauce |
| 2 tbsp vegetable oil |
| 150 g/$5^1/_2$ oz broccoli florets |
| 1 tbsp light soy sauce |
| 150 ml/$^1/_4$ pint beef stock |
| 2 tsp cornflour |
| 4 tsp water |
| carrot strips, to garnish |

**1** Cut the steak into thin strips and place in a shallow glass dish. Mix together the garlic, chilli sauce, ginger, five-spice powder and soy sauce in a bowl. Pour the mixture over the steak, tossing to coat the strips evenly.

**2** Heat 1 tablespoon of the oil in a preheated wok. Add the broccoli and stir-fry for 4–5 minutes. Remove from the wok with a slotted spoon and set aside.

**3** Heat the remaining oil in the wok. Add the steak, together with the marinade, and stir-fry for 2–3 minutes, until the beef is sealed. Return the broccoli to the wok and stir in the soy sauce and stock.

**4** Blend the cornflour with the water to form a smooth paste and stir it into

the wok. Bring to the boil, stirring constantly until thickened and clear. Cook for 1 further minute. Transfer to a warm serving dish, garnish with the carrot strips arranged in a lattice pattern on top and serve immediately.

### COOK'S TIP

Marinate the beef for several hours for a fuller flavour. Cover and marinate in the refrigerator if preparing in advance.

# Beef & Chilli Black Bean Sauce

It is not necessary to use the expensive cuts of steak
for this recipe: the meat will be tender as it is cut
into small, thin slices and marinated.

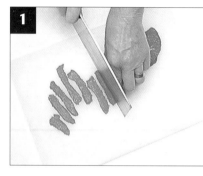

| Serves 4 |
| --- |
| 225–275 g/8–9$\frac{1}{2}$ oz steak (such as rump) |
| 1 small onion |
| 1 small green pepper, seeded |
| about 300 ml/$\frac{1}{2}$ pint vegetable oil |
| 1 spring onion, cut into short sections |
| a few small slices of fresh ginger root |
| 1–2 small green or red chillies, seeded and sliced |
| 2 tbsp crushed black bean sauce |

| MARINADE |
| --- |
| $\frac{1}{2}$ tsp bicarbonate of soda or baking powder |
| $\frac{1}{2}$ tsp sugar |
| 1 tbsp light soy sauce |
| 2 tsp Chinese rice wine or dry sherry |
| 2 tsp Cornflour Paste (see page 16) |
| 2 tsp sesame oil |

**4** Pour off the excess oil, leaving about 1 tablespoon in the wok. Add the spring onion, ginger, chillies, onion and green pepper and stir-fry for about 1 minute. Add the black bean sauce and stir until smooth. Return the steak strips to the wok, blend well and stir-fry for another minute. Transfer to a warm serving dish and serve immediately.

**1** Cut the steak into small thin strips. Mix together all the marinade ingredients in a shallow dish, add the steak strips, turn to coat and marinate for at least 2–3 hours.

**2** Cut the onion and green pepper into small equal-size squares.

**3** Heat the oil in a preheated wok. Add the steak strips and stir-fry for about 1 minute, or until the colour changes. Remove with a slotted spoon and drain on kitchen paper.

# Peppered Beef Cashew

A simple but stunning dish of tender strips of beef mixed with
crunchy cashew nuts, coated in a hot sauce.
Serve with rice noodles.

| Serves 4 |
| --- |
| 1 tbsp peanut or sunflower oil |
| 1 tbsp sesame oil |
| 1 onion, sliced |
| 1 garlic clove, crushed |
| 1 tbsp grated fresh ginger root |
| 450 g/1 lb fillet or rump steak, cut into thin strips |
| 2 tsp palm sugar or demerara sugar |
| 2 tbsp light soy sauce |
| 1 small yellow pepper, seeded and sliced |
| 1 red pepper, seeded and sliced |
| 4 spring onions, finely chopped |
| 2 celery stalks, chopped |
| 4 large open-cap mushrooms, thinly sliced |
| 4 tbsp roasted cashew nuts |
| 3 tbsp stock or white wine |
| rice noodles, to serve |

**1** Heat the peanut or sunflower oil
and the sesame oil in a preheated
wok or large, heavy-based frying pan.
Add the onion, garlic and ginger,
and stir-fry for about 2 minutes,
until the onion is softened and
lightly coloured.

**2** Add the steak strips and stir-fry for
a further 2–3 minutes, until the meat
has browned all over.

**3** Add the sugar and soy sauce,
mixing thoroughly. Stir in the
peppers, spring onions, celery,
mushrooms and cashews.

**4** Add the stock or wine and stir-fry
for 2–3 minutes, until the steak is
cooked through and the vegetables are
tender-crisp. Transfer to a warm
serving dish and serve immediately
with rice noodles.

### COOK'S VARIATION

The cashews could be replaced with the
same quantity of unsalted, roasted
peanuts.

# Chinese Beef

This dish is quick to cook, but benefits
from a lengthy marinating, as this
tenderizes and flavours the meat.

### Serves 4

| |
| --- |
| 225 g/8 oz lean steak, cut into 2.5-cm/1-inch cubes |
| 1 tbsp light soy sauce |
| 1 tsp sesame oil |
| 2 tsp Chinese rice wine or dry sherry |
| 1 tsp caster sugar |
| 2 tsp hoi-sin sauce |
| 1 garlic clove, crushed |
| 1/2 tsp cornflour |
| green pepper matchsticks, to garnish |
| rice or noodles, to serve |

### SAUCE

| |
| --- |
| 2 tbsp dark soy sauce |
| 1 tsp caster sugar |
| 1/2 tsp cornflour |
| 3 tbsp oyster sauce |
| 8 tbsp water |
| 2 tbsp vegetable oil |
| 3 garlic cloves, crushed |
| 1-cm/1/2-inch piece fresh ginger root, grated |
| 8 baby corn cobs, halved lengthways |
| 1/2 green pepper, seeded and thinly sliced |
| 25 g/1 oz canned bamboo shoots, drained |

**1** Put the steak in a shallow glass bowl. Mix together the soy sauce, sesame oil, rice wine or sherry, sugar, hoi-sin sauce, garlic and cornflour and pour on the steak, turning it to coat completely. Cover and marinate for at least 1 hour.

**2** Meanwhile, make the sauce. Mix the dark soy sauce with the sugar,

cornflour, oyster sauce and water. Heat the oil in a preheated wok. Add the steak, together with the marinade, and stir-fry for about 2–3 minutes, until sealed.

**3** Add the garlic, ginger, baby corn cobs, pepper and bamboo shoots. Stir in the oyster sauce mixture and bring to the boil, reduce the heat and cook

for a further 2–3 minutes. Garnish with green pepper matchsticks and serve with rice or noodles.

### COOK'S TIP

For a fuller flavour, marinate the beef in the refrigerator overnight.

# Crispy Shredded Beef

A very popular Szechuan dish served
in most Chinese restaurants
all over the world.

| Serves 4 |
| --- |
| 275–350 g/9¹/₂–12 oz beef steak (such as topside or rump) |
| 2 eggs |
| ¹/₄ tsp salt |
| 4–5 tbsp plain flour |
| vegetable oil, for deep-frying |
| 2 medium carrots, cut into matchstick strips |
| 2 spring onions, finely shredded |
| 1 garlic clove, finely chopped |
| 2–3 small fresh green or red chillies, seeded and finely shredded |
| 4 tbsp sugar |
| 3 tbsp rice vinegar |
| 1 tbsp light soy sauce |
| 2–3 tbsp Chinese Stock (see page16) or water |
| 1 tsp Cornflour Paste (see page 16) |

**1** Cut the steak across the grain into thin strips. Beat the eggs in a bowl with the salt and flour, adding a little water if necessary. Add the steak and mix until coated with the batter.

**2** Heat the oil in a preheated wok until smoking. Add the steak strips and deep-fry for 4–5 minutes, stirring to separate the shreds. Remove with a slotted spoon and drain on kitchen paper.

**3** Add the carrots to the wok and deep-fry for about 1–1½ minutes, then remove with a slotted spoon and drain on kitchen paper.

**4** Pour off the excess oil, leaving about 1 tablespoon in the wok. Add the spring onions, garlic, chillies and carrots, stir-fry for about 1 minute. Add the sugar, vinegar, soy sauce and stock or water, blend well and bring to the boil.

**5** Stir in the cornflour paste and simmer for a few minutes to thicken the sauce. Return the steak to the wok and stir until the shreds of meat are well coated with the sauce. Transfer to a warm serving dish and serve immediately.

# Sweet & Sour Pork

This has to be the most popular Chinese dish all over
the world. To vary, replace pork with fish,
prawns, chicken or vegetables.

| Serves 4 |
| --- |
| 225–275 g/8–9¹/₂ oz lean pork |
| 2 tsp brandy or whisky |
| vegetable oil, for deep-frying |
| 1 egg, beaten |
| 2 tbsp plain flour |
| salt and pepper |
| SAUCE |
| 1 tbsp vegetable oil |
| 1 small onion, diced |
| 1 small carrot, diced |
| ¹/₂ small green pepper, seeded and diced |
| 1 tbsp light soy sauce |
| 3 tbsp sugar |
| 3 tbsp wine vinegar |
| 1 tbsp tomato purée |
| about 3–4 tbsp Chinese Stock (see page 16) or water |
| 1 tbsp Cornflour Paste (see page 16) |

**1** Cut the pork into bite-size cubes. Place in a dish with the salt, pepper and brandy or whisky and marinate for 15–20 minutes.

**2** Heat the oil in a preheated wok or deep-fryer. Place the pork cubes in a bowl with the beaten egg and turn to coat. Sprinkle the flour over them and turn the pork cubes until they are well coated.

**3** Deep-fry the pork cubes in batches for about 3–4 minutes, stirring gently to separate the pieces. Remove with a slotted spoon and drain on kitchen paper. Reheat the oil and return the meat to the wok for 1–2 minutes, until golden brown. Remove with a slotted spoon and drain on kitchen paper.

**4** To make the sauce, heat the oil in a preheated wok, add the vegetables and stir-fry for about 1 minute. Add the seasonings and tomato purée with the stock or water, bring to the boil and thicken with the cornflour paste.

**5** Add the pork and blend well so that each piece of meat is coated with the sauce. Serve immediately.

# Spare Ribs with Chilli

For the best results, chop the spare ribs
into bite-size pieces or ask your
butcher to do this for you.

| Serves 4 |
| --- |
| 450 g/1 lb pork spare ribs |
| 1 tsp caster sugar |
| 1 tbsp light soy sauce |
| 1 tsp Chinese rice wine or |
| dry sherry |
| 1 tsp cornflour |
| about 600 ml/1 pint |
| vegetable oil |
| 1 garlic clove, finely chopped |
| 1 spring onion, |
| cut into short sections |
| 1 small fresh green or red chilli |
| seeded and thinly sliced |
| 2 tbsp black bean sauce |
| about 150 ml/$^1$/$_4$ pint |
| Chinese Stock (see page 16) |
| or water |
| 1 small onion, diced |
| 1 green pepper, |
| seeded and diced |

**1** Trim any excess fat from the ribs,
and chop each one into 3–4 bite-size
pieces. Place the ribs in a shallow dish
with the sugar, soy sauce, rice wine or
sherry and cornflour and marinate for
35–45 minutes.

**2** Heat the oil in a preheated wok.
Add the spare ribs and deep-fry for
2–3 minutes, until light brown.
Remove with a slotted spoon and
drain on kitchen paper.

**3** Pour off the oil, leaving about
1 tablespoon in the wok. Add the
garlic, spring onion, chilli and black
bean sauce and stir-fry for 30–40
seconds.

**4** Add the spare ribs, blend well, then
add the stock or water. Bring to the
boil, reduce the heat, cover and braise
for 8–10 minutes, stirring occasionally.

**5** Add the onion and green pepper.
Increase the heat to high, and stir,
uncovered, for about 2 minutes to
reduce the sauce a little. Serve hot.

# Deep-fried Pork with a Soy Dipping Sauce

Small pieces of pork are coated in a light batter and deep-fried in this recipe – the pork is delicious dipped in a soy and honey sauce.

| Serves 4 |
| --- |
| 450 g/1 lb pork fillet |
| 2 tbsp peanut oil |
| 200 g/7 oz plain flour |
| 2 tsp baking powder |
| 1 egg, beaten |
| 225 ml/8 fl oz milk |
| pinch of chilli powder |
| vegetable oil, for deep-frying |

| SAUCE |
| --- |
| 2 tbsp dark soy sauce |
| 3 tbsp clear honey |
| 1 tbsp wine vinegar |
| 1 tbsp chopped chives |
| 1 tbsp tomato purée |
| chives, to garnish |

**1** Cut the pork into 2.5-cm/1-inch cubes. Heat the peanut oil in a preheated wok. Add the pork and stir-fry for 2–3 minutes, until sealed. Remove the meat with a slotted spoon and set aside.

**2** Sift the flour and baking powder into a bowl and make a well in the centre. Beat in the egg, milk and chilli powder to make a thick batter.

**3** Heat the oil for deep-frying in a wok until almost smoking, then reduce the heat slightly. Toss the pork pieces in the batter to coat thoroughly and deep-fry until golden brown. Remove the cooked pork from the wok with a slotted spoon and drain on absorbent kitchen paper.

**4** Meanwhile, make the sauce. Mix together the soy sauce, honey, vinegar chives and tomato purée and spoon into a small serving bowl.

**5** Serve the sauce with the hot pork cubes, garnished with chives.

### COOK'S TIP

Be careful when heating the oil for deep-frying. It must be heated so that it is almost smoking, then the heat must be reduced immediately.

# Fish-flavoured Shredded Pork

'Fish-flavoured' (yu-xiang in Chinese) is a Szechuan
cookery term meaning that the dish contains
seasonings normally used in fish dishes.

### Serves 4

about 2 tbsp dried wood ears

225–275 g/8–9$^{1}/_{2}$ oz pork fillet

1 tsp salt

2 tsp Cornflour Paste
(see page 16)

3 tbsp vegetable oil

1 garlic clove, finely chopped

$^{1}/_{2}$ tsp finely chopped ginger root

2 spring onions,
finely chopped, with the white
and green parts separated

2 celery sticks, thinly sliced

$^{1}/_{2}$ tsp sugar

1 tbsp light soy sauce

1 tbsp chilli bean sauce

2 tsp rice vinegar

1 tsp Chinese rice wine or
dry sherry

a few drops of sesame oil

**1** Soak the wood ears in warm water
for 20 minutes, then rinse in cold
water until the water is clear. Drain
well, then cut into thin shreds.

**2** Cut the pork into thin shreds and
mix in a bowl with a pinch of the
salt and about half the cornflour
paste until well coated.

**3** Heat 1 tablespoon of oil in a
preheated wok. Add the pork strips
and stir-fry for about 1 minute, or
until the colour changes. Remove
with a slotted spoon.

**4** Heat the remaining oil in the wok.
Add the garlic, ginger, the white parts
of the spring onions, the wood ears

and celery. Stir-fry for about 1 minute.
Return the pork strips to the wok,
together with the sugar, soy sauce,
chilli bean sauce, vinegar, rice wine or
sherry and remaining salt. Continue
stirring for another minute.

**5** Finally add the green parts of
the spring onions and blend in the
remaining cornflour paste and
sesame oil. Stir until the sauce has
thickened. Transfer to a serving dish
and serve immediately.

# Red Spiced Beef

A spicy stir-fry flavoured with paprika,
chilli and tomato, with a crisp bite
to it from the celery strips.

| Serves 4 |
| --- |
| 500 g/1 lb 2 oz sirloin or rump steak |
| 2 tbsp paprika |
| 2–3 tsp mild chilli powder |
| ½ tsp salt |
| 6 celery sticks |
| 4 tomatoes, peeled, seeded and sliced |
| 6 tbsp stock or water |
| 2 tbsp tomato purée |
| 2 tbsp clear honey |
| 3 tbsp wine vinegar |
| 1 tbsp Worcestershire sauce |
| 2 tbsp sunflower oil |
| 4 spring onions, thinly sliced diagonally |
| 1–2 garlic cloves, crushed |
| celery leaves, to garnish (optional) |
| Chinese noodles, to serve |

**1** Cut the steak across the grain into narrow strips 1 cm/½ inch thick and place in a bowl.

**2** Combine the paprika, chilli powder and salt. Add to the steak and mix thoroughly until the meat strips are evenly coated with the spice mixture. Cover and marinate in a cool place for a minimum of 30 minutes.

**3** Cut the celery into 5-cm/2-inch lengths, then slice into strips about 5 mm/¼ inch thick. Combine the stock, tomato purée, honey, vinegar and Worcestershire sauce.

**4** Heat the oil in a preheated wok. Add the spring onions (scallions),

celery, tomatoes and garlic, and stir-fry for about 1 minute, until the vegetables are beginning to soften. Then add the steak strips and stir-fry over a high heat for 3–4 minutes, until the meat is well sealed.

**5** Add the sauce to the wok and continue to stir-fry briskly until thoroughly coated and sizzling.

**6** Serve with noodles and garnish with celery leaves, if desired.

# Pork with Plum Sauce

Plum sauce is often used in Chinese cooking
with duck or rich, fattier meat
to counteract the flavour.

| Serves 4 |
| --- |
| 1 tbsp cornflour |
| 2 tbsp light soy sauce |
| 2 tbsp Chinese rice wine or dry sherry |
| 4 tsp light brown sugar |
| pinch of ground cinnamon |
| 450 g/1 lb pork fillet, sliced |
| 5 tsp vegetable oil |
| 2 garlic cloves, crushed |
| 2 spring onions chopped |
| 4 tbsp plum sauce |
| 1 tbsp hoi-sin sauce |
| 150 ml/¼ pint water |
| dash of chilli sauce |
| fried plum quarters and spring onions, to garnish |

**1** Mix the cornflour, soy sauce, Chinese rice wine or sherry, sugar and cinnamon together. Place the pork in a single layer in a shallow non-metallic dish and pour the marinade over it. Cover and marinate for a minimum of 30 minutes. Remove the pork from the dish, reserving the marinade.

**2** Heat the oil in a preheated wok. Add the pork and stir-fry for 3–4 minutes, until lightly browned.

**3** Stir in the garlic, spring onions, plum sauce, hoi-sin sauce, water and chilli sauce. Bring the sauce to the boil, cover, lower the heat and simmer for 8–10 minutes, or until the pork is cooked through.

**4** Stir in the reserved marinade and cook for a further 5 minutes. Transfer to a serving dish, garnish with fried plum quarters and spring onions and serve immediately.

### VARIATION

Strips of boneless duck meat may be used instead of the pork.

# Stir-fried Pork with Vegetables

This is another basic meat and vegetable recipe that
can be varied with chicken, beef or lamb, and
vegetables according to seasonal availability.

| Serves 4 |
| --- |
| 250 g/9 oz pork fillet |
| 1 tsp sugar |
| 1 tbsp light soy sauce |
| 1 tsp Chinese rice wine or dry sherry |
| 1 tsp Cornflour Paste (see page 16) |
| 1 small carrot |
| 1 small green pepper, seeded |
| about 175 g/6 oz Chinese leaves |
| 4 tbsp vegetable oil |
| 1 spring onion, cut into short sections |
| a few small slices of peeled fresh ginger root |
| 1 tsp salt |
| 2–3 tbsp Chinese Stock (see page 16) or water |
| a few drops of sesame oil |

**4** Add the carrot, pepper, Chinese leaves, spring onion and ginger and stir-fry for about 2 minutes. Add the salt and remaining sugar. Return the pork to the wok and add the remaining soy sauce and the stock or water. Blend thoroughly and stir for a further 1–2 minutes, until hot. Sprinkle with the sesame oil. Transfer the pork and vegetables to a warm serving dish and serve immediately.

**1** Thinly slice the pork fillet into small pieces and place in a shallow dish. Add half the sugar, half the the soy sauce, the Chinese rice wine or sherry and cornflour paste. Set aside to marinate in the refrigerator for 10–15 minutes.

**2** Cut the carrot, green pepper and Chinese leaves into thin slices roughly the same length and width as the pork pieces.

**3** Heat the oil in a preheated wok and stir-fry the pork for about 1 minute to seal in the flavour. Remove with a slotted spoon and keep warm.

# Braised Pork & Tofu

This is a typical example of the way Chinese
cuisine harmonizes and contrasts
flavours and textures.

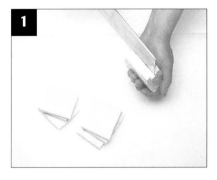

| Serves 4 |
| --- |
| 3 cakes tofu |
| 115 g/4 oz boneless pork |
| 1 leek |
| 1–2 spring onions, cut into short sections |
| a few small dried whole chillies, soaked |
| vegetable oil, for deep-frying |
| 2 tbsp yellow bean sauce |
| 1 tbsp light soy sauce |
| 2 tsp Chinese rice wine or dry sherry |
| a few drops of sesame oil |

wine or sherry and braise for 2–3
minutes, stirring very gently to blend
everything well. Sprinkle on the
sesame oil. Transfer to a warm serving
dish and serve immediately.

**VARIATION**

The pork can be replaced by chicken
or prawns.

**1** Split each cake of tofu into 3 slices
crossways, then cut each slice
diagonally into 2 triangles.

**2** Cut the pork into shreds. Cut the
leek into thin strips. Drain the
chillies, remove the seeds using the
tip of a knife, then cut the flesh into
small shreds.

**3** Heat the oil in a preheated wok
until smoking. Deep-fry the tofu
triangles for 2–3 minutes, or until
golden brown all over. Remove with a
slotted spoon and drain on kitchen
paper.

**4** Pour off the hot oil, leaving about
1 tablespoon in the wok. Add the pork
strips, spring onions and chillies and
stir-fry for 1 minute, or until the pork
changes colour.

**5** Add the leek, tofu, yellow bean
sauce, soy sauce and Chinese rice

# Vegetable Dishes

No Chinese meal can be regarded as complete without a freshly cooked, colourful vegetable dish on the table, quite separate from the vegetables included as an integral part of other dishes.

Flavour, texture, colour and nutrients are all preserved by such cooking techniques as steaming. stir-frying or brief braising. Vegetables should be as fresh as possible –

Chinese cooks buy them daily. Vegetables are washed just before cutting or slicing and cooked immediately

afterwards to minimize the loss of flavour, texture and nutrients.

Besides forming an essential part of a Chinese meal, many of the recipes in this chapter would provide a special and unusual accompaniment to a western-style grill or roast. Try Stir-fried Mixed Vegetables, Stir-fried Cucumber with Ginger and Chilli, or Garlic Spinach.

# Vegetable Chop Suey

Make sure that the vegetables are all cut into pieces
of a similar size in this recipe, so that they cook
within the same amount of time.

| Serves 4 |
| --- |
| 1 yellow pepper, seeded |
| 1 red pepper, seeded |
| 1 carrot |
| 1 courgette |
| 1 fennel bulb |
| 1 onion |
| 50 g/1¾ oz mangetout, sliced diagonally |
| 2 tbsp peanut oil |
| 3 garlic cloves, crushed |
| 1 tsp grated fresh ginger root |
| 115 g/4 oz beansprouts |
| 2 tsp light brown sugar |
| 2 tbsp light soy sauce |
| 125 ml/4 fl oz vegetable stock |

**1** Cut the peppers, carrot, courgette and fennel into thin slices. Quarter the onion and then cut each piece in half. Slice the mangetouts diagonally.

**2** Heat the oil in a preheated wok until almost smoking. Add the garlic and ginger and stir-fry for 30 seconds.

**3** Add the onion and stir-fry for a further 30 seconds.

**4** Add the peppers, carrot, courgette, fennel and mangetout and stir-fry for 2 minutes.

**5** Add the beansprouts and stir in the sugar, soy sauce and stock. Reduce the heat to low and simmer for a further 1–2 minutes, or until the vegetables are tender and thoroughly coated in the sauce.

**6** Transfer the vegetable chop suey to a warm serving dish and serve immediately.

### COOK'S TIP

Use any combination of colourful vegetables that you have to hand for this versatile dish.

# Sweet & Sour Vegetables

Make your choice of vegetables from the suggested list,
including spring onions and garlic. For a hotter,
spicier sauce add chilli sauce.

---

| Serves 4 |
| --- |
| 5–6 vegetables from the following: |
| 1 pepper, seeded and sliced |
| 115 g/4 oz French beans, cut into 2–3 pieces |
| 115 g/4 oz mangetout, cut into 2–3 pieces |
| 225 g/8 oz broccoli or cauliflower florets |
| 225 g/8 oz courgettes, cut into 5-cm/2-inch lengths |
| 175 g/6 oz carrots, cut into julienne strips |
| 115 g/4 oz baby corn cobs, sliced thinly |
| 175 g/6 oz parsnip or celeriac, finely diced |
| 13 celery sticks, thinly sliced crosswise |
| 4 tomatoes, peeled, quartered and seeded |
| 115 g/4 oz button mushrooms, sliced |
| 7-cm/3-inch length of cucumber, diced |
| 200 g/7 oz can water chestnuts or bamboo shoots, drained and sliced |
| 400 g/14 oz can beansprouts, drained |
| 4 spring onions, thinly sliced |
| 1 garlic clove, crushed |
| 2 tbsp sunflower oil |

### SWEET & SOUR SAUCE

| |
| --- |
| 2 tbsp wine vinegar |
| 2 tbsp clear honey |
| 1 tbsp tomato purée |
| 2 tbsp soy sauce |
| 2 tbsp Chinese rice wine or dry sherry |
| 1–2 tsp sweet chilli sauce (optional) |
| 2 tsp cornflour |

**1** Prepare the selected vegetables, cutting them into uniform lengths.

**2** Combine the sauce ingredients in a bowl, blending well together.

**3** Heat the oil in a preheated wok. Add the spring onions and garlic and stir-fry for 1 minute.

**4** Add the prepared vegetables – the harder and firmer ones first – and stir-fry for 2 minutes. Then add the softer ones such as mushrooms, mangetout and tomatoes and continue to stir-fry for 2 minutes.

**5** Add the sauce to the wok. Bring to the boil, tossing until the vegetables are thoroughly coated. Serve hot.

# Stir-fried Mixed Vegetables

The Chinese never mix ingredients indiscriminately –
they are carefully selected to achieve a harmonious
balance of colours and textures.

| Serves 4 |
| --- |
| 50 g/1³/₄ oz mangetout |
| 1 small carrot |
| 115 g/4 oz Chinese leaves |
| 115 g/4 oz fresh beansprouts |
| 50 g/1³/₄ oz black or white mushrooms |
| 50 g/1³/₄ oz canned bamboo shoots, drained |
| 3–4 tbsp vegetable oil |
| 1 tsp salt |
| 1 tsp sugar |
| 1 tbsp oyster sauce or light soy sauce |
| a few drops of sesame oil (optional) |
| dipping sauce, to serve (optional) |

**1** Prepare the vegetables. Top and tail the mangetout, and cut the carrot, Chinese leaves, mushrooms and bamboo shoots into roughly the same shape and size as the mangetout.

**2** Heat the oil in a preheated wok, and add the carrot. Stir-fry for a few seconds, then add the mangetout and Chinese leaves and stir-fry for about 1 minute.

**3** Add the beansprouts, mushrooms and bamboo shoots and stir-fry for another minute.

**4** Add the salt and sugar, continue stirring for another minute, then add the oyster sauce or soy sauce. Blend well and sprinkle with sesame oil (if using). Transfer to a warm serving dish and serve immediately or let cool and serve cold, with a dipping sauce, if wished.

## COOK'S TIP

Many ready-made sauces, both hotly spiced and mild, are available from Chinese supermarkets.

# Braised Bamboo Shoots

This dish has a wonderfully strong ginger flavour which is integral
to Chinese cooking. The mixed peppers give the otherwise
insipid bamboo shoots a burst of colour.

| Serves 4 |
| --- |
| 2 tbsp peanut oil |
| 225 g/8 oz can bamboo shoots, drained |
| 2.5-cm/1-inch piece fresh ginger root, finely chopped |
| 1 small red pepper, seeded and thinly sliced |
| 1 small green pepper, seeded and thinly sliced |
| 1 small yellow pepper, seeded and thinly sliced |
| 1 leek, sliced |
| 125 ml/4 fl oz vegetable stock |
| 1 tbsp light soy sauce |
| 2 tsp light brown sugar |
| 2 tsp Chinese rice wine or dry sherry |
| 1 tsp cornflour |
| 2 tsp water |
| 1 tsp sesame oil |

**1** Heat the oil in a preheated wok. Add the bamboo shoots, ginger, peppers and leek and stir-fry for 2–3 minutes.

**2** Stir in the stock, soy sauce, sugar and Chinese rice wine or sherry and bring to the boil, stirring constantly. Reduce the heat and simmer for 4–5 minutes, until the vegetables begin to soften.

**3** Blend the cornflour with the water to form a smooth paste and stir into the wok. Bring to the boil, stirring until the sauce thickens and clears.

**4** Sprinkle the sesame oil over the vegetables and cook for 1 further minute.

**5** Transfer to a warm serving dish and serve immediately.

**COOK'S TIP**

Add a chopped fresh red chilli or a few drops of chilli sauce for a spicier dish.

# Golden Needles with Bamboo Shoots

Golden needles are the dried flower buds of the tiger lily.
Available at specialist shops and Chinese supermarkets,
they impart a unique musky flavour.

| Serves 4 |
| --- |
| 25 g/1 oz dried lily flowers |
| 2 × 215 g/7$\frac{1}{2}$ oz cans bamboo shoots, drained |
| 50 g/1$\frac{3}{4}$ oz cornflour |
| vegetable oil, for deep-frying |
| 1 tbsp vegetable oil |
| 450 ml/$\frac{3}{4}$ pint vegetable stock |
| 1 tbsp dark soy sauce |
| 1 tbsp Chinese rice wine or dry sherry |
| 1 tsp sugar |
| 1 large garlic clove, sliced |
| $\frac{1}{2}$ each red, green and yellow peppers, seeded and thinly sliced |

**1** Soak the lily flowers in hot water for 30 minutes.

**2** Coat the bamboo shoots in cornflour. Heat the oil for deep-frying in a large heavy-based saucepan. Deep-fry the bamboo shoots, in batches, until just beginning to colour. Remove with a slotted spoon and drain on kitchen paper.

**3** Drain the lily flowers and trim off the hard ends. Heat the oil in a preheated wok or large frying pan. Add the lily flowers, bamboo shoots, stock, soy sauce, rice wine or sherry, sugar and garlic.

**4** Add the peppers to the wok or pan. Bring to the boil, stirring constantly, then reduce the heat and simmer for 5 minutes. Add extra water or stock if necessary.

# Chinese Braised Vegetables

This colourful selection of braised vegetables
makes a splendid accompaniment
to a main dish.

| Serves 4–6 |
| --- |
| 3 tbsp sunflower oil |
| 1 garlic clove, crushed |
| 1 head Chinese leaves, coarsely shredded |
| 2 onions, cut into wedges |
| 225 g/8 oz broccoli florets |
| 2 large carrots, cut into julienne strips |
| 12 baby corn cobs, halved if large |
| 50 g/1¾ oz mangetout, halved |
| 75 g/2¾ oz Chinese or oyster mushrooms, sliced |
| 1 tbsp grated fresh ginger root |
| 175 ml/6 fl oz vegetable stock |
| 2 tbsp light soy sauce |
| 1 tbsp cornflour |
| salt and pepper |
| ½ tsp sugar |

**1** Heat the oil in a preheated wok or large, heavy-based frying pan. Add the garlic, Chinese leaves, onions, broccoli, carrots, corn, mangetout, mushrooms and ginger and stir-fry for 2 minutes.

**2** Add the stock, cover and cook for a further 2–3 minutes.

**3** Blend the soy sauce with the cornflour, and add salt and pepper to taste.

**4** Remove the braised vegetables from the pan with a slotted spoon and keep warm. Add the soy sauce

mixture to the pan juices, mixing well. Bring to the boil, stirring constantly, until the mixture thickens slightly. Stir in the sugar.

**5** Return the vegetables to the pan and toss in the slightly thickened sauce. Cook gently to heat through, transfer to a warm serving dish and serve immediately.

# Stir-Fried Cucumber with Ginger & Chilli

Warm cucumbers are absolutely delicious, especially when combined
with the heat of chilli and the flavour of ginger.

| Serves 4 |
| --- |
| 2 medium cucumbers |
| 2 tsp salt |
| 1 tbsp vegetable oil |
| 2 garlic cloves, crushed |
| 1-cm/$\frac{1}{2}$-inch fresh ginger root, grated |
| 2 spring onions, chopped |
| 2 fresh red chillies, chopped |
| 1 tsp yellow bean sauce |
| 1 tbsp clear honey |
| 125 ml/4 fl oz water |
| 1 tsp sesame oil |

**1** Peel the cucumbers and cut them in
half lengthways. Scrape the seeds
from the centre, using a teaspoon,
and discard.

**2** Cut the cucumber into strips and
sprinkle the salt over them. Place in a
colander for 20 minutes. Rinse well
under cold running water and pat dry
with kitchen paper.

**3** Heat the oil in a preheated wok
until almost smoking. Lower the heat
slightly and add the garlic, ginger,
chilli and spring onions and stir-fry
for 30 seconds.

**4** Add the cucumbers to the wok,
together with the yellow bean sauce
and honey. Stir-fry for a further
30 seconds and add the water.

**5** Cook over a high heat until most of
the water has evaporated. Sprinkle in
the sesame oil and serve immediately.

### COOK'S VARIATION

You could use Asian squashes, such as
dudi or tindoori, in this recipe.

### COOK'S TIP

The cucumber is salted and left to
stand to draw out the excess water.

# Stir-Fried Beansprouts

Be sure to use fresh beansprouts, rather
than the canned variety, for this
crunchy-textured dish.

| Serves 4 |
| --- |
| 225 g/8 oz fresh beansprouts |
| 2–3 spring onions |
| 1 red chilli |
| 3 tbsp vegetable oil |
| $^1/_2$ tsp salt |
| $^1/$ tsp sugar |
| 1 tbsp light soy sauce |
| a few drops of sesame oil (optional) |

**1** Rinse the beansprouts in cold water, discarding any husks or small pieces that float to the top. Drain well on kitchen paper.

**2** Cut the spring onions into short sections. Shred the chilli, if using, discarding the seeds.

**3** Heat the oil in a preheated wok. Add the beansprouts, spring onions and chilli, if using, and stir-fry for about 2 minutes.

**4** Add the salt, sugar, soy sauce and sesame oil, if using. Stir well to blend. Serve hot or cold.

### COOK'S TIP

Beansprouts are extremely easy to grow yourself and this ensures the freshest supply. You can grow them in a clean jar or a special sprouter.

# Beansprouts with Peppers

This dish is served cold as a salad or appetizer
and is very easy to make. It is a
form of cold chop suey.

| Serves 4 |
| --- |
| 450 g/1 lb beansprouts |
| 2 fresh red chillies |
| 1 red pepper, seeded and thinly sliced |
| 1 green pepper, seeded and thinly sliced |
| 50 g/1¾ oz canned water chestnuts, drained and quartered |
| 1 celery stick, sliced |
| 3 tbsp rice wine vinegar |
| 2 tbsp light soy sauce |
| 2 tbsp chopped chives |
| 1 garlic clove, crushed |
| pinch of Chinese curry powder |

**1** Place the beansprouts, chilli, peppers, water chestnuts and celery in a bowl and mix well.

**2** Mix together the rice wine vinegar, soy sauce, chives, garlic and Chinese curry powder and pour on top of the vegetables. Toss to mix thoroughly.

**3** Cover the salad and chill for at least 3 hours. Drain the vegetables well, spoon into a serving dish and serve.

## COOK'S TIP

If wished, top the salad with a nest of crisp-fried Chinese rice noodles for a more substantial dish.

# Vegetables in Black Bean Sauce

This recipe, as the title suggests, is a colourful mixture
of eight vegetables, cooked in a
black bean and soy sauce.

| Serves 4 |
| --- |
| 2 tbsp peanut oil |
| 6 spring onions, sliced |
| 3 garlic cloves, crushed |
| 1 green pepper, seeded and diced |
| 1 red pepper, seeded and diced |
| 1 fresh red chilli, sliced |
| 2 tbsp drained canned chopped water chestnuts |
| 1 courgette, chopped |
| 125 g/4$^1/_2$ oz oyster mushrooms |
| 3 tbsp black bean sauce |
| 2 tsp Chinese rice wine or dry sherry |
| 4 tbsp dark soy sauce |
| 1 tsp dark brown sugar |
| 2 tbsp water |
| 1 tsp sesame oil |

**1** Heat the oil in a preheated wok until it is almost smoking. Lower the heat slightly, add the spring onions and garlic and stir-fry for 30 seconds.

**2** Add the peppers, chilli, water chestnuts and courgette and stir-fry for 2–3 minutes, until the vegetables begin to soften.

**3** Add the mushrooms, black bean sauce, Chinese rice wine or sherry, soy sauce, sugar and water and stir-fry for a further 4 minutes. Sprinkle with sesame oil. Transfer to a warm serving dish and serve immediately.

### COOK'S TIP

If you cannot obtain oyster mushrooms, use canned Chinese straw mushrooms instead.

### VARIATION

Add 225 g/8 oz diced, marinated tofu to this recipe for a main meal for 4 people.

# Vegetable & Nut Stir-Fry

A colourful selection of vegetables are stir-fried
in a creamy peanut sauce and
sprinkled with nuts to serve.

| Serves 4 |
| --- |
| 3 tbsp crunchy peanut butter |
| 150 ml/¼ pint water |
| 1 tbsp light soy sauce |
| 1 tsp sugar |
| 1 carrot |
| ½ red onion |
| 4 baby courgettes |
| 1 red |
| pepper, seeded |
| 225 g/8 oz egg thread noodles |
| 25g/1 oz peanuts, |
| chopped roughly |
| 2 tbsp vegetable oil |
| 1 tsp sesame oil |
| 1 small green chilli, |
| seeded and thinly sliced |
| 1 garlic clove, thinly sliced |
| 200 g/7 oz can water chestnuts, |
| drained and sliced |
| 175 g/6 oz beansprouts |
| salt |

**1** In a small bowl, gradually blend the peanut butter with the water. Stir in the soy sauce and sugar.

**2** Cut the carrot into thin matchsticks and slice the onion. Slice the courgettes on the diagonal and cut the pepper into chunks.

**3** Bring a large pan of water to the boil and add the egg noodles. Remove from the heat immediately and set aside for 4 minutes, stirring occasionally to divide the noodles.

**4** Heat a wok or large frying pan, add the peanuts and dry-fry until they are

beginning to brown. Remove the peanuts and set aside.

**5** Heat the oils in the wok or pan. Add the carrot, onion, courgette, pepper, chilli and garlic and stir-fry for 2–3

minutes. Add the water chestnuts, beansprouts and peanut sauce. Bring to the boil and heat thoroughly. Season to taste. Drain the noodles and serve with the stir-fry, sprinkled with the peanuts.

# Chinese Green Bean Stir-fry

These beans are simply cooked
in a spicy, hot sauce for a
tasty and easy recipe.

| Serves 4 |
| --- |
| 2 tbsp peanut oil |
| 450 g/1 lb thin green beans, cut in half |
| 2 fresh red chillies, sliced |
| $\frac{1}{2}$ tsp ground star anise |
| 1 garlic clove crushed |
| 2 tbsp light soy sauce |
| 2 tsp clear honey |
| $\frac{1}{2}$ tsp sesame oil |

**1** Heat the oil in a preheated wok
until almost smoking. Lower the heat
slightly, add the beans and stir-fry for
1 minute.

**2** Add the chillies, star anise and
garlic and stir-fry for a further
30 seconds.

**3** Mix together the soy sauce,
honey and sesame oil and stir into
the wok. Cook for 2 minutes, tossing
the beans in the sauce to coat.

**4** Transfer to a warm serving dish
and serve immediately.

### COOK'S TIP

This dish makes a great accompaniment
to fish or lightly cooked meats with a
mild flavour.

# Stir-fried Greens

The basis of this recipe is pak choi, sometimes known as
bok choy or Chinese greens. If unavailable, use Swiss chard
or Savoy cabbage in its place.

| Serves 4 |
| --- |
| 2 tbsp peanut oil |
| 2 garlic cloves, crushed |
| $\frac{1}{2}$ tsp ground star anise |
| 1 tsp salt |
| 350 g/12 oz pak choi, roughly shredded |
| 225 g/8 oz baby spinach |
| 25 g/1 oz mangetout |
| 1 celery stick, sliced |
| 1 green pepper, seeded and sliced |
| 50 ml/2 fl oz vegetable stock |
| 1 tsp sesame oil |

**1** Heat the oil in a preheated wok.
Add the garlic and stir-fry for
30 seconds. Stir in the salt, pak choi,
spinach, mangetout, celery and
pepper and stir-fry for 3–4 minutes.

**2** Add the stock, cover and cook for
3–4 minutes.

**3** Remove the lid from the wok and
stir in the sesame oil. Mix well,
transfer to a warm serving dish and
serve immediately.

### COOK'S TIP

Serve this dish as part of a vegetarian
meal or with roast meats for non-
vegetarians.

# Tofu & Vegetables with Black Bean Sauce

Chunks of smoked tofu are stir-fried with a delicious mixture
of vegetables and black bean sauce.

| Serves 4 |
| --- |
| 275 g/9$^{1}$/$_2$ oz smoked tofu, cubed |
| 2 tbsp soy sauce |
| 1 tbsp Chinese rice wine or dry sherry |
| 1 tsp sesame oil |
| 4 dried Chinese mushrooms, soaked in warm water for 30 minutes |
| 2 tbsp peanut oil |
| 1 carrot, cut into thin sticks |
| 1 celery stalk, cut into thin sticks |
| 115 g/4 oz (16–18) baby corn cobs, halved lengthways |
| 1 courgette, sliced |
| 4 spring onions, chopped |
| 115 g/4 oz mangetout, each cut into 3 pieces |
| 2 tbsp black bean sauce |
| 1 tsp cornflour |
| salt and pepper |
| 1 tbsp toasted sesame seeds, to garnish |
| egg noodles, to serve |

**1** Marinate the tofu in the soy sauce,
Chinese rice wine or sherry and
sesame oil for 30 minutes.

**2** Drain the mushrooms, reserving
1 tbsp of the liquid. Squeeze out
excess water from the mushrooms
and discard the hard stalks. Thinly
slice the caps.

**3** Heat the oil in a preheated wok.
Add the carrot, celery and corn and
stir-fry for 2 minutes. Alternatively,
place in a large bowl, cover and
microwave on HIGH power for
1 minute.

**4** Add the mushrooms, courgette,
spring onions and mangetout and stir-
fry for 4–5 minutes, until just tender.
Or, cover and microwave on HIGH
power for 4 minutes, stirring every
minute.

**5** Add the black bean sauce. Mix the
cornflour with the reserved
mushroom water and stir it into the
vegetables, together with the tofu and
marinade. Stir-fry or cover and
microwave on HIGH power for 2–3
minutes, until heated through and the
sauce has thickened slightly. Season.
Garnish and serve.

# Vegetable & Tofu Casserole

This colourful Chinese-style casserole
is made with tofu, vegetables
and black bean sauce.

| Serves 4 |
|---|
| 6 Chinese dried mushrooms, soaked in warm water for 30 minutes |
| 275 g/9³/₄ oz tofu |
| 3 tbsp vegetable oil |
| 1 carrot, cut into thin strips |
| 115 g/4 oz mangetout |
| 115 g/4 oz baby corn cobs, halved lengthways |
| 200 g/7 oz can bamboo shoots, drained and sliced |
| 1 red pepper, seeded and diced |
| 115 g/4 oz Chinese leaves, shredded |
| 1 tbsp soy sauce |
| 1 tbsp black bean sauce |
| 1 tsp sugar |
| 1 tsp cornflour |
| vegetable oil for deep-frying |
| 225 g/8 oz Chinese rice noodles |
| salt |

**1** Drain the mushrooms, reserving the liquid. Squeeze out the excess. Remove the stems and slice the caps.

**2** Cut the tofu into cubes. Boil in lightly salted water for 2–3 minutes to firm up. Drain well.

**3** Heat half the oil in a large saucepan. Add the tofu and fry until lightly browned all over. Remove with a slotted spoon and drain on kitchen paper.

**4** Add the remaining oil and stir-fry the mushrooms, carrot, mangetout, corn, bamboo shoots and pepper for 2–3 minutes. Add the Chinese leaves and tofu, and stir-fry for 2 minutes.

**5** Stir in the soy sauce, black bean sauce and sugar and season with salt. Add 6 tablespoons of the reserved mushroom liquid mixed with the cornflour. Bring the mixture to the boil, reduce the heat, cover and braise for 2–3 minutes until thickened.

**6** Heat the oil for deep-frying in a large saucepan. Add the noodles in batches and deep-fry until puffed up and lightly golden. Drain and serve with the casserole.

# Stir-Fried Mushrooms, Cucumber & Smoked Tofu

Chunks of cucumber and smoked tofu are stir-fried with straw mushrooms,
mangetouts and corn in a yellow bean sauce.

| Serves 4 |
| --- |
| 1 large cucumber |
| 1 tsp salt |
| 225 g/8 oz smoked tofu |
| 2 tbsp vegetable oil |
| 50 g/1³/₄ oz mangetout |
| 115 g/4 oz baby corn cobs, halved if large |
| 1 celery stick, sliced diagonally |
| 400 g/14 oz can straw mushrooms, drained |
| 2 spring onions, cut into strips |
| 1-cm/¹/₂-inch piece fresh ginger root, chopped |
| 1 tbsp yellow bean sauce |
| 1 tbsp light soy sauce |
| 1 tbsp Chinese rice wine or dry sherry |

**1** Cut the cucumber in half
lengthways. Remove the seeds, using
a teaspoon, and discard. Cut the flesh
into cubes, place in a colander and
sprinkle with the salt. set aside to
drain for 10 minutes. Rinse
thoroughly in cold water to remove
the salt and drain thoroughly.

**2** Cut the smoked tofu into 2.5-cm/1-
inch cubes. Heat the oil in a
preheated wok or large heavy-based
frying pan. Add the tofu, mangetout ,
baby corn cobs and celery. Stir-fry
until the tofu is lightly browned.

**3** Add the straw mushrooms, spring
onions and ginger, and stir-fry for a
further minute. Stir in the cucumber,

yellow bean sauce, soy sauce, Chinese
rice wine or sherry and 2 tablespoons
of water. Stir-fry the entire mixture for
1 further minute.

**4** Transfer to a warm serving dish and
serve immediately.

# Deep-Fried Tofu with Chinese Five Spice

A marinated tofu is ideal in this recipe for added flavour,
although the spicy coating is very tasty with plain tofu.

| Serves 4 |
| --- |
| 1 tbsp sea salt |
| 4½ tsp Chinese five-spice powder |
| 3 tbsp light brown sugar |
| 2 garlic cloves, crushed |
| 1 tsp grated fresh ginger root |
| 2 x 225 g/8 oz cakes tofu |
| vegetable oil, for deep-frying |
| 2 leeks, shredded and halved |
| fresh shredded leek, to garnish |

**1** Mix the salt, Chinese five-spice, sugar, garlic and ginger in a bowl and then spread the mixture out on a plate. Cut the tofu cakes in half diagonally to form two triangles. Cut each triangle in half and then in half again until a total of 16 triangles is formed.

**2** Gently roll the tofu triangles in the spice mixture, turning to coat thoroughly. Set aside to marinate for 1 hour.

**3** Heat the oil for deep-frying in a preheated wok until almost smoking. Reduce the heat slightly, add the tofu triangles and fry for 5 minutes, until golden brown. Remove from the wok with a slotted spoon and keep warm.

**4** Add the leeks to the wok and stir-fry for 1 minute. Remove with a slotted spoon and drain on absorbent kitchen paper.

**5** Arrange the leeks on a warm serving plate and place the fried tofu triangles on top.

**6** Garnish the triangles with the fresh shredded leek and serve immediately.

**COOK'S TIP**

Fry the tofu in batches and keep each batch warm until all of the tofu has been fried and is ready to serve.

# Braised Vegetables with Tofu

Also called Lo Han Zhai or Buddha's Delight, the original recipe
uses 18 vegetables to represent the 18 Buddhas (Lo Han) –
but nowadays 6–8 are acceptable.

| Serves 4 |
| --- |
| 5 g/$\frac{1}{4}$ oz dried wood ears |
| 1 cake tofu |
| 50 g/1$\frac{3}{4}$ oz mangetout |
| 115 g/4 oz Chinese leaves |
| 1 small carrot |
| 75 g/2$\frac{3}{4}$ oz canned baby corn cobs, drained |
| 75 g/2$\frac{3}{4}$ oz canned straw mushrooms, drained |
| 50 g/1$\frac{3}{4}$ oz canned water chestnuts, drained |
| 300 ml/$\frac{1}{2}$ pint vegetable oil |
| 1 tsp salt |
| $\frac{1}{2}$ tsp sugar |
| 1 tbsp light soy sauce or oyster sauce |
| 2–3 tbsp Chinese Stock (see page 16) or water |
| a few drops of sesame oil |

**1** Put the wood ears in a bowl and cover with warm water. Soak for 25–30 minutes, then rinse thoroughly in cold water and drain, discarding any hard stalks, and leave to dry on kitchen paper.

**2** Cut the cake of tofu into about 18 small pieces. Top and tail the mangetouts. Cut the Chinese leaves and the carrot into slices roughly the same size and shape as the mangetout. Cut the baby corn, the straw mushrooms and the water chestnuts in half.

**3** Heat the oil in a preheated wok.

Add the tofu and deep-fry for about 2 minutes, until it turns slightly golden. Remove with a slotted spoon and drain thoroughly.

**4** Pour off the excess oil, leaving about 2 tablespoons in the wok. Add the carrot, Chinese leaves and mangetout and stir-fry for 1 minute.

**5** Add the corn, mushrooms and water chestnuts. Stir for 2 minutes, then add the salt, sugar, soy sauce and stock or water. Bring to the boil and cook for 1 more minute. Sprinkle with sesame oil and serve hot or cold.

# Aubergine in Chilli Sauce

Strips of aubergine are deep-fried, then served in a
fragrant chilli sauce with carrot matchsticks
and spring onions.

| Serves 4 |
| --- |
| 1 large aubergine |
| vegetable oil, for deep-frying |
| 2 carrots |
| 4 spring onions |
| 2 large garlic cloves |
| 1 tbsp vegetable oil |
| 2 tsp chilli sauce |
| 1 tbsp soy sauce |
| 1 tbsp Chinese rice wine or dry sherry |

**1** Slice the aubergine and then cut it into strips about the size of regular potato chips.

**2** Heat enough oil in a wok or large heavy-based saucepan to deep-fry the aubergine in batches until just browned. Remove the strips with a slotted spoon and drain well on kitchen paper.

**3** Cut the carrots into thin matchsticks. Trim and slice the spring onions diagonally. Slice the garlic cloves thinly.

**4** Heat 1 tablespoon of oil in a wok or large frying pan. Add the carrot matchsticks and stir-fry for 1 minute. Add the chopped spring onions and garlic and stir-fry for 1 further minute.

**5** Stir in the chilli sauce, soy sauce and wine or sherry, then stir in the drained aubergine. Stir well until the vegetables are thoroughly heated through before serving.

# Spicy Aubergines

Try to obtain the smaller Chinese aubergines for this dish,
as they have a slightly sweeter taste, but the recipe
is delicious with the larger variety as well.

### Serves 4

450 g/1 lb aubergines,
washed

2 tsp salt

3 tbsp vegetable oil

2 garlic cloves, crushed

2.5-cm/1-inch piece
fresh ginger root, chopped

1 onion, halved and sliced

1 fresh red chilli, sliced

2 tbsp dark soy sauce

1 tbsp hoi-sin sauce

1/2 tsp chilli sauce

1 tbsp dark brown sugar

1 tbsp wine vinegar

1 tsp ground
Szechuan pepper

300 ml/1/2 pint
vegetable stock

**1** Cut the aubergines into cubes if
you are using the larger variety, or cut
the smaller type in half. Place the
aubergines in a colander and sprinkle
with the salt. Let stand for 30
minutes. Rinse the aubergines under
cold running water and pat dry with
kitchen paper.

**2** Heat the oil in a preheated wok and
add the garlic, ginger, onion and fresh
chilli. Stir-fry for 30 seconds and add
the aubergines. Continue to cook for
1–2 minutes.

**3** Add the remaining ingredients to
the wok, reduce the heat and simmer,
uncovered, for 10 minutes, until the
aubergines are cooked. Increase the
heat to high and bring to the boil.

Cook until the the sauce has
thickened slightly and is coating the
aubergines completely.

**4** Transfer the spicy aubergines to a
warm serving dish and serve
immediately.

### COOK'S TIP

Sprinkling the aubergines with salt and
letting them stand removes the bitter
juices, which would otherwise taint the
flavour of the dish.

# Aubergine in Black Bean Sauce

Stir-fried aubergine is served in a black bean sauce with garlic and spring onions. This is good served with plain boiled rice.

| Serves 4 |
| --- |
| 50 g/1¾ oz |
| dried black beans |
| 425 ml/¾ pint |
| vegetable stock |
| 1 tbsp malt vinegar |
| 1 tbsp Chinese rice wine or dry sherry |
| 1 tbsp soy sauce |
| 1 tbsp sugar |
| 1½ tsp cornflour |
| 1 red chilli, seeded and chopped |
| 1-cm/½-inch piece |
| fresh ginger root, chopped |
| 2 aubergines |
| 2 tsp salt |
| 3 tbsp vegetable oil |
| 2 garlic cloves, sliced |
| 4 spring onions, |
| sliced diagonally |
| shredded radishes, to garnish |

**1** Soak the beans overnight in plenty of cold water. Drain and place in a saucepan. Cover with cold water, bring to the boil and boil rapidly, uncovered, for 10 minutes. Drain. Return the beans to the saucepan with the stock and bring to the boil.

**2** Blend together the vinegar, rice wine or sherry, soy sauce, sugar, cornflour, chilli and ginger in a small bowl. Add to the beans, then cover and simmer for 40 minutes, or until the beans are tender and the sauce has thickened. Stir occasionally.

**3** Cut the aubergines into chunks and place in a colander. Sprinkle with the salt and let drain for 30 minutes.

Rinse well and dry on kitchen paper.

**4** Heat the oil in a preheated wok or large frying pan. Add the aubergine and garlic. Stir-fry for 3–4 minutes until the aubergine has started to brown.

**5** Add the sauce to the aubergine, with the spring onions. Heat thoroughly and garnish with radish shreds.

# Spicy Mushrooms

A mixture of mushrooms common in Western cooking, have been used
in this recipe for a richly flavoured dish. If Chinese dried mushrooms
are available, add a small quantity.

| Serves 4 |
| --- |
| 2 tbsp peanut oil |
| 2 garlic cloves, crushed |
| 3 spring onions, chopped |
| 300 g/10½ oz button mushrooms |
| 2 large open-cap mushrooms, thinly sliced |
| 115 g/4 oz oyster mushrooms, torn into pieces or fresh shiitake mushrooms, finely chopped |
| 1 tsp chilli sauce |
| 1 tbsp dark soy sauce |
| 1 tbsp hoi-sin sauce |
| 1 tbsp wine vinegar |
| ½ tsp ground Szechuan pepper |
| 1 tbsp dark brown sugar |
| 1 tsp sesame oil |
| chopped parsley, to garnish |

**1** Heat the oil in a preheated wok until almost smoking. Reduce the heat slightly, add the garlic and spring onions and stir-fry for 30 seconds.

**2** Add the button, open-cap and oyster or shiitake mushrooms, chilli sauce, soy sauce, hoi-sin sauce, wine vinegar, pepper and brown sugar and stir-fry for 4–5 minutes, until the mushrooms are cooked.

**3** Sprinkle the sesame oil on top. Transfer to a warm serving dish and serve immediately, garnished with the fresh parsley.

### COOK'S TIP

Follow the lines of the gills when tearing oyster mushrooms.

### COOK'S TIP

This dish is ideal served with rich meat or fish dishes.

# Money Bags

These steamed dumplings are filled with mushroom and sweetcorn.
Try dipping them in a mixture of soy sauce, Chinese rice wine
or dry sherry and slivers of fresh ginger root.

| Serves 4 |
| --- |
| 3 Chinese dried mushrooms or thinly sliced open-cup mushrooms |
| 225 g/8 oz plain flour |
| 1 egg, beaten |
| 75 ml/3 fl oz water |
| 1 tsp baking powder |
| $^3/_4$ tsp salt |
| 2 tbsp vegetable oil |
| 2 spring onions, chopped |
| 75 g/2$^3/_4$ oz sweetcorn kernels |
| $^1/_2$ red chilli, seeded and chopped |
| 1 tbsp brown bean sauce |

**1** Place the dried mushrooms in a small bowl, cover with warm water and soak for 20–25 minutes.

**2** To make the wrappers, sift the flour into a bowl. Add the egg and mix lightly. Stir in the water, baking powder and salt. Mix to a soft dough. Knead lightly until smooth on a floured board. Cover with a damp cloth and set aside for 5–6 minutes. This allows the baking powder time to activate, so that the dumplings swell when they are steamed.

**3** Drain the mushrooms, squeezing them dry. Remove the tough stalks and chop the caps.

**4** Heat the oil in a wok or large heavy-based frying pan. Add the

mushrooms, spring onions, sweetcorn and chilli and stir-fry for 2 minutes. Stir in the brown bean sauce and remove the wok or pan from the heat.

**5** Roll the dough out on a lightly floured surface into a large sausage and cut into 24 even-size pieces.

**6** Roll each piece out into a thin round and place a teaspoonful of the filling in the centre. Gather up the edges, pinch together and twist to seal.

**7** Stand the dumplings in an oiled steaming basket. Place over a saucepan of simmering water, cover and steam for 12–14 minutes before serving.

# Steamed Vegetable Cabbage Rolls

In this recipe a mixed vegetable stuffing is wrapped in
Chinese leaves and steamed until tender. Serve with chilli
or soy sauce for a really tasty meal.

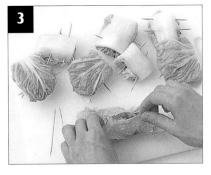

| Serves 4 |
| --- |
| 8 large Chinese leaves |
| **FILLING** |
| 2 baby corn cobs, sliced |
| 1 carrot, finely chopped |
| 1 celery stick, chopped |
| 4 spring onions, chopped |
| 4 water chestnuts, chopped |
| 2 tbsp chopped unsalted cashew nuts |
| 1 garlic clove, chopped |
| 1 tsp grated fresh ginger root |
| 25 g/1 oz canned bamboo shoots, drained and chopped |
| 1 tsp sesame oil |
| 2 tsp soy sauce |

**1** Put the Chinese leaves in a large
bowl and pour boiling water over
them to soften the leaves. Leave for 1
minute and drain well.

**2** Make the filling. Mix together the
corn, carrot, celery, spring onions,
water chestnuts, cashews, garlic,
ginger, bamboo shoots, sesame oil and
soy sauce in a bowl. Spread out the
Chinese leaves on a board and spoon
an equal quantity of the filling
mixture on to each one.

**3** Roll the leaves up, folding in the
sides, and secure with cocktail sticks.

**4** Place the filled rolls in a small
heatproof dish in a steamer, cover and
cook for 15–20 minutes, until the
parcels are cooked through.

**5** Transfer the filled rolls to a warm
serving dish and serve immediately
with chilli or soy sauce, according to
your choice.

**COOK'S TIP**

Make the parcels in advance,
cover and store in the refrigerator until
required and then steam
as in step 4.

# Creamy Cabbage & Leeks

This dish is very quick to make. The Chinese leaves complement the leek perfectly.
A dash of cream is added to the sauce, but this may be omitted if preferred.

| Serves 4 |
| --- |
| 450 g/1 lb Chinese leaves, shredded |
| 2 tbsp peanut oil |
| 2 leeks, shredded |
| 4 garlic cloves, crushed |
| 300 ml/$\frac{1}{2}$ pint vegetable stock |
| 1 tbsp light soy sauce |
| 2 tsp cornflour |
| 4 tsp water |
| 2 tbsp single cream or natural yogurt |
| 1 tbsp chopped fresh coriander, to garnish |

**1** Blanch the Chinese leaves in boiling water for 30 seconds, then drain well, rinse under cold water and drain again. Heat the peanut oil in a preheated wok and add the Chinese leaves, leeks and garlic. Stir-fry for 2–3 minutes.

**2** Add the stock and soy sauce to the wok, reduce the heat to low, cover and simmer for 10 minutes, or until the vegetables are tender.

**3** Remove the vegetables with a slotted spoon, set aside and keep warm. Bring the stock to the boil and boil vigorously to reduce by half. Blend the cornflour with the water and stir it into the stock. Bring to the boil, stirring until thickened and clear.

**4** Reduce the heat and return the vegetables to the wok. Add the cream or yogurt and cook the mixture over a gentle heat for at least 1 minute.

**5** Transfer to a warm serving dish, sprinkle with the chopped coriander to garnish and serve.

### COOK'S TIP

Do not boil the sauce once the cream or yogurt has been added, as it will separate on boiling.

# Lemon Chinese Leaves

Stir-fried Chinese leaves are served with a tangy sauce
made of grated lemon rind, lemon juice and fresh ginger.

| Serves 4 |
| --- |
| 450 g/1 lb Chinese leaves |
| 3 tbsp vegetable oil |
| 1-cm/¹/₂-inch piece fresh ginger root, grated |
| 1 tsp salt |
| 1 tsp sugar |
| 125 ml/4 fl oz water or vegetable stock |
| 1 tsp grated lemon rind |
| 1 tbsp cornflour |
| 1 tbsp lemon juice |

**1** Separate the Chinese leaves, wash and drain thoroughly. Pat dry with kitchen paper. With a sharp knife, cut into 5-cm/2-inch wide slices.

**2** Heat the oil in a preheated wok or frying pan. Add the ginger and Chinese leaves and stir-fry for 2–3 minutes, or until the leaves begin to wilt. Add the salt and sugar, and mix well until the leaves soften. Remove with a slotted spoon and set aside.

**3** Add the water or vegetable stock and grated lemon zest and bring to the boil. Meanwhile, mix the cornflour to a smooth paste with the lemon juice, then add to the water or stock in the pan. Simmer, stirring constantly, for about 1 minute to make a smooth sauce.

**4** Return the cooked leaves to the pan and mix thoroughly. Arrange on a serving plate and serve immediately.

# Chinese Leaves Stir-fried in Soy & Honey

Chinese leaves (cabbage) are rather similar to lettuce in that they are delicate with a sweet flavour.

| Serves 4 |
| --- |
| 450 g/1 lb Chinese leaves |
| 1 tbsp peanut oil |
| 1-cm/$\frac{1}{2}$-inch piece fresh ginger root, grated |
| 2 garlic cloves, crushed |
| 1 fresh red chilli, sliced |
| 1 tbsp Chinese rice wine or dry sherry |
| 4$\frac{1}{2}$ tsp light soy sauce |
| 1 tbsp clear honey |
| 125 ml/4 fl oz orange juice |
| 1 tbsp sesame oil |
| 2 tsp sesame seeds |
| orange zest, to garnish |

**1** Separate the Chinese leaves and shred finely. Heat the oil in a preheated wok. Add the ginger, garlic and chilli and stir-fry for 30 seconds.

**2** Add the Chinese leaves, rice wine or sherry, soy sauce, honey and orange juice. Reduce the heat and simmer for 5 minutes.

**3** Add the sesame oil, sprinkle in the sesame seeds and mix thoroughly. Transfer to a warm serving dish, garnish with the orange zest and serve immediately.

### COOK'S TIP

Use a western cabbage, such as Savoy, in place of Chinese leaves if they are unavailable.

# Lentil Balls with Sweet & Sour Sauce

Crisp golden lentil balls are served in a sweet-and-sour sauce
with peppers and pineapple chunks.

### Serves 4

225 g/8 oz red lentils, washed

450 ml/16 fl oz water

$^1/_2$ green chilli, seeded and chopped

4 spring onions, finely chopped

1 garlic clove, crushed

1 tsp salt

4 tbsp pineapple juice from can

1 egg, beaten

vegetable oil, for deep-frying

rice or noodles, to serve

### SAUCE

3 tbsp white wine vinegar

2 tbsp sugar

2 tbsp tomato purée

1 tsp sesame oil

1 tsp cornflour

$^1/_2$ tsp salt

6 tbsp water

2 canned pineapple rings

2 tbsp vegetable oil

$^1/_2$ red pepper, seeded and diced

$^1/_2$ green pepper, seeded and diced

**1** Put the lentils in a pan with the
water and bring to the boil. Skim and
boil rapidly for 10 minutes. Lower the
heat and simmer for 5 minutes.

**2** Remove the lentils from the heat
and stir in the chilli, spring onions,
garlic, salt and pineapple juice. Cool
for 10 minutes.

**3** To make the sauce, mix together
the vinegar, sugar, tomato purée,
sesame oil, cornflour, salt and water,
and set aside. Cut the pineapple
into chunks.

**4** Add the egg to the lentil mixture.
Heat the oil in a wok and deep-fry
tablespoons of the mixture in batches
until crisp and golden. Remove with a
slotted spoon and drain.

**5** Heat the 2 tablespoons oil in a wok
or frying pan. Stir-fry the peppers for

2 minutes. Add the sauce mixture
with the pineapple chunks. Bring to
the boil, reduce the heat and simmer
for 1 minute, stirring constantly, until
the sauce has thickened. Add the
lentil balls and heat through, taking
care not to break them up. Serve with
rice or noodles.

# Crisp Fried Pak Choi & Almonds

This can be served on its own as an appetizer
or as a delicious accompaniment to grilled fish or meat.

| Serves 4 |
| --- |
| 900 g/2 lb pak choi |
| 700 ml/1¹/₄ pints vegetable oil |
| 1 tbsp light brown sugar |
| 1 tsp salt |
| pinch of ground cinnamon |
| 75 g/2³/₄ oz blanched almonds |

**1** Separate and wash the pak choi leaves. Dry thoroughly with kitchen paper and shred into thin strips.

**2** Heat the oil in a preheated wok until almost smoking. Reduce the heat and add the shredded pak choi. Cook for 2–3 minutes, or until the leaves begin to float in the oil and have become crisp.

**3** Remove the leaves from the oil with a slotted spoon and drain thoroughly on absorbent kitchen paper. Add the almonds to the oil and cook for 30 seconds. Remove from the oil with a slotted spoon.

**4** Mix the salt, sugar and cinnamon together and sprinkle on to the pak choi leaves, toss in the almonds, transfer to a large serving dish and serve immediately.

### COOK'S VARIATION
You could also prepare this dish with spring greens, rather like crispy seaweed.

### COOK'S TIP
Fry the almonds very briefly, as they will brown almost immediately and can easily burn and become bitter.

# Broccoli with Ginger & Orange

Thinly sliced broccoli florets are lightly stir-fried and
served in a ginger and orange sauce.

| Serves 4 |
| --- |
| 675 g/1¹/₂ lb broccoli |
| 2 thin slices fresh ginger root |
| 2 garlic cloves |
| 1 orange |
| 2 tsp cornflour |
| 1 tbsp light soy sauce |
| ¹/₂ tsp caster sugar |
| 2 tbsp vegetable oil |

**1** Divide the broccoli into small
florets. Peel the stems, using a
vegetable peeler. Cut the stems into
thin slices. Cut the ginger root into
matchsticks and slice the garlic.

**2** Peel 2 long strips of zest from the
orange and cut into thin strips. Place
the strips in a bowl, cover with cold
water and set aside. Squeeze the juice
from the orange and mix with the
cornflour, soy sauce, sugar and 4
tablespoons water.

**3** Heat the oil in a preheated wok or
large frying pan. Add the sliced
broccoli stems and stir-fry for
2 minutes. Add the ginger, garlic and
broccoli florets, and stir-fry for a
further 3 minutes.

**4** Stir in the orange sauce mixture
and cook, stirring constantly, until the
sauce has thickened and the broccoli
is thoroughly coated.

**5** Drain the reserved orange rind and
stir it in. Transfer the ginger and
sauce to a warm serving dish and
serve immediately.

# Broccoli in Oyster Sauce

Some Cantonese restaurants use only the stalks of the broccoli
for this dish, for the crunchy texture.

| Serves 4 |
|---|
| 300 g/10$^{1}$/$_{2}$ oz broccoli |
| 3 tbsp vegetable oil |
| 3–4 small slices fresh ginger root |
| $^{1}$/$_{2}$ tsp salt |
| $^{1}$/$_{2}$ tsp sugar |
| 3–4 tbsp Chinese Stock (see page 16) or water |
| 1 tbsp oyster sauce |

**1** Cut the broccoli into small florets. Trim the stalks, peel off the rough skin, and cut the stalks diagonally into diamond-shaped chunks.

**2** Heat the oil in a preheated wok and add the pieces of stalk and the ginger. Stir-fry for 30 seconds, then add the broccoli florets and continue to stir-fry for another 2 minutes.

**3** Add the salt, sugar and stock or water, and continue stirring for another 1–2 minutes.

**4** Blend in the oyster sauce. Transfer to a warm serving dish and serve hot. Alternatively, let cool and serve cold.

### COOK'S TIP

For a vegetarian version of this dish, substitute dark soy sauce for the oyster sauce.

# Garlic Spinach

This has to be one of the simplest recipes, yet it is so tasty. Spinach is quickly fried
with garlic and lemon grass and tossed in a little soy sauce and sugar.

| Serves 4 |
| --- |
| 900 g/2 lb fresh spinach |
| 2 tbsp peanut oil |
| 2 garlic cloves, crushed |
| 1 tsp chopped lemon grass |
| pinch of salt |
| 1 tbsp dark soy sauce |
| 2 tsp brown sugar |

**1** Remove the stems from the
spinach. Wash the leaves and drain
very well, patting dry with absorbent
kitchen paper.

**2** Heat the oil in a preheated wok
until almost smoking. Reduce the
heat slightly, add the garlic and lemon
grass and stir-fry for 30 seconds.

**3** Add the spinach and salt and stir-
fry for 2–3 minutes, until the spinach
has wilted.

**4** Stir in the soy sauce and sugar and
cook for a further 3–4 minutes.
Transfer to a warm serving dish and
serve immediately.

## COOK'S TIP

Use baby spinach if possible, as the
leaves have a better flavour and look
more appealing. In this case, the stems
may be left intact.

# Spinach with Straw Mushrooms

Straw mushrooms, available in cans from supermarkets and Chinese foodstores, are served with spinach, raisins and pine nuts.

| Serves 4 |
| --- |
| 25 g/1 oz pine nuts |
| 450 g/1 lb fresh spinach |
| 3 tbsp vegetable oil |
| 1 red onion, sliced |
| 2 garlic cloves, sliced |
| 400 g/14 oz can straw mushrooms, drained |
| 25 g/1 oz raisins |
| 2 tbsp soy sauce |
| salt |

**1** Heat a wok or large frying pan and dry-fry the pine nuts, stirring constantly, until lightly browned. Remove and set aside.

**2** Wash the spinach thoroughly, picking the leaves over and removing any long stalks. Drain and pat dry with kitchen paper.

**3** Heat the oil in a preheated wok or frying pan. Add the onion and garlic, and stir-fry for 1 minute.

**4** Add the spinach and mushrooms, and stir-fry until the leaves have wilted. Drain off any excess liquid.

**5** Stir in the raisins, the reserved pine nuts and the soy sauce. Stir-fry until thoroughly heated and well mixed. Season with salt to taste, transfer to a warm serving dish and serve immediately.

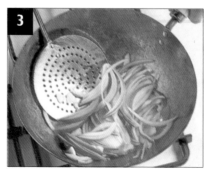

# Chinese Potato Sticks

These sticks are a variation on the great Western favourite,
being flavoured with soy sauce and chilli.

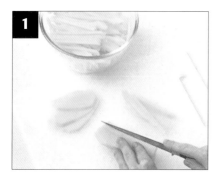

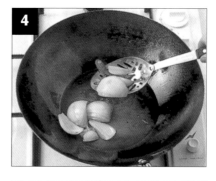

| Serves 4 |
|---|
| 675 g/1¹/₂ lb medium-size maincrop potatoes |
| 8 tbsp vegetable oil |
| 1 fresh red chilli, halved |
| 1 small onion, quartered |
| 2 garlic cloves, halved |
| 2 tbsp soy sauce |
| pinch of salt |
| 1 tsp wine vinegar |
| 1 tbsp coarse sea salt |
| pinch of chilli powder |

**1** Peel the potatoes and cut into thin slices along their length. Cut the slices into matchsticks.

**2** Blanch the potato sticks in boiling water for 2 minutes and drain well. Dry on absorbent kitchen paper.

**3** Heat the oil in a preheated wok until almost smoking.

**4** Add the chilli, onion and garlic to the wok and stir-fry for 30 seconds. Remove and discard the chilli, onion and garlic.

**5** Add the potato sticks to the oil and fry for 3–4 minutes, until golden.

**6** Add the soy sauce, salt and vinegar, reduce the heat and fry for 1 further minute, or until the potatoes are crisp. Remove the potatoes with a slotted spoon and leave to drain thoroughly on absorbent kitchen paper.

**7** Transfer the potato sticks to a serving bowl.

**8** Sprinkle the potato sticks with the sea salt and chilli powder and serve immediately.

**COOK'S TIP**

Sprinkle other flavourings, such as curry powder, over the cooked potato sticks or serve with a chilli dip.

# Rice Dishes

Rice is a staple food throughout much of China and is served with most meals. Plain boiled rice is the usual everyday accompaniment to family meals, but it can easily be enlivened by steaming or frying it with other ingredients, such as peppers, peas, spring onions or mushrooms. While rice has a fairly bland flavour, it provides a complementary texture to many other

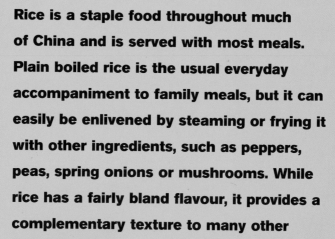

ingredients and absorbs the stronger flavours of other dishes, as well as providing the essential bulk required for satisfying the appetite.

Some of the recipes in this chapter could be adapted to make a quick and easy main meal. Try Chicken & Rice Casserole, Rice with Crab & Mussels or Fried Rice with Pork, Tomatoes, Peas & Mushrooms.

White long-grain rice is most frequently served with savoury dishes, although brown long-grain rice may also be used.

# Chinese Fried Rice

The rice for this dish may be cooked in the wok
or in a saucepan, but it is essential to use cold,
dry rice with separate grains for success.

| Serves 4 |
| --- |
| 700 ml/1¼ pints water |
| ½ tsp salt |
| 300 g long-grain rice |
| 2 eggs |
| 4 tsp cold water |
| 3 tbsp sunflower oil |
| 4 spring onions, sliced diagonally |
| 1 red, green or yellow pepper, seeded and thinly sliced |
| 3–4 lean bacon slices, cut into strips |
| 200 g/7 oz beansprouts |
| 115 g/4 oz frozen peas, thawed |
| 2 tbsp light soy sauce (optional) |
| salt and pepper |

**1** Bring the water to the boil with the
salt in a wok. Rinse the rice under
cold water until it runs clear, drain
and add to the wok. Stir, cover tightly
and simmer gently for 12–13 minutes.
(Do not remove the lid during cooking
or the steam will escape and the rice
will not be cooked.)

**2** Stir the rice and spread out on a
large plate or baking sheet to cool
and dry.

**3** Beat each egg separately with salt
and pepper and 2 teaspoons cold
water. Heat 1 tablespoon of oil in a
preheated wok. Pour in 1 egg, swirl it
around and cook until set. Remove to
a board and cook the second egg. Cut
the omelettes into thin slices.

**4** Heat the remaining oil in the wok.
When it is hot, add the spring onions

and pepper slices and stir-fry for 1–2
minutes. Add the bacon and continue
to stir-fry for a further 1–2 minutes.
Add the beansprouts and peas and
toss together thoroughly. Stir in the
soy sauce if using.

**5** Add the rice and season to taste
with salt and pepper. Stir-fry for
1–2 minutes. Add the strips of
omelette and continue to stir for
about 2 minutes, or until the rice is
piping hot. Transfer to a warm serving
dish and serve at once.

# Vegetable Fried Rice

This dish can be served as part of a substantial
meal for a number of people or as a
vegetarian meal in itself for four.

| Serves 4 |
| --- |
| 150 g/5 oz long-grain white rice |
| 3 tbsp peanut oil |
| 2 garlic cloves, crushed |
| $^{1}/_{2}$ tsp Chinese five-spice powder |
| 50 g/1$^{3}/_{4}$ oz green beans |
| 1 green pepper, seeded and chopped |
| 4 baby corn cobs, sliced |
| 25 g/1 oz canned bamboo shoots drained and chopped |
| 3 tomatoes, peeled, seeded and chopped |
| 50 g/1$^{3}/_{4}$ oz cooked peas |
| 1 tsp sesame oil |

**1** Cook the rice in lightly salted boiling water for 15 minutes. Drain, rinse under cold running water and drain well again.

**2** Heat the peanut oil in a preheated wok. Add the garlic and Chinese five-spice powder and stir-fry for 30 seconds.

**3** Add the green beans, pepper and corn cobs and stir-fry for about 2 minutes.

**4** Stir in the bamboo shoots, tomatoes, peas and rice and stir-fry for 1 further minute. Sprinkle with sesame oil.

**5** Transfer to a warm serving dish and serve immediately.

### COOK'S TIP

When cooking rice by the non-absorption method, as here, stir it once only. Stirring more frequently will break up the grains and the cooked rice will be sticky.

### COOK'S TIP

Use a selection of vegetables of your choice in this recipe, cutting them to a similar size in order to ensure that they cook in the same amount of time.

# Fragrant Steamed Rice in Lotus Leaves

The fragrance of the lotus leaves flavours the rice. Lotus leaves are available from Chinese foodstores, but the cabbage or spinach leaves can be substituted.

| Serves 4 |
| --- |
| 2 lotus leaves |
| 4 Chinese dried mushrooms |
| 175 g/6 oz long-grain rice |
| 1 cinnamon stick |
| 6 cardamom pods |
| 4 cloves |
| 1 tsp salt |
| 2 eggs |
| 1 tbsp vegetable oil |
| 2 spring onions, chopped |
| 1 tbsp light soy sauce |
| 2 tbsp Chinese rice wine or dry sherry |
| 1 tsp sugar |
| 1 tsp sesame oil |

**1** Unfold the lotus leaves and cut along the fold to divide each leaf in half. Lay on a large baking sheet and pour over enough hot water to cover. Soak for about 30 minutes, or until softened.

**2** Place the mushrooms in a small bowl and cover with warm water. Soak for 20–25 minutes.

**3** Cook the rice in boiling water with the cinnamon stick, cardamom pods, cloves and salt for about 10 minutes, until partially cooked. Drain and remove the cinnamon stick.

**4** Beat the eggs lightly. Heat the oil in a preheated wok or heavy-based frying pan. Add the eggs and cook quickly, stirring constantly until set. Remove the mixture from the wok or pan and set aside.

**5** Drain the mushrooms, squeezing out the excess water. Remove the stalks and chop the caps. Place the rice in a bowl. Stir in the mushrooms, eggs, spring onions, soy sauce, rice wine or sherry, sugar and sesame oil. Season with salt to taste.

**6** Drain the lotus leaves and divide the rice mixture into 4 portions. Place a portion in the centre of each leaf and fold up to form a parcel. Place in a steamer, cover and steam for 20 minutes. To serve, cut the tops of the leaves open to expose the filling.

# Green Fried Rice with Spinach

Spinach is used in this recipe to give the rice a wonderful
green colouring. Tossed with the carrot strips,
it is a really appealing dish.

| Serves 4 |
| --- |
| 150 g/5¹/₂ oz long-grain rice |
| 2 tbsp vegetable oil |
| 2 garlic cloves, crushed |
| 1 tsp grated fresh ginger root |
| 1 carrot, cut into matchsticks |
| 1 courgette, diced |
| 225 g/8 oz baby spinach |
| 2 tsp light soy sauce |
| 2 tsp light brown sugar |
| salt |

**1** Cook the rice in lightly salted boiling water for 15 minutes. Drain, rinse under cold running water and rinse thoroughly again.

**2** Heat the oil in a preheated wok. Add the garlic and ginger and stir-fry for 30 seconds. Add the carrot and courgette and stir-fry for 2 minutes.

**3** Stir in the baby spinach and stir-fry for 1 minute, until wilted. Add the rice, soy sauce and sugar and mix well. Transfer to a warm serving dish and serve immediately.

**VARIATION**

Chinese leaves may be used in place of the spinach, giving a lighter green colour to the dish.

# Egg Fried Rice with Chilli

This version of fried rice is given extra
punch with hot red chillies,
spring onions and fish sauce.

| Serves 4 |
| --- |
| 225 g/8 oz basmati rice |
| 3 tbsp sunflower oil |
| 1 hot red chilli, seeded and finely chopped |
| 2 tsp fish sauce |
| 3 spring onions, chopped |
| 1 large egg, beaten |
| 1 tbsp chopped fresh parsley or coriander |
| 1 tbsp light soy sauce |
| 1 tsp sugar |
| salt and pepper |

**1** Cook the rice in lightly salted
boiling water for about 10 minutes,
until tender. Drain, rinse with boiling
water and drain again thoroughly.
Spread out on a large plate or baking
sheet to dry.

**2** Heat the oil in a preheated wok or
large, heavy-based frying pan. Add the
chilli, fish sauce and spring onions
and stir-fry for 1–2 minutes.

**3** Add the beaten egg and stir-fry
quickly so that the egg scrambles into
small fluffy pieces.

**4** Fork through the rice to separate
the grains, then add to the wok or pan
and stir-fry for about
1 minute to mix thoroughly and to
heat through.

**5** Sprinkle a little of the chopped
parsley or coriander over the rice. Mix
the soy sauce with the sugar and

remaining chopped parsley or
coriander and stir into the rice
mixture, tossing well to mix.

**6** Transfer to a warm serving dish and
serve immediately.

**COOK'S TIP**

It is often difficult to identify chillies.
As a general rule, sharply pointed, thin
chillies tend to be hotter than short,
blunt ones.

# Egg Fried Rice

The rice used for frying should not be too soft.
Ideally, the rice should have been slightly undercooked
and thoroughly cooled before frying.

| Serves 4 |
| --- |
| 3 eggs |
| 1 tsp salt |
| 2 spring onions, finely chopped |
| 2–3 tbsp vegetable oil |
| 450 g/1 lb cooked rice, well drained and cooled |
| 115 g/4 oz cooked peas |

**1** Lightly beat the eggs with a pinch of salt and 1 tablespoon of the spring onions.

**2** Heat the oil in a preheated wok, add the eggs and stir until lightly scrambled. (The eggs should be cooked only until they start to set, so that they are still moist.)

**3** Add the cold rice and stir to make sure that each grain is separated. Make sure the oil is really hot, otherwise the rice will become heavy and greasy.

**4** Add the remaining salt, spring onions and peas. Blend well and serve hot or cold.

# Egg Fu Yong with Rice

Cooked rice mixed with scrambled eggs, Chinese mushrooms,
bamboo shoots and water chestnuts – a great
way of using up leftover cooked rice.

| Serves 2-4 |
| --- |
| 175 g/6 oz long grain rice |
| 2 Chinese dried mushrooms (or thinly sliced open-cup mushrooms) |
| 3 eggs |
| 3 tbsp vegetable oil |
| 4 spring onions, sliced |
| ½ green pepper, seeded and chopped |
| 50 g/1¾ oz canned bamboo shoots, drained |
| 50 g/1¾ oz canned water chestnuts, drained and sliced |
| 115 g/4 oz beansprouts |
| 2 tbsp light soy sauce |
| 2 tbsp Chinese rice wine or dry sherry |
| 2 tsp sesame oil |
| salt and pepper |

**1** Cook the rice in lightly salted boiling water for about 10 minutes, until almost tender. Drain, rinse, drain again and set aside to cool.

**2** Place the dried mushrooms in a small bowl, cover with warm water and soak for 20–25 minutes.

**3** Beat the eggs with a little salt. Heat 1 tablespoon of the oil in a wok or frying pan. Add the eggs and stir until set. Remove and set aside.

**4** Drain the mushrooms and squeeze out the excess water. Remove the tough stalks and chop the caps.

**5** Heat the remaining oil in a clean wok or frying pan. Add the mushrooms, spring onions and green pepper, and stir-fry for 2 minutes. Add the bamboo shoots, water chestnuts and beansprouts. Stir-fry for 1 minute.

**6** Add the rice to the wok or pan, together with the soy sauce, Chinese rice wine or sherry and sesame oil. Mix well, heating the rice thoroughly. Season to taste with salt and pepper. Stir in the reserved eggs, transfer to a serving dish and serve.

# Special Fried Rice

This dish is a popular choice in Chinese restaurants. Ham and prawns
are mixed with vegetables in a soy-flavoured rice.

| Serves 4 |
| --- |
| 150 g/5¹/₂ oz |
| long-grain rice |
| 2 tbsp vegetable oil |
| 2 eggs, beaten |
| 2 garlic cloves, crushed |
| 1 tsp grated fresh ginger root |
| 3 spring onions, |
| sliced |
| 75 g/2³/₄ oz cooked peas |
| 150 g/5¹/₂ oz |
| beansprouts |
| 225 g/8 oz |
| shredded ham |
| 150 g/5¹/₂ oz peeled, |
| cooked prawns |
| 2 tbsp light soy sauce |
| salt |

**1** Cook the rice in lightly salted
boiling water for 15 minutes. Drain,
rinse under cold water and drain
thoroughly again.

**2** Heat 1 tbsp of the oil in a
preheated wok and add the beaten
eggs and a further 1 teaspoon of oil.
Tilt the wok so that the egg covers the
base to make a thin omelette. Cook
until lightly browned on the
underside, flip the omelette and cook
on the other side for 1 minute.
Remove from the wok and let cool.

**3** Heat the remaining oil in the wok.
Add the garlic and ginger and stir-fry
for 30 seconds. Add the spring onions,
peas, beansprouts, ham and prawns
and stir-fry for 2 minutes.

**4** Stir in the soy sauce and rice and
cook for a further 2 minutes. Slice the
omelette very thinly and sprinkle it on
to the dish. Transfer the special fried
rice to a warm serving dish and serve
immediately.

## COOK'S TIP

As this recipe contains meat and fish, it
is ideal served with simpler vegetable
dishes.

# Fried Rice with Prawns

Use either large peeled prawns
or tiger prawns for
this rice dish.

| Serves 4 |
| --- |
| 275 g/9$\frac{1}{2}$ oz |
| long-grain rice |
| 2 eggs |
| 4 tsp cold water |
| 3 tbsp sunflower oil |
| 4 spring onions, |
| thinly sliced diagonally |
| 1 garlic clove, crushed |
| 115 g/4 oz closed-cup or button |
| mushrooms, thinly sliced |
| 2 tbsp oyster or anchovy sauce |
| 200g/7 oz can water chestnuts, |
| drained and sliced |
| 225 g/8 oz peeled prawns, |
| thawed if frozen |
| $\frac{1}{2}$ bunch of watercress, |
| roughly chopped |
| salt and pepper |
| watercress sprigs, |
| to garnish (optional) |

**1** Cook the rice in lightly salted boiling salted water, following the instructions given in Chinese Fried Rice (see page 176) and keep warm.

**2** Beat each egg separately with 2 teaspoons of cold water and salt and pepper to taste. Heat 2 teaspoons of oil in a preheated wok. Pour in the first egg, swirl it around, and cook undisturbed until set. Remove to a plate or board and repeat with the second egg. Cut the omelettes into 2.5-cm/1-inch squares.

**3** Heat the remaining oil in the wok and when really hot add the spring onions and garlic, and stir-fry for 1 minute. Add the mushrooms and continue to cook for a further 2 minutes.

**4** Stir in the oyster or anchovy sauce and seasoning. Add the water chestnuts and prawns and stir-fry for 2 minutes.

**5** Stir in the cooked rice and stir-fry for 1 minute. Add the watercress and omelette squares and stir-fry for a further 1–2 minutes, until piping hot.

**6** Transfer to a warm serving dish, garnish with sprigs of watercress, if desired, and serve immediately.

# Chicken & Rice Casserole

This is a spicy casserole of rice, chicken, vegetables and chilli in a soy and ginger flavoured sauce. Although called a casserole, it requires only approximately 30 minutes cooking time.

| Serves 4 |
|---|
| 150 g/5$^{1}/_{2}$ oz long grain rice |
| 2 tsp salt |
| 1 tbsp Chinese rice wine or dry sherry |
| 2 tbsp light soy sauce |
| 2 tbsp dark soy sauce |
| 2 tsp dark brown sugar |
| 1 tsp sesame oil |
| 900 g/2 lb skinless, boneless chicken meat, diced |
| 850 ml/1$^{1}/_{2}$ pints chicken stock |
| 2 open-cap mushrooms, thinly sliced |
| 50 g/1$^{3}/_{4}$ oz canned water chestnuts, drained and halved |
| 75 g/2$^{3}/_{4}$ oz broccoli florets |
| 1 yellow pepper, seed and sliced |
| 4 tsp grated fresh ginger root |
| 2 tbsp chopped chives |

**1** Cook the rice in lightly salted boiling water for 15 minutes. Drain, rinse under cold water and drain again thoroughly.

**2** Mix together the Chinese rice wine or sherry, soy sauce, sugar and sesame oil in a large bowl. Season to taste with salt. Stir the chicken into the mixture, turning to coat well, and marinate for 30 minutes.

**3** Bring the stock to the boil, add the chicken, together with the marinade, mushrooms, water chestnuts, broccoli, pepper and ginger.

**4** Stir in the rice, reduce the heat, cover and cook for 25–30 minutes, until the chicken and vegetables are cooked through.

**5** Transfer to a warm serving dish and serve as a meal in itself.

### VARIATION

This dish would work equally well with beef or pork. Chinese dried mushrooms may be used instead of the open-cap mushrooms.

# Special Fried Rice with Cashew Nuts

In this simple recipe, cooked rice is fried with vegetables
and cashew nuts. It can be eaten on its own
or served as an accompaniment.

| Serves 4 |
| --- |
| 175 g/6 oz |
| long grain rice |
| 50 g/1³/₄ oz/¹/₂ cup cashew nuts |
| 1 carrot |
| ¹/₂ cucumber |
| 1 yellow pepper |
| 2 spring onions |
| 2 tbsp vegetable oil |
| 1 garlic clove, crushed |
| 115 g/4 oz frozen |
| peas, thawed |
| 1 tbsp light soy sauce |
| 1 tsp salt |
| coriander leaves, |
| to garnish |

**1** Bring a large pan of lightly salted
water to the boil. Add the rice and
simmer for 15 minutes. Strain and
rinse, drain thoroughly and set aside
to cool.

**2** Heat a wok or large frying pan, add
the cashew nuts and dry-fry until
lightly browned. Remove and set
aside.

**3** Cut the carrot in half along the
length, then slice thinly into semi-
circles. Halve the cucumber, remove
the seeds, using a teaspoon, and
discard. Dice the flesh. Seed and slice
the pepper and chop the spring
onions.

**4** Heat the oil in a preheated wok or
large frying pan. Add the prepared
vegetables and the garlic. Stir-fry for 3
minutes.

**5** Add the rice, peas, soy sauce and
salt. Continue to stir-fry until well-
mixed and thoroughly heated. Stir in
the reserved cashew nuts. Transfer the
special fried rice to a serving dish and
serve garnished with coriander leaves.

## VARIATION

You could substitute blanched almonds
or pine nuts for the cashews in this
recipe, if wished.

# Fried Rice & Prawns

When you've got one eye on the clock and a meal to make, try this!
Quickly made yet simply stunning to look at,
its taste belies its simplicity.

| Serves 4 |
| --- |
| 50 g/1³/₄ oz butter |
| 3 tbsp vegetable oil |
| 450 g/1 lb cold cooked basmati rice |
| 6 spring onions, sliced finely |
| 115 g/4 oz mangetout, halved |
| 1 carrot, cut into julienne strips |
| 115 g/4 oz canned water chestnuts, drained and sliced |
| 1 small crisp lettuce, shredded |
| 350 g/12 oz peeled cooked tiger prawns |
| 1 large red chilli, seeded and sliced diagonally |
| 3 egg yolks |
| 4 tsp sesame oil |
| salt and pepper |

**1** Heat the butter and the oil in a wok or large, heavy-based frying pan. Add the cooked rice and stir-fry for 2 minutes.

**2** Add the spring onions, mangetout, carrot and water chestnuts and season to taste with salt and pepper. Mix thoroughly. Stir-fry over a medium heat for a further 2 minutes.

**3** Add the shredded lettuce, prawns and chilli and stir-fry for a further 2 minutes.

**4** Beat the egg yolks with the sesame oil and stir into the wok or pan, coating the rice and vegetable mixture. Cook for about 2 minutes to set the egg mixture.

**5** Transfer to a large serving dish and serve at once.

### COOK'S VARIATION

You could substitute pak choi for the lettuce and a thinly sliced red pepper for the carrot.

# Rice with Crab & Mussels

Shellfish makes an ideal partner for rice.
Mussels and crab add flavour
and texture to this spicy dish.

| Serves 4 |
| --- |
| 275 g/9¹/₂ oz long-grain rice |
| 175 g/6 oz crabmeat, fresh, canned or frozen (thawed if frozen), or 8 crab sticks, thawed if frozen |
| 2 tbsp sesame or sunflower oil |
| 2.5-cm/1-inch pieced fresh ginger root, grated |
| 4 spring onions, thinly sliced diagonally |
| 115 g/4 oz mangetout, cut into 2–3 pieces |
| ¹/₂ tsp turmeric |
| 1 tsp ground cumin |
| 2 x 200g/7 oz jars mussels, well drained, or 350 g/12 oz frozen mussels, thawed |
| 400 g/14 oz can beansprouts, well drained |
| salt and pepper |
| **TO GARNISH** |
| crab claws or legs (optional) |
| 8 mangetout, blanched |

**1** Cook the rice in boiling salted water, following the instructions given in Chinese Fried Rice (see page 176).

**2** Meanwhile, flake the fresh crabmeat, if using. If using crab sticks, cut them into 3 or 4 pieces.

**3** Heat the oil in a preheated wok. Add the ginger and spring onions and stir-fry for 1–2 minutes. Add the mangetout and continue to cook for a further minute.

**4** Sprinkle the turmeric and cumin over the vegetables and mix thoroughly. Season to taste with salt and pepper. Add the crabmeat or crab sticks and mussels and stir-fry for 1 minute.

**5** Stir in the cooked rice and beansprouts and stir-fry for 2 minutes, or until really hot and well mixed.

**6** Serve very hot, garnished with crab claws and mangetout.

# Fried Rice with Pork, Tomatoes, Peas & Mushrooms

This dish is a meal in itself, containing pieces of pork,
fried with rice, peas, tomatoes and mushrooms.

| Serves 4 |
| --- |
| 150 g/5¹/₂ oz long-grain rice |
| 3 tbsp peanut oil |
| 1 large onion, cut into eight |
| 225 g/8 oz pork fillet, thinly sliced |
| 2 open-cap mushrooms, sliced |
| 2 garlic cloves, crushed |
| 1 tbsp light soy sauce |
| 1 tsp light brown sugar |
| 2 tomatoes, peeled, seeded and chopped |
| 50 g/1³/₄ oz cooked peas |
| 2 eggs, beaten |
| salt |

**1** Cook the rice in lightly salted boiling water for 15 minutes, until tender, but not soft. Drain, rinse under cold running water and drain again thoroughly.

**2** Heat the oil in a preheated wok. Add the onion and pork and stir-fry for 3–4 minutes, until the meat is beginning to colour.

**3** Add the mushrooms and garlic and stir-fry for 1 minute. Add the soy sauce and sugar and stir-fry for a further 2 minutes

**4** Stir in the rice, tomatoes and peas, mixing well. Transfer to a warmed dish and keep warm.

**5** Stir the eggs into the wok and cook, stirring, for 2–3 minutes, until beginning to set.

**6** Return the rice mixture to the wok and mix well. Heat through.

**7** Transfer to a warm serving dish and serve immediately.

**COOK'S TIP**

Cook the rice in advance and chill or freeze until required.

# Noodle Dishes

Noodles are to northern China what rice is to the south and are served at every occasion from birthdays to weddings. They are served hot or cold and combined with fish, seafood, meat, poultry or vegetables.

There are numerous varieties of noodles, including egg noodles made from wheat flour, egg and water, transparent noodles made from ground mung beans, and rice noodles made from ground rice. They come in fine threads, strings or flat ribbons.

Most types of dried noodles require little more than rehydration. They can then be served plain, boiled, braised, fried, deep-fried or in combination with other ingredients. Chow Mein is probably the most famous noodle dish in the world, but other specialities in this chapter include Curried Prawn Noodles and Singapore-style Rice Noodles. These would all make a substantial snack or light lunch served on their own.

# Chow Mein

This is a basic recipe for Chow Mein. Additional
ingredients, such as chicken, pork or prawns,
can be added if desired.

| Serves 4 |
| --- |
| 275 g/9¹/₂ oz egg noodles |
| 3–4 tbsp vegetable oil |
| 1 small onion, finely sliced |
| 115 g/4 oz fresh beansprouts |
| 1 spring onion, finely shredded |
| 2 tbsp light soy sauce |
| a few drops of sesame oil |

**1** Cook the noodles in salted boiling
water according to the instructions on
the packet.

**2** Drain and rinse the noodles in cold
water. Drain well again, then toss
with a little vegetable oil.

**3** Heat the remaining oil in a
preheated wok. Stir-fry the onion for
about 30–40 seconds, then add the
beansprouts and noodles, stir and
toss for 1 more minute.

**4** Add the spring onion and soy sauce
and blend well. Sprinkle with the
sesame oil, transfer to a warm serving
dish and serve.

## COOK'S TIP

Egg noodles can be cooked up to
24 hours in advance and kept in a bowl
of cold water in the refrigerator until
required.

# Fried Vegetable Noodles

In this recipe, noodles are first boiled and then
deep-fried for a crisply textured dish,
and tossed with fried vegetables.

| Serves 4 |
| --- |
| 350 g/12 oz |
| dried egg noodles |
| 2 tbsp peanut oil |
| 2 garlic cloves, crushed |
| $^1/_2$ tsp ground star anise |
| 1 carrot, cut into matchsticks |
| 1 green pepper, |
| seeded and cut into matchsticks |
| 1 onion, quartered and sliced |
| 125 g/4$^1/_2$ oz broccoli florets |
| 75 g/2$^3/_4$ oz canned bamboo |
| shoots, drained and sliced |
| 1 celery stick, sliced |
| 1 tbsp light soy sauce |
| 150 ml/$^1/_4$ pint |
| vegetable stock |
| 1 tsp cornflour |
| 2 tsp water |
| oil, for deep-frying |

**1** Cook the noodles in boiling water
for 1–2 minutes. Drain well and rinse
under cold running water. Let drain
in a colander.

**2** Heat the oil in a preheated wok
until almost smoking. Reduce the
heat slightly, add the garlic and star
anise and stir-fry for 30 seconds. Add
the carrot, pepper, onion, broccoli,
bamboo shoots and celery and stir-fry
for 1–2 minutes.

**3** Add the soy sauce and stock to the
wok and cook over a low heat for
5 minutes.

**4** Heat the oil for deep-frying to
180°C/350°F, or until a cube of bread

browns in 30 seconds. Add the
drained noodles, in batches, and cook
until crisp. Drain on absorbent
kitchen paper.

**5** Blend the cornflour with the water
to form a paste and stir it into the

wok. Bring to the boil, stirring until
the sauce is thickened and clear.

**6** Arrange the noodles on a warm
serving plate, spoon the vegetables on
top and serve immediately.

# Mixed Vegetable Chow Mein

Egg noodles are fried with a colourful
variety of vegetables to make
this well-known dish.

| Serves 4 |
| --- |
| 450 g/1 lb egg noodles |
| 4 tbsp vegetable oil |
| 1 onion, thinly sliced |
| 2 carrots, cut into thin matchsticks |
| 115 g/4 oz button mushrooms, quartered |
| 115 g/4 oz mangetout |
| 1/2 cucumber, cut into thin matchsticks |
| 115 g/4 oz spinach, shredded |
| 115 g/4 oz fresh beansprouts |
| 2 tbsp dark soy sauce |
| 1 tbsp Chinese rice wine or dry sherry |
| 1 tsp salt |
| 1 tsp sugar |
| 1 tsp cornflour |
| 1 tsp sesame oil |

**1** Cook the noodles according to the packet instructions. Drain well and rinse under running cold water until cool. Drain thoroughly again and set aside.

**2** Heat 3 tablespoons of the vegetable oil in a preheated wok or large frying pan. Add the onion and carrots, and stir-fry for 1 minute. Add the mushrooms, mangetout and cucumber, and stir-fry for a further minute.

**3** Stir in the remaining vegetable oil and add the drained noodles, together with the spinach and beansprouts.

**4** In a bowl, blend together the soy sauce, Chinese rice wine or sherry, salt, sugar, cornflour and sesame oil and pour the mixture over the noodles and vegetables. Stir well to mix.

**5** Stir-fry for a further 1–2 minutes, until thoroughly heated through.

**6** Transfer the vegetable chow mein to a warm serving dish and serve immediately.

# Transparent Noodles with Yellow Bean Sauce

Transparent or thread noodles are excellent re-heated, unlike most other noodles which must be served as soon as they are ready.

| Serves 4 |
| --- |
| 175 g/6 oz transparent noodles |
| 1 tbsp peanut oil |
| 1 leek, sliced |
| 2 garlic cloves, crushed |
| 450 g/1 lb minced chicken |
| 450 ml/16 fl oz chicken stock |
| 1 tsp chilli sauce |
| 2 tbsp yellow bean sauce |
| 4 tbsp light soy sauce |
| 1 tsp sesame oil |
| chopped chives, to garnish |

**COOK'S TIP**

Chilli sauce is made from chillies, vinegar, sugar and salt. Tabasco sauce can be substituted.

**COOK'S TIP**

Cellophane noodles are available from many supermarkets and all Chinese supermarkets.

**1** Put the noodles in a bowl, cover with boiling water and soak for 15 minutes. Drain and cut into short lengths with a pair of kitchen scissors.

**2** Heat the oil in a preheated wok. Add the leek and garlic and stir-fry for 30 seconds.

**3** Add the chicken and stir-fry for 4–5 minutes, until cooked.

**4** Add the chicken stock, chilli sauce, yellow bean sauce and soy sauce and cook for 3–4 minutes.

**5** Add the drained noodles and sesame oil and cook for 4–5 minutes, until heated through.

**6** Spoon into warm bowls, sprinkle with chopped chives and serve immediately.

# Homemade Noodles with Stir-Fried Vegetables

These noodles are simple to make; you do not need a pasta-making machine, as they are rolled out by hand.

| Serves 4 |
| --- |
| **NOODLES** |
| 115 g/4 oz plain flour |
| 2 tbsp cornflour |
| 1/2 tsp salt |
| 125 ml/4 fl oz boiling water |
| 5 tbsp vegetable oil |
| **STIR-FRY** |
| 1 courgette, cut into matchsticks |
| 1 celery stick, cut into matchsticks |
| 1 carrot, cut into matchsticks |
| 115 g/4 oz open-cup mushrooms, thinly sliced |
| 1 leek, thinly sliced |
| 115 g/4 oz broccoli, divided into florets and stalks thinly sliced |
| 115 g/4 oz fresh beansprouts |
| 1 tbsp soy sauce |
| 2 tsp rice wine vinegar |
| 1/2 tsp sugar |

**3** Heat 3 tablespoons of oil in a preheated wok. Add the noodles and fry over a high heat for 1 minute. Reduce the heat and cook for a further 2 minutes. Remove and drain on kitchen paper.

**4** Heat the remaining oil. Stir-fry the courgette, celery and carrot for 1 minute. Add the mushrooms, broccoli and leek, and stir-fry for 1 minute. Stir in the remaining ingredients, heat through and serve.

**1** Sift the flour, cornflour and salt into a bowl. Make a well in the centre and pour in the boiling water and 1 teaspoon of the oil. Mix quickly with a wooden spoon, to make a soft dough. Cover and leave for 5–6 minutes.

**2** Make the noodles by rolling small balls of dough across a very lightly oiled work surface with the palm of your hand to form thin noodles. Do not worry if some of the noodles break. Set aside.

# Transparent Noodles with Prawns

In this recipe tiger prawns are cooked with orange juice, peppers,
soy and vinegar and served on a bed of transparent
noodles for a truly wonderful dish.

| Serves 4 |
| --- |
| 175 g/6 oz transparent noodles |
| 1 tbsp vegetable oil |
| 1 garlic clove, crushed |
| 2 tsp grated fresh ginger root |
| 24 raw tiger prawns, peeled and deveined |
| 1 red pepper, seeded and thinly sliced |
| 1 green pepper, seeded and thinly sliced |
| 1 onion, chopped |
| 2 tbsp light soy sauce |
| juice of 1 orange |
| 2 tsp wine vinegar |
| pinch of brown sugar |
| 150 ml/¹⁄₄ pint fish stock |
| 1 tbsp cornflour |
| 2 tsp water |
| coriander sprigs and orange rind, to garnish |

**1** Cook the noodles in boiling water for 1 minute. Drain, rinse under cold water and drain thoroughly again.

**2** Heat the oil in a preheated wok. Add the garlic and ginger and stir-fry for 30 seconds. Add the prawns and stir-fry for 2 minutes. Remove the prawns with a slotted spoon and keep warm.

**3** Add the peppers and onion and stir-fry for 2 minutes. Stir in the soy sauce, orange juice, vinegar, sugar and stock. Return the prawns to the wok and cook for 8-10 minutes, until cooked through.

**4** Blend the cornflour with the water and add to the wok. Bring to the boil. Add the noodles and cook for 1–2 minutes. Serve garnished with coriander sprigs and orange rind.

**VARIATION**

Lime or lemon juice and rind may be used instead of the orange. Use 3-5¹⁄₂ teaspoons of these juices.

# Seafood Chow Mein

Use whatever seafood is available for this
delicious noodle dish – mussels or
crab would be suitable.

| Serves 4 |
| --- |
| 75 g/2³/₄ oz squid, cleaned |
| 3–4 fresh scallops |
| 75 g/2³/₄ oz raw prawns, peeled and deveined |
| ¹/₂ egg white, beaten lightly |
| 1 tbsp Cornflour Paste (see page 16) |
| 275 g/9¹/₂ oz egg noodles |
| 5–6 tbsp vegetable oil |
| 2 tbsp light soy sauce |
| 50 g/1³/₄ oz mangetout |
| ¹/₂ tsp salt |
| ¹/₂ tsp sugar |
| 1 tsp Chinese rice wine or dry sherry |
| 2 spring onions, finely shredded |
| a few drops of sesame oil |

**1** Open up the squid and score the inside in a criss-cross pattern. Cut into small pieces. Soak the squid in boiling water until all the pieces curl up. Rinse thoroughly in cold water and drain.

**2** Cut each scallop into 3–4 slices. Cut the prawns in half lengthways if large. Mix the scallops and prawns with the egg white and cornflour paste.

**3** Cook the noodles in boiling water according to the instructions on the packet, then drain and rinse under cold water. Drain well, then toss with 1 tablespoon of oil.

**4** Heat 3 tablespoons of oil in a preheated wok. Add the noodles and 1 tablespoon of the soy sauce and stir-fry for 2–3 minutes. Remove to a large warm serving dish.

**5** Heat the remaining oil and stir-fry the mangetout and seafood for 2 minutes. Stir in the salt, sugar, Chinese rice wine or sherry, the remaining soy sauce and about half the spring onion.

**6** Pour the seafood mixture on top of the noodles and sprinkle with sesame oil. Garnish with the remaining spring onions and serve.

# Curried Prawn Noodles

These noodles have a fairly strong flavour and are almost a meal
in themselves. If served as an accompaniment, they are
ideal with plain vegetable or fish dishes.

| Serves 4 |
| --- |
| 225 g/8 oz rice noodles |
| 4 tbsp vegetable oil |
| 1 onion, sliced |
| 2 ham slices, shredded |
| 2 tbsp Chinese curry powder |
| 150 ml/¼ pint fish stock |
| 225 g/8 oz peeled and deveined, raw prawns |
| 2 garlic cloves, crushed |
| 6 spring onions, chopped |
| 1 tbsp light soy sauce |
| 2 tbsp hoi-sin sauce |
| 1 tbsp Chinese rice wine or dry sherry |
| 2 tsp lime juice |
| snipped chives, to garnish |

**1** Cook the rice noodles in boiling
water for 3–4 minutes. Drain, rinse
under cold water and drain
thoroughly again.

**2** Heat 2 tablespoons of the oil in a
preheated wok. Add the onion and
ham and stir-fry for 1 minute. Add
the curry powder and stir-fry for a
further 30 seconds.

**3** Stir the noodles and fish stock into
the wok and cook for 2–3 minutes.
Remove from the wok, set aside and
keep warm.

**4** Heat the remaining oil in the wok
and add the prawns, garlic and spring
onions. Stir-fry for 1 minute, then add
the soy sauce, hoi-sin sauce, Chinese
rice wine or sherry and lime juice and
heat through. Pour this mixture over
the noodles.

**5** Serve immediately, garnished with
freshly snipped chives.

COOK'S TIP

If cooked prawns are used, toss them
into the mixture at the last minute,
just long enough for them to heat right
through.

# Singapore-Style Rice Noodles

Rice noodles, or vermicelli, are also known as rice sticks.
Egg noodles can be used for this dish, but it
will not taste quite the same.

| Serves 4 |
| --- |
| 200 g/7 oz rice vermicelli |
| 115 g/4 oz boneless cooked chicken or pork |
| 50 g/1³/₄ oz peeled cooked prawns, thawed if frozen |
| 4 tbsp vegetable oil |
| 1 onion, thinly sliced |
| 115 g/4 oz fresh beansprouts |
| 1 tsp salt |
| 1 tbsp mild curry powder |
| 2 tbsp light soy sauce |
| 2 spring onions, thinly shredded |
| 1–2 small fresh green or red chillies, seeded and thinly shredded |

**1** Soak the rice vermicelli in boiling water for 8–10 minutes, then rinse in cold water and drain well.

**2** Thinly slice the cooked meat. Dry the prawns on kitchen paper.

**3** Heat the oil in a preheated wok. Add the onion and stir-fry until translucent. Add the beansprouts and stir-fry for 1 minute.

**4** Add the noodles, together with the meat and prawns, and continue stirring for another minute.

**5** Blend in the salt, curry powder and soy sauce, followed by the spring onions and chillies. Stir-fry for 1 more minute. Transfer to a serving dish and serve immediately.

# Cantonese Fried Noodles

This dish is usually served as a snack or light meal.
It may also be served as an accompaniment
to plain meat and fish dishes.

| Serves 4 |
| --- |
| 350 g/12 oz egg noodles |
| 675 g/1¹/₂ lb lean steak, cut into thin strips |
| 3 tbsp vegetable oil |
| 75 g/2³/₄ oz canned bamboo shoots, drained and sliced |
| 6 spring onions, sliced |
| 25 g/1 oz green beans, cut in half |
| 115 g/4 oz green cabbage, shredded |
| 1 tbsp dark soy sauce |
| 2 tbsp beef stock |
| 1 tbsp Chinese rice wine or dry sherry |
| 1 tbsp light brown sugar |
| 2 tbsp chopped parsley, to garnish |

**1** Cook the noodles in boiling water for 2–3 minutes. Drain, rinse under cold running water and drain thoroughly again.

**2** Heat 1 tablespoon of the oil in a preheated wok. Add the noodles and stir-fry for 1–2 minutes. Drain and set aside.

**3** Heat the remaining oil in the wok. Add the steak and stir-fry for 2–3 minutes. Add the bamboo shoots, spring onions, beans and cabbage and stir-fry for 1–2 minutes.

**4** Add the soy sauce, stock, Chinese rice wine or sherry and sugar to the wok, mixing well.

**5** Stir the noodles into the wok, mixing. Heat through for 1–2 minutes.

**6** Transfer to a warm serving dish and serve immediately, sprinkled with chopped parsley.

### VARIATION

Use lean pork or chicken instead of the steak in this recipe and alter the stock accordingly.

# Chicken Noodles

Rice noodles are used in this recipe. They are available
in some supermarkets or Chinese supermarkets. If unavailable,
egg noodles may be used in their place.

| Serves 4 |
| --- |
| 225 g/8 oz rice noodles |
| 2 tbsp peanut oil |
| 225 g/8 oz skinless, boneless chicken breast, sliced |
| 2 garlic cloves, crushed |
| 1 tsp grated fresh ginger root |
| 1 tsp Chinese curry powder |
| 1 red pepper, seeded and thinly sliced |
| 75 g/1¾ oz mangetout, shredded |
| 1 tbsp light soy sauce |
| 2 tsp Chinese rice wine or dry sherry |
| 2 tbsp chicken stock |
| 1 tsp sesame oil |
| 1 tbsp chopped fresh coriander |

**1** Soak the rice noodles for 4 minutes in warm water. Drain thoroughly and set aside.

**2** Heat the oil in a preheated wok. Add the chicken and stir-fry for 2–3 minutes.

**3** Add the garlic, ginger and curry powder and stir-fry for a further 30 seconds. Add the pepper and mangetout and stir-fry for 2–3 minutes.

**4** Add the noodles, soy sauce, Chinese rice wine or sherry and chicken stock to the wok, mix thoroughly and cook, stirring constantly, for 1 minute.

**5** Sprinkle the sesame oil and coriander over the dish.

**6** Transfer to a warm serving dish and serve immediately.

## VARIATION

Use pork or duck in this recipe instead of the chicken.

# Chicken on Crispy Noodles

Blanched noodles are fried in the wok until crisp and brown,
and then topped with a shredded chicken sauce
for a delightfully tasty dish.

| Serves 4 |
| --- |
| 225 g/8 oz skinless, boneless chicken breasts, shredded |
| 1 egg white |
| 5 tsp cornflour |
| 225 g/8 oz thin egg noodles |
| 325 ml/11 fl oz vegetable oil |
| 600 ml/1 pint chicken stock |
| 2 tbsp Chinese rice wine or dry sherry |
| 2 tbsp oyster sauce |
| 1 tbsp light soy sauce |
| 1 tbsp hoi-sin sauce |
| 1 red pepper, seeded and thinly sliced |
| 2 tbsp water |
| 3 spring onions, chopped |

**1** Mix the chicken, egg white and 2 teaspoons of the cornflour in a bowl. Let stand for at least 30 minutes.

**2** Blanch the noodles in boiling water for 2 minutes, then drain. Heat the vegetable oil in a preheated wok. Add the noodles, spreading them to cover the base. Cook over a low heat for 5 minutes, until the browned on the underside. Flip them over and brown the other side. Remove from the wok and keep warm. Drain the oil from the wok.

**3** Add 300 ml/½ pint of the stock to the wok, remove from the heat and stir in the chicken. Return to the heat and cook for 2 minutes. Drain, discarding the stock.

**4** Wipe the wok with kitchen paper and return to the heat.

**5** Add the wine or sherry, sauces, pepper and the remaining chicken stock. Bring to the boil. Blend the remaining cornflour with the water to form a paste and stir it into the mixture.

**6** Return the chicken to the wok and cook over a low heat for 2 minutes.

**7** Put the noodles on top and sprinkle with spring onions and serve immediately.

# Pork Chow Mein

When time is short, serve this quick-and-easy
dish with a green salad for a
delicious light lunch.

| Serves 4 |
| --- |
| 225 g/8 oz egg noodles |
| 4–5 tbsp vegetable oil |
| 115 g/4 oz French beans |
| 225 g/8 oz cooked pork fillet |
| 2 tbsp light soy sauce |
| 1 tsp salt |
| 1/2 tsp sugar |
| 1 tbsp Chinese rice wine or dry sherry |
| 2 spring onions, finely shredded |
| a few drops of sesame oil |
| chilli sauce, to serve (optional) |

**1** Cook the noodles in boiling water according to the instructions on the packet. Drain and rinse under cold water. Drain again then toss with 1 tablespoon of the oil.

**2** Slice the pork into thin shreds. Top and tail the beans.

**3** Heat 3 tablespoons of the vegetable oil in a preheated wok. Add the noodles and stir-fry for 2–3 minutes, together with 1 tablespoon of the soy sauce. Remove to a warm serving dish. Keep warm.

**4** Heat the remaining vegetable oil in the wok. Add the beans and the pork and stir-fry for approximately 2 minutes. Add the salt, sugar, Chinese rice wine or sherry, the remaining soy sauce and about half the spring onions.

**5** Blend the mixture thoroughly and add a little stock if necessary. Pour the mixture on top of the noodles and sprinkle with sesame oil and the remaining spring onions.

**6** Serve immediately with chilli sauce, if desired.

**VARIATION**

This chow mein can also be made with 225 g/8 oz shredded cooked chicken or turkey breast. It is especially tasty served cold as a salad.

# Beef Chow Mein

Wafer-thin strips of lean steak are cooked with a
colourful selection of vegetables and
served with noodles in a rich sauce.

| Serves 4 |
| --- |
| 450 g/1 lb egg noodles |
| 4 tbsp peanut oil |
| 450 g/1 lb lean steak, cut into thin strips |
| 2 garlic cloves, crushed |
| 1 tsp grated fresh ginger root |
| 1 green pepper, seeded and thinly sliced |
| 1 carrot, thinly sliced |
| 2 celery sticks, sliced |
| 8 spring onions |
| 1 tsp dark brown sugar |
| 1 tbsp Chinese rice wine or dry sherry |
| 2 tbsp dark soy sauce |
| few drops chilli sauce |

**1** Cook the noodles in boiling salted
water for 4–5 minutes. Drain, rinse
under cold running water and drain
thoroughly again. Toss them in
1 tablespoon of the oil.

**2** Heat the remaining oil in a
preheated wok. Add the strips of
steak and stir-fry for 3–4 minutes,
until browned and sealed. Add the
garlic and ginger and stir-fry for a
further 30 seconds.

**3** Add the pepper, carrot, celery and
spring onions and stir-fry for 2
minutes.

**4** Add the sugar, Chinese rice wine or
sherry, soy sauce chilli sauce to taste
and cook, stirring constantly, for
1 minute.

**5** Stir in the noodles, mixing well,
and cook until warmed through.

**6** Transfer to a warm serving dish and
serve immediately.

**COOK'S VARIATION**

Add drained canned straw mushrooms
for extra texture.

# Fried Noodles with Mushrooms & Pork

This dish benefits from the use of coloured oyster mushrooms.
If these are unavailable, plain grey mushrooms will suffice.

| Serves 4 |
|---|
| 450 g/1 lb thin egg noodles |
| 2 tbsp peanut oil |
| 350 g/12 oz pork fillet, sliced |
| 2 garlic cloves, crushed |
| 1 onion, quartered |
| 225 g/8 oz oyster mushrooms, torn into pieces |
| 4 tomatoes, peeled, seeded and thinly sliced |
| 2 tbsp light soy sauce |
| 50 ml/2 fl oz pork stock or Chinese Stock (see page 16) |
| 1 tbsp chopped fresh coriander |

**1** Cook the noodles in boiling water for 2–3 minutes. Drain, rinse under cold running water and drain thoroughly again.

**2** Heat 1 tablespoon of the oil in a preheated wok. Add the noodles and stir-fry for 2 minutes. Remove from the wok with a slotted spoon and set aside.

**3** Heat the remaining oil in the wok. Add the pork and stir-fry for about 4–5 minutes, until lightly coloured and sealed.

**4** Stir the garlic and onion into the wok and stir-fry for a further 2–3 minutes.

**5** Add the mushrooms, tomatoes, soy sauce and pork or Chinese stock.

**6** Return the noodles to the wok. Stir well and cook for 1–2 minutes until heated through.

**7** Transfer to a warm serving dish, sprinkle with coriander and serve immediately.

### COOK'S TIP

For crisper noodles, fry them in 2 tablespoons oil for 5-6 minutes, spreading them thinly in the wok and turning half way through.

# Lamb with Transparent Noodles

Lamb is quick fried, coated in a soy sauce and served on a bed of transparent noodles for a richly flavoured dish.

| Serves 4 |
| --- |
| 150 g/5½ oz transparent noodles |
| 450 g/1 lb boneless lean lamb, thinly sliced |
| 2 tbsp peanut oil |
| 2 garlic cloves, crushed |
| 2 leeks, sliced |
| 3 tbsp dark soy sauce |
| 250 ml/9 fl oz lamb stock |
| dash of chilli sauce |

**1** Bring a large pan of water to the boil. Add the noodles and cook for 1 minute. Drain well, rinse under cold running water and drain well again.

**2** Heat the oil in a preheated wok. Add the lamb and stir-fry for 2 minutes. Add the garlic and leeks to the wok and stir-fry for a further 2 minutes.

**3** Stir in the soy sauce, stock and chilli sauce and cook for 3–4 minutes, until the meat is cooked through.

**4** Add the noodles and cook for 1 minute, until heated through. Serve immediately.

## COOK'S TIP

Transparent noodles are available in Chinese foodstores. If they are unavailable, use egg noodles instead, and cook them according to the packet instructions.

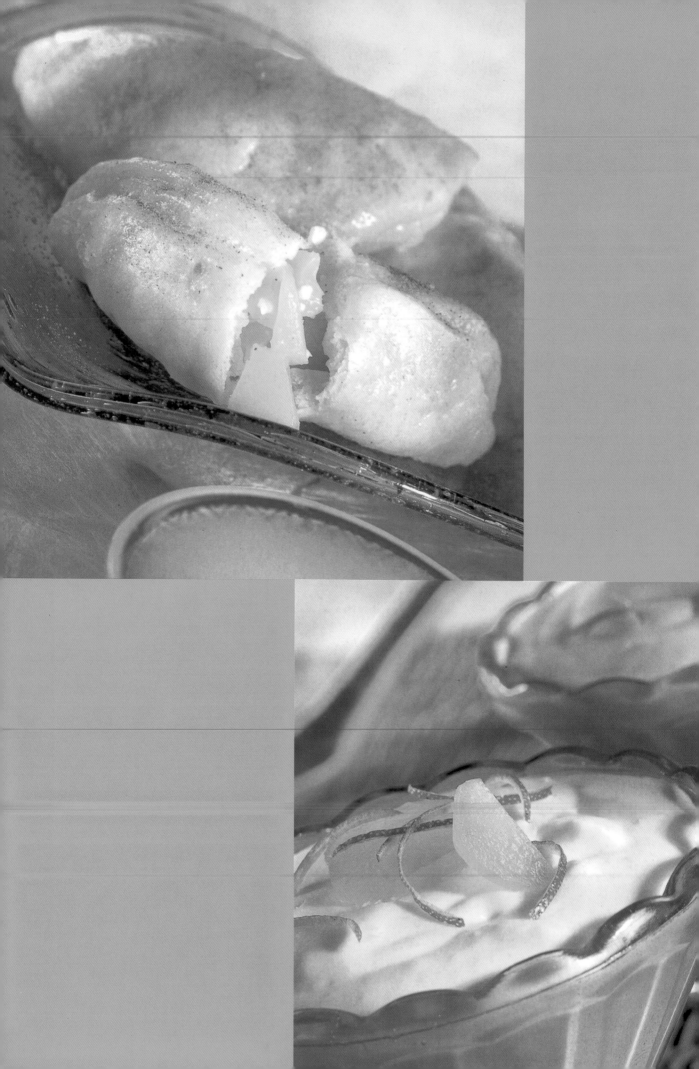

# Desserts

Family meals in China usually end with fresh fruit. Desserts are served only at banquets and on very special occasions, although sweet snacks are often nibbled between meal times. Nevertheless, when Chinese cooks do prepare a dish for the sweet-toothed, at the New Year festival, for example, there are no half measures.

Just as northern China is well known for wontons and dumplings containing a melt-in-the mouth savoury filling, it is also famous for wonderfully self-indulgent parcels of sweetly spiced dried or fresh fruit. Rice, too, is used for preparing desserts, often pressed into a mould and concealing a delicious surprise in the centre. Cutting the first slice from Sweet Rice is truly a revelation. However, fruit reigns supreme and, with such a vast choice available, this is hardly surprising. Try Mango Mousse or Ginger Lychees with Orange Sorbet.

# Sweet Fruit Wontons

Sweet wontons are very adaptable and may be
filled with whole, small fruits or a spicy
chopped mixture, as in this recipe.

| Serves 4 |
| --- |
| 12 wonton wrappers |
| oil, for deep-frying |
| 2 tbsp clear honey |
| **FILLING** |
| 175 g/6 oz chopped, dried, stoned dates |
| 2 tsp dark brown sugar |
| $^1/_2$ tsp ground cinnamon |
| 2 tsp cornflour |
| 6 tsp cold water |

**1** First start making the filling. Mix together the chopped dates, sugar and cinnamon in a bowl.

**2** Spread out the wonton wrappers on a chopping board and spoon a little of the filling into the centre of each wrapper.

**3** Mix together the cornflour and water and brush this around the edges of the wrappers.

**4** Fold the wrappers over the filling, bringing the edges together, then bring the two corners together, sealing with the cornflour mixture.

**5** Heat the oil for deep-frying in a wok to 180°C/350°F, or until a cube of stale bread browns in 30 seconds. Fry the wontons, in batches, for about 2–3 minutes, until golden. Remove from the oil with a slotted spoon and drain on absorbent kitchen paper.

**6** Place the honey in a bowl and stand it in warm water until it has become quite runny.

**7** Drizzle the honey over the wontons, transfer to a serving dish and serve immediately.

**COOK'S TIP**

Wonton wrappers may be found in Chinese supermarkets. Alternatively, make the dough as described for Wonton Soup (see page 55).

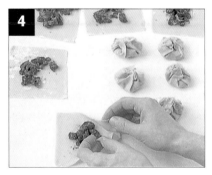

# Banana Pastries

These pastries require a little time to prepare, but are
well worth the effort. A sweet banana filling
is wrapped in dough and baked.

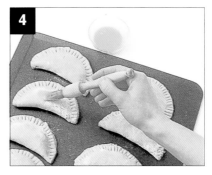

| Serves 4 |
| --- |
| **DOUGH** |
| 450 g/1 lb plain flour |
| 50 g/1³/₄ oz/4 tbsp lard |
| 50 g/1³/₄ oz/4 tbsp unsalted butter |
| 125 ml/4 fl oz water |
| **FILLING** |
| 2 large bananas |
| 75 g/2³/₄ oz finely chopped no-need-to-soak dried apricots |
| pinch of nutmeg |
| dash of orange juice |
| 1 egg yolk, beaten |
| icing sugar, for dusting |

**1** First make the dough. Sift the flour
into a large mixing bowl. Add the lard
and butter and rub into the flour with
the fingertips until the mixture
resembles breadcrumbs. Gradually
blend in the water to make a soft
dough. Wrap in clear film and chill in
the refrigerator for 30 minutes.

**2** Mash the bananas in a bowl with a
fork and stir in the apricots, nutmeg
and orange juice, mixing well.

**3** Roll the dough out on a lightly
floured surface and cut out
16 x 10-cm/4-inch rounds. Spoon a
little of the banana filling on to one
half of each round and fold the dough
over the filling to make semi-circles.
Pinch the edges together and seal by
pressing with the prongs of a fork.

**4** Arrange the pastries on a non-stick
baking sheet and brush with the
beaten egg. Cut a small slit in each
pastry and cook in a preheated oven at
180°C/350°F/Gas 4 for 25 minutes, or
until golden brown.

**5** Dust with icing sugar and serve with
cream or ice cream.

# Mango Dumplings

Fresh mango and canned lychees fill these
small steamed dumplings, making a
really colourful and tasty treat.

| Serves 4 |
| --- |
| DOUGH |
| 150 ml/¼ pint milk |
| 150 ml/¼ pint water |
| 2 tsp baking powder |
| 1 tbsp caster sugar |
| 400 g/14 oz plain flour |
| 1 small mango |
| 115 g/4 oz can lychees, drained |
| 1 tbsp ground almonds |
| 4 tbsp orange juice |
| ground cinnamon and icing sugar, for dusting |

**1** Mix together the water and milk
and stir into the baking powder and
sugar in a mixing bowl. Gradually stir
in the flour to make a soft dough. Set
aside in a warm place for 1 hour.

**2** Peel the mango and cut the flesh
from the stone. Roughly chop and
reserve half. Chop the lychees and
add to half the chopped mango,
together with the ground almonds.
Let stand for 20 minutes.

**3** Meanwhile, blend the remaining
mango, together with the orange
juice, in a food processor until
smooth. Press through a plastic
strainer to make a smooth sauce.

**4** Divide the dough into 16 equal
pieces. Roll each piece out on a lightly
floured surface into 7.5-cm/ 3-inch
rounds. Spoon a little of the mango
and lychee mixture on to the centre
of each round and bring the dough up

around the fruit to the top, and pinch
together to make "purses".

**5** Place the mango and lychee
dumplings in a single layer on a
heatproof plate in a steamer, cover

and steam for about 20–25 minutes,
until cooked through.

**6** Remove from the steamer, dust
with cinnamon and icing sugar and
serve with the mango sauce.

# Sweet Rice

This dessert is served at banquets and
celebratory meals in China, as it
looks wonderful when sliced.

| Serves 4 |
| --- |
| 175 g/6 oz pudding rice |
| 25 g/1 oz/2 tbsp unsalted butter |
| 1 tbsp caster sugar |
| 8 dried dates, pitted and chopped |
| 1 tbsp raisins |
| 5 walnut halves |
| 5 glacé cherries, halved |
| 5 pieces angelica, chopped |
| 115 g/4 oz canned chestnut purée |
| **SYRUP** |
| 4$\frac{1}{2}$ tsp light brown sugar |
| 150 ml/$\frac{1}{4}$ pint water |
| 2 tbsp orange juice |
| 1$\frac{1}{2}$ tsp cornflour |

**1** Put the rice in a saucepan and cover with cold water. Bring to the boil, cover and simmer for 15 minutes, until the water has been absorbed. Stir in the butter and sugar.

**2** Lightly grease a 600-ml/1-pint pudding basin. Cover the base and sides with a thin layer of the rice, pressing it on with the back of a spoon.

**3** Mix the fruit and nuts together and press them into the rice, again using the back of a spoon.

**4** Spread a thicker layer of rice over this and fill the centre with the chestnut purée. Cover with the remaining rice, pressing it down.

**5** Cover the basin with pleated greaseproof paper and foil. Secure

with string. Place in a steamer or stand it in a pan and add hot water until it reaches halfway up the sides. Cover and steam for 45 minutes. Let stand for 10 minutes.

**6** Before serving, dissolve the sugar for the syrup in the water and orange

juice over a gentle heat. Bring to the boil. Blend the cornflour to a smooth paste with 1 tbsp of cold water and stir into the boiling syrup. Cook for 1 minute until thickened.

**7** Turn out the pudding. Pour the syrup over the top and serve.

# Honeyed Rice Puddings

These small rice puddings are quite sweet, but have
a wonderful flavour because of the combination
of ginger, honey and cinnamon.

| Serves 4 |
| --- |
| 300 g/10½ oz pudding rice |
| 2 tbsp clear honey |
| large pinch of ground cinnamon |
| 3 pieces stem ginger, drained and chopped |
| 15 no-need to soak dried apricots, chopped |
| honey, for drizzling |

**1** Put the rice in a saucepan and add just enough cold water to cover. Bring to the boil, reduce the heat, cover and cook for 15 minutes, or until the water has been absorbed.

**2** Stir the honey and cinnamon into the rice.

**3** Lightly grease 4 x 150-ml/¼-pint ramekin dishes.

**4** Put the apricots and ginger in a food processor and process to make a paste. Divide the paste into 4 equal portions and shape each into a flat round to fit into the circumference of the ramekin dishes.

**5** Divide half the rice among the ramekins and place the apricot paste on top.

**6** Cover the apricot mixture with the remaining rice. Cover the ramekins with greaseproof paper and foil. Place the ramekins in a steamer and steam for 30 minutes, or until set.

**7** Remove the ramekins from the steamer and let stand for 5 minutes.

**8** Turn the puddings out on to warm serving plates and drizzle with clear honey. Serve immediately.

### COOK'S TIP

The puddings may be chilled in their dishes, turned out and served with ice cream or cream.

# Mango Mousse

This is a light, softly set and tangy mousse,
which is perfect for clearing the palate
after a meal of mixed flavours.

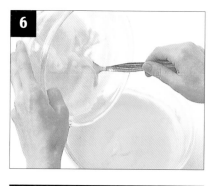

| Serves 4 |
|---|
| 400 g/14 oz can mangoes in syrup |
| 2 pieces stem ginger, chopped |
| 200 ml/7 fl oz double cream |
| 20 g/³/₄ oz/4 tsp powdered gelatine |
| 2 tbsp water |
| 2 egg whites |
| 1¹/₂ tbsp light brown sugar |
| chopped mango and stem ginger, to decorate |

**6** Beat the sugar into the egg whites and then gently fold into the mango and cream mixture with a metal spoon.

**7** Spoon the mousse into individual serving dishes and decorate with chopped mango and stem ginger. Serve immediately.

**COOK'S TIP**

The gelatine must be stirred into the mango mixture in a gentle stream to prevent it from setting in lumps when it comes into contact with the cold mixture.

**1** Drain the mangoes, reserving the syrup. Put the mango pieces and ginger in a food processor or blender and process for 30 seconds, or until a smooth purée. Measure the quantity of purée and make up to 300 ml/ ¹/₂ pint with the reserved mango syrup. Place the mango mixture in a measuring jug.

**2** In a separate bowl, whip the cream until it forms soft peaks.

**3** Carefully fold the mango mixture into the whipped cream until fully combined.

**4** Dissolve the gelatine in the water, cool slightly and pour it into the mango and cream mixture in a steady stream, stirring constantly. Leave to chill in the refrigerator for about 30 minutes, until almost set.

**5** Beat the egg whites in a clean bowl until they form peaks.

# Poached Allspice Pears

These pears are moist and delicious after poaching
in a sugar and allspice mixture. They are
wonderful served hot or cold.

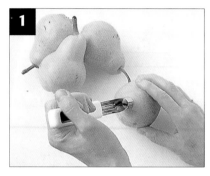

| Serves 4 |
| --- |
| 4 large, ripe pears |
| 300 ml/¹/₂ pint |
| orange juice |
| 2 tsp ground allspice |
| 50 g/1³/₄ oz raisins |
| 2 tbsp light brown sugar |

**1** Peel, core and halve the pears.

**2** Place the pear halves in a saucepan
together with the orange juice,
allspice, raisins and sugar. Heat gently
to dissolve the sugar.

**3** Once the sugar has dissolved, bring
the mixture to the boil for 1 minute.

**4** Reduce the heat to low and simmer
for 10 minutes, until the pears are
cooked, but still fairly firm – test by
inserting the tip of a knife.

**5** Serve the pears hot with the syrup
or cool and chill in the refrigerator
before serving cold.

### VARIATION

Use cinnamon instead of the allspice
and decorate with cinnamon sticks and
mint sprigs.

# Chinese Custard Tarts

These small tarts are irresistible – a custard is baked
in a rich, sweet pastry. The tarts may
be served warm or cold.

| Makes 15 |
| --- |
| **DOUGH** |
| 175 g/6 oz plain flour |
| 3 tbsp caster sugar |
| 50 g/1³/₄ oz/4 tbsp unsalted butter |
| 25 g/1 oz/2 tbsp lard |
| 2 tbsp water |
| **CUSTARD** |
| 2 small eggs, separated |
| 50 g/1³/₄ oz caster sugar |
| 175 ml/6 fl oz pint milk |
| ¹/₂ tsp ground nutmeg |
| nutmeg, for sprinkling |
| cream, to serve |

**1** First make the pastry. Sift the flour into a bowl, add the sugar and rub in the butter and lard until the mixture resembles breadcrumbs. Mix in the water to make a firm dough.

**2** Transfer the dough to a lightly floured surface and knead for 5 minutes, until smooth. Cover with clear film and chill in the refrigerator while you are preparing the filling.

**3** Beat the eggs and sugar together and gradually beat in the milk. Add the nutmeg.

**4** Separate the dough into 15 even-size pieces. Flatten into rounds and press into shallow patty tins.

**5** Spoon the custard into the pastry cases and cook in a preheated oven at 150°C/300°F/Gas 2 for 25–30 minutes. Cool slightly before removing from the tins. Transfer to a wire rack and sprinkle with nutmeg. Serve accompanied with cream.

**COOK'S TIP**

Make the dough in advance, cover and chill in the refrigerator until required. Make the custard filling and continue from step 5.

# Ginger Lychees With Orange Sorbet

This dish is truly delicious. The fresh flavour
of the sorbet perfectly complements
the spicy lychees.

| Serves 4 |
| --- |
| **SORBET** |
| 225 g/8 oz caster sugar |
| 450 ml/16 fl oz cold water |
| 350 g/12 oz can mandarins in natural juice |
| 2 tbsp lemon juice |
| **STUFFED LYCHEES** |
| 425 g/15 oz can lychees, drained |
| 50 g/1³/₄ oz stem ginger, drained |
| mandarin slices and chopped stem ginger or orange zest, to decorate |

**1** First make the sorbet. Place the sugar and water in a saucepan and stir over a low heat until the sugar has dissolved. Bring to the boil and boil vigorously for 2–3 minutes.

**2** Meanwhile, process the mandarins in a food processor or blender until smooth. Press through a plastic strainer and stir into the syrup, together with the lemon juice. Set aside to cool.

**3** Pour the mixture into a rigid, plastic container suitable for the freezer and freeze until set, stirring from time to time.

**4** Meanwhile, drain the lychees on absorbent kitchen paper. Finely chop the ginger and spoon into the centre of the lychees to stuff them.

**5** Arrange the lychees on serving plates and serve with scoops of the orange sorbet.

### COOK'S TIP

Let the sorbet stand in the refrigerator for 10 minutes before scooping to serve.

# Chinese Fruit Salad

The syrup for this colourful dish
is filled with Chinese flavours
for a refreshing dessert.

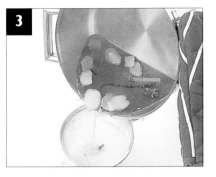

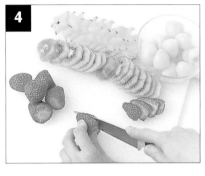

### Serves 4

| |
| --- |
| 75 ml/3 fl oz Chinese rice wine or dry sherry |
| juice and rind of 1 lemon |
| 850 ml/1½ pints water |
| 225 g/8 oz caster sugar |
| 2 cloves |
| 2.5-cm/1-inch piece cinnamon stick, bruised |
| 1 vanilla pod |
| pinch of mixed spice |
| 1 star anise pod |
| 2.5-cm/1-inch piece fresh ginger root, sliced |
| 2 mint sprigs |
| 50 g/1¾ oz unsalted cashew nuts |
| 2 kiwi fruits, halved and sliced |
| 1 star fruit, sliced |
| 400 g/14 oz can lychees in syrup, drained |
| 115 g/4 oz strawberries, hulled and sliced |
| 1 piece stem ginger, drained and sliced |
| mint sprigs, to decorate |

**1** Put the Chinese rice wine or sherry, lemon rind and juice and water in a saucepan. Add the sugar, cloves, cinnamon, vanilla pod, mixed spice, star anise and fresh ginger root.

**2** Heat gently, stirring constantly, until the sugar has dissolved and then bring to the boil. Reduce the heat and simmer for 5 minutes. Set aside to cool completely.

**3** Strain the syrup, discarding the flavourings. Stir in the cashew nuts, cover and chill.

**4** Prepare the fruits and spoon into a dish. Pour the syrup over them, decorate with mint sprigs and serve.

### COOK'S TIP

Make the syrup in advance, cover and chill in the refrigerator overnight before straining, for a fuller flavour.

# Index

## A

alcoholic drinks 19
allspice pears, pached 216
almonds:
broccoli, pepper & almond salad 49
chicken soup with almonds 69
crisp fried pak choi & almonds 168
appetizers 21-39
aromatic & crispy duck 112
aubergines:
aubergine in black bean sauce 160
aubergine in chilli sauce 158
spicy aubergines 159

## B

bacon
Chinese ried rice 176
baked crab with ginger 90
bamboo shoots 12
braised bamboo shoots 143
golden needles with bamboo shoots 144
noodles in soup 58
pork dim sum 34
pot sticker dumplings 37
banana pastries 211
barbecue pork (char siu) 36
barbecue spare ribs 35
basil 12
bean sauce 12
beansprouts 12
beansprouts with peppers 148
chicken chop suey 107
chicken with beansprouts 97
Chinese chicken salad 96
Chinese fried rice 176
Chinese hot salad 44
chow mein 192
cucumber & beansprout salad 48
egg fu yong with rice 182
Oriental salad 45
rice with crab & mussels 188
Singapore-style rice noddles 200
special fried rice 183
spring rolls 25
stir-fried beansprouts 147
vegetable chop suey 140
beef 117
beef & chilli black bean sauce 126
beef & pak choi 124
beef & vegetable noodle soup 57
beef chow mein 205
peppered beef cashew 127
Cantonese fried noodles 201
Chinese beef 128
crispy shredded beef 129
oyster sauce beef 123

red spiced beef 134
spicy beef & broccoli stir-fry 125
black bean sauce:
aubergine in black bean sauce 160
beef & chilli black bean sauce 126
fish with black bean sauce 75
fried squid flowers 92
spare ribs with chilli 131
tofu & vegetables with black bean sauce 153
vegetables in black bean sauce 149
black beans 12
bok choy see pak choi
braised bamboo shoots 143
braised chicken 101
braised fish fillets 77
braised pork & tofu 137
braised vegetables with tofu 157
braising 15
bread:
sesame prawn toasts 31
broccoli:
broccoli, pepper & almond salad 49
broccoli in oyster sauce 170
broccoli with ginger & orange 169
clear chicken & egg soup 76
peanut sesame chicken 100
spicy beef & broccoli stir-fry 125
stir-fried duck with broccoli & peppers 111

## C

cabbage:
Cantonese fried noodles 201
steamed cabbage rolls 28
see also Chinese leaves
Cantonese cooking 10
Cantonese fried noodles 201
Cantonese prawns 88
cardamom 12
carp:
fish in Szechuan hot sauce 79
carrots:
Chinese hot salad 44
flowers 17
shrimp fu yong 87
cashew nuts 12
peppered beef cashew 127
chicken with celery & cashew nuts 110
Kung Po chicken with cashew nuts 98
sizzled chilli prawns 85
special fried rice with cashew nuts 186
casseroles:
chicken & rice casserole 185
vegetable & tofu casserole 154
cauliflower:
duck in spicy sauce 113
celery:
chicken with celery & cashew nuts 110

red spiced beef 134
char siu 36
Chekiang cooking 10
chestnut purée:
sweet rice 213
chicken 95
braised chicken 101
chicken & rice casserole 185
chicken chop suey 107
chicken fu yong 104
chicken noodles 202
chicken on crispy noodles 203
chicken soup with almonds 69
chicken with beansprouts 97
chicken with pepper 102
chicken with celery & cashew nuts 110
chicken with mushrooms 108
chicken with yellow bean sauce 99
chilli chicken 105
Chinese chicken salad 96
Chinese omelette 39
Chinese stock 16
clear chicken & egg soup 68
crispy chicken 109
curried chicken & sweetcorn soup 65
Kung Po chicken with cashew nuts 98
noodles in soup 58
peanut sesame chicken 100
pot sticker dumplings 37
Singapore-style rice noodles 200
spicy peanut chicken 103
steamed cabbage rolls 28
Szechuan chilli chicken 106
three-flavour soup 70
transparent noodles with yellow bean sauce 195
chilli bean paste 12
chilli oil 72
chilli pork with chilli & garlic sauce 33
chilli powder:
red spiced beef 134
Chilli sauce 12
aubergine in chilli sauce 158
chillies 12
beansprouts with peppers 148
beef & chilli black bean sauce 126
braised pork & tofu 137
Chinese green bean stir-fry 151
Chinese potato sticks 173
crispy fish with chillies 76
crispy shredded beef 129
egg fried rice with chilli 180
flowers 17
hot & sour duck salad 47
hot lamb 119
Kung Po chicken with cashew nuts 98
Singapore-style rice noodles 200
sizzled chilli prawns 85
spare ribs with chilli 131

spicy peanut chicken 103
stir-fried cucumber with ginger & chilli 146
Szechuan chilli chicken 106
Szechuan prawns 84
Chinese beef 128
Chinese braised vegetables 145
Chinese cabbage
    see Chinese leaves
Chinese chicken salad 96
Chinese custard tarts 217
Chinese five-spice powder 12
    deep-fried tofu with Chinese fice spice 156
    five-spiced lamb 121
Chinese fried rice 176
Chinese fruit salad 219
Chinese green bean stir-fry 151
Chinese greens see pak choi
Chinese hot salad 44
Chinese leaves 12
    Chinese cabbage soup 54
    Chinese leaves stir-fried in soy & honey 166
    creamy cabbage and leeks 164
    lamb meatballs in soy sauce 118
    lemon Chinese leaves 165
    Oriental salad 45
    Peking duck soup 67
    steamed vegetable cabbage rolls 163
    pork pancake rolls 26
Chinese omelette 39
Chinese pancakes 12
Chinese potato sticks 183
Chinese stock 16
chives:
    Chinese omelette 39
chop suey 97
    chicken 107
    vegetable 140
chopping 15
chopsticks 14
chow mein 192
    beef 205
    mixed vegetable 194
    pork 204
    seafood 198
cilantro 12
clear chicken & egg soup 68
cleavers 14
cooking techniques 15
coriander 12
corn cobs 12
    beef & pak choi 124
    chinese beef 128
    curried chicken & sweetcorn soup 65
    peanut sesame chicken 100
    see also sweetcorn
cornflower paste 16
courgettes
    Chinse hot salad 44
crabmeat:
    baked crab with ginger 90
    crab & ginger soup 63
    rice with crab & mussels 188
creamy cabbage and leeks 164
crisp fried pak choi & almonds 168
crispy chicken 109
crispy fish with chillies 76
crispy seaweed 23
crispy shredded beef 129
crispy wontons with piquant dipping sauce 22

cucumber:
    cucumber & beansprout salad 48
    fans 17
    mushroom & cucumber noodle soup 59
    pickled cucumber 46
    prawn stir-fry with lemon grass 86
    stir-fried cucumber with ginger & chilli 146
    stir-fried mushrooms. cucumber & smoked
        tofu 155
    sweet & sour cucumber 43
curries:
    curried chicken & sweetcorn soup 65
    curried prawn noodles 199
custard tarts. Chinese 217

D

dates:
    sweet fruit wontons 210
    sweet rice 213
deep-fried pork with a soy dipping sauce 132
deep-fried prawns 30
deep-fried spare ribs 32
deep-fried tofu with Chinese five spice 156
deep-frying 15
desserts 209-219
dim sum. pork 34
dipping sauces 17
drinks:
    alcoholic 19
    tea 18
duck 95
    aromatic & crispy duck 112
    duck in spicy sauce 113
    duck with mangoes 115
    honey & soy glazed duck 114
    hot & sour duck salad 47
    Peking duck soup 67
    steamed duck buns 38
    stir-fried duck with broccoli & peppers 111
dumplings:
    mango dumplings 212
    money bags 162
    pot sticker dumplings 37
    shrimp dumpling soup 62
    steamed duck buns 38

E

Eastern Chinese cooking 10
egg noodles see noodles
eggs:
    Cantonese prawns 88
    chicken fu yong 104
    Chinese fried rice 176
    Chinese omelette 39
    clear chicken & egg soup 68
    egg fried rice 181
    egg fried rice with chilli 180
    egg fu yong with rice 182
    shrimp fu yong 87
equipment 14

F

fennel:

hot lamb 119
fish & seafood 73-93
    braised fish fillets 77
    crispy fish with chillies 76
    fish & ginger stir-fry 93
    fish in Szechuan hot sauce 79
    fish soup with wontons 60
    fish with black bean sauce 75
    mullet with ginger 78
    seafood combination 83
    steamed snapper with fruit & ginger stuffing
        80
    trout with pineapple 74
fish-flavoured shredded pork 133
fish sauce:
    hot & sour duck salad 47
five-spiced lamb 121
flowers, vegetable garnishes 17
fragrant steamed rice in lotus leaves 178
French beans:
    Chinese green bean stir-fry 151
    Chinese hot salad 44
    five-spiced lamb 121
fried noodles with mushrooms & pork 206
fried rice & prawns 187
fried rice with pork, tomatoes, peas &
    mushrooms 189
frid rice with prawns 184
fried squid flowers 92
fried vegetable noodles 183
fruit:
    Chinese fruit salad 219
    see also lychees. mangoes etc
fu yong:
    chicken 104
    egg with rice 182
    shrimp 87
Fukien cooking 10

G

garlic 12
    Cantonese prawns 88
    creamy cabbage and leeks 164
    garlic spinach 171
    lamb in garlic sauce 122
    lamb meatballs in soy sauce 118
    pork with chilli & garlic sauce 33
garnishes 17
ginger 12
    baked crab with ginger 90
    braised bamboo shoots 143
    broccoli with ginger & orange 169
    crab & ginger soup 63
    fish & ginger stir-fry 93
    ginger lychees with orange sorbet 218
    steamed snapper with fruit & ginger stuffing
        80
    stir-fried cucumber with ginger & chilli 146
golden needles with bamboo shoots 144
green fried frice with spinach 179

H

ham:
    special fried rice 183
    three-flavour soup 64

hoi-sin suace 13
homemate noodles with stir-fried vegetables 196
Honan cooking 10
honey:
    Chinese leaves stir-fried in soy & honey 166
    crispy chicken 109
    deep-fried pork with a soy dipping sauce 132
    honey & soy glazed duck 114
    honeyed rice puddings 214
    sweet & sour cucumber 43
hot & sour duck salad 47
vegetarian hot & sour soup 53
hot lamb 119

I

ingredients 12-13

K

Kiangsu cooking 10
Kung Po chicken with cashew nuts 98

L

lamb 117
    five-spiced lamb 121
    hot lamb 119
    lamb & rice soup 70
    lamb in garlic sauce 122
    lamb meatballs in soy sauce 118
    lamb with transparent noodles 207
    stir-fried lamb with sesame seeds 120
leeks:
    creamy cabbage and leeks 164
    deep-fried tofu with Chinese five spice 156
    lamb with transparent noodles 207
lemon:
    lemon Chinese leaves 165
lemon grass 13
    prawn stir-fry with lemon grass 86
lentil balls with sweet & sour sauce 167
lettuce-wrapped minced meat 27
lily buds 13
lotus leaves 13
    fragrant steamed rice in lotus leaves 178
lychees:
    ginger lychees with orange sorbet 218
    mango dumplings 212

M

mandarins:
    ginger lychees with orange sorbet 218
mangetout 13
    beef & pak choi 124
    Oriental salad 45
    spiced scallops 81
manoes:
    duck with mangoes 115
    mango dumplings 212
    mango mousse 215
Mao Tai 19
marmalade:
    sweet & sour sauce 17

meals 11
meat 117-137
    see also beef, pork etc
meatballs:
    lamb meatballs in soy sauce 118
    spinach meatballs 24
mixed pickled vegetables 46
mixed vegetable chow mein 199
mixed vegetable soup 52
money bags 162
mousse, mango 215
mullet with ginger 78
mushrooms 13
    chicken with mushrooms 108
    fried noodles with mushrooms & pork 206
    fried rice with prawns 184
    money bags 162
    mushroom & cucumber noodle soup 59
    prawn stir-fry with lemon grass 86
    spiced scallops 81
    spicy mushrooms 161
    spinach with straw mushrooms 172
    stir-fried mushrooms, cucumber & smoked tofu 155
mussels:
    rice with crab & mussels 188

N

noodles 13, 191-207
    beef & vegetable noodle soup 57
    beef chow mein 205
    Cantonese fried noodles 201
    chicken noodles 202
    chicken on crispy noodles 203
    chow mein 192
    curried prawn noodles 199
    fried noodles with mushrooms & pork 206
    fried vegetable noodles 193
    homemade noodles with stir-fried vegetables 196
    lamb with transparent noodles 207
    mixed vegetable chow mein 194
    mushroom & cucumber noodle soup 59
    noodles in soup 58
    pork chow mein 204
    seafood chow mein 198
    Singapore-style rice noodles 200
    transparent noodles with yellow bean sauce 195
    vegetable & nut stir-fry 150
    vegetable & tofu casserole 154
Northern Chinese cooking 10

O

omelette, Chinese 39
orange:
    broccoli with ginger & orange 169
    chinese leaves stir-fried in soy & honey 166
    ginger lychees with orange sorbet 218
    Oriental salad 45
    peanut sesame chicken 100
    poached allspice pears 216
    steamed snapper with fruit & ginger stuffing 80
    transparent noodles with prawns 197

Oriental salad 49
oyster sauce 13
    broccoli in oyster sauce 170
    chicken on crispy noodles 203
    oyster sauce beef 123
    squid in oyster sauce & vegetables 91

P

pak choi 13
    beef & pak choi 124
    crisp fried pak choi & almonds 168
    stir-fried greens 152
pancakes:
    aromatic & crispy duck 112
    pork pancake rolls 26
paprika:
    red spiced beef 134
pastries, banana 211
peanut butter:
    vegetable & nut stir-fry 150
peanuts:
    peanut sesame chicken 100
    spicy peanut chicken 103
    vegetable & nut stir-fry 150
pears:
    poached allspice pears 216
peas:
    chicken fu yong 104
    Chinese fried rice 176
    egg fried rice 181
    fried rice with pork, tomatoes, peas & mushrooms 189
Peking duck soup 67
peppercorns
    see Szechuan peppercorns
peppers:
    beansprouts with peppers 170
    beef & pak choi 142
    braised bamboo shoots 143
    broccoli, pepper & almond salad 49
    chicken on crispy noodles 203
    chicken with pepper 102
    chilli chicken 105
    Chinese chicken salad 96
    Chinese fried rice 176
    Chinese hot salad 44
    five-spiced lamb 121
    fried squid flowers 92
    golden needles with bamboo shoots 144
    lentil balls with sweet & sour sauce 167
    peanut sesame chicken 100
    peppered beef cashew 127
    pot sticker dumplings 37
    seafood combination 83
    spicy peanut chicken 103
    stir-fried duck with broccoli & peppers 111
    transparent noodles with prawns 197
pickles 45
    mixed pickled vegetables 46
    pickled cucumber 46
pine nuts:
    spinach with straw mushrooms 172
pineapple:
    lentil balls with sweet & sour sauce 167
    trout with pineapple 74
piquant dipping sauce 22
plum sauce 13

pork with plum sauce 135
pached allspice pears 216
pork 117
    barbecue pork (char sui) 36
    barbecue spare ribs 35
    braised pork & tofu 137
    Cantonese prawns 88
    Chinese stock 16
    deep-fried pork with a soy dipping sauce 132
    deep-fried spare ribs 32
    fish-flavoured shredded pork 133
    fried noodles with mushrooms & pork 206
    fried rice with pork, tomatoes, peas &
    mushrooms 189
    lettuce-wrapped minced meat 27
    pork & Szechuan vegetable soup 71
    pork chow mein 204
    pork dim sum 34
    pork pancake rolls 26
    pork with chilli & garlic sauce 33
    pork with plum sauce 135
    shrimp dumpling soup 62
    spare ribs with chilli 131
    spinach meatballs 24
    stir-fried pork with vegetables 136
    sweet & sour pork 130
pot sticker dumplings 37
potatoes:
    Chinese potato sticks 173
poultry 95-115
prawns:
    Cantonese prawns 88
    Chinese omelette 39
    curried prawn noodles 199
    deep-fried prawns 30
    fish soup with wontons 60
    fried rice with prawns 184, 187
    prawn crackers 17
    prawn soup 66
    prawn stir-fry with lemon grass 86
    rice paper parcels 29
    seafood combination 83
    sesame prawn toasts 31
    Singapore-style rice noodles 200
    sizzled chilli prawns 85
    special fried rice 183
    steamed cabbage rolls 28
    stir-fried prawns & vegetables 82
    sweet & sour prawns 89
    Szechuan prawns 84
    three-flavour soup 64
    transparent noodles with prawns 197

R

radishes:
    flowers 17
    roses 17
ravioli, Chinese 30
red spiced beef 134
rice 13, 175-189
    chicken & rice casserole 185
    Chinese fried rice 176
    egg fried rice 181
    egg fried rice with chilli 180
    egg fu yong with rice 182
    fragrant steamed rice in lotus leaves 178
    fried rice & prawns 187

fried rice with pork, tomatoes, peas &
    mushrooms 189
fried rice with prawns 184
green fried rice with spinach 179
honeyed rice puddings 214
lamb & rice soup 70
plain rice 16
rice with crab & mussels 188
special fried rice 183
special fried rice with cashew nuts 186
sweet rice 213
vegetable fried rice 177
rice noodles see noodles
rice paper parcels 29
rice vinegar 13
    sweet & sour cucumber 43
rice wine 13, 19
roasting 15
roses, vegetable garnishes 17

S

salads 41-49
    broccoli, pepper & almond salad 49
    Chinese chicken salad 96
    Chinese hot salad 44
    cucumber & beansprout salad 48
    hot & sour duck salad 47
    Oriental salad 45
    sweet & sour cucumber 43
    sweet & sour tofu salad 42
salt & pepper sauce 17
sauces:
    chilli & garlic 33
    piquant dipping 22
    salt & pepper 17
    spring onion 17
    sweet & sour 17, 141
    Szechuan hot 79
Scallions see spring onions
scallops:
    spiced scallops 81
sea bass:
    fish with black bean sauce 75
seafood & fish 73-93
    seafood & tofu soup 61
    seafood chow mein 198
    seafood combination 83
    see also crabmeat, prawns etc
seaweed, crispy 23
sesame oil 13
sesame seeds 13
    peanut sesame chicken 100
    sesame prawn toasts 31
    stir-fried lamb with sesame seeds 120
shallots 13
Shantung cooking 10
shrimp:
    shrimp dumpling soup 62
    shrimp fu yong 87
    see also prawns
Singapore-style rice noodles 200
sizzled chilli prawns 85
snapper:
    steamed snapper with fruit & ginger stuffing
    80
snow peas see mangetout
sorbet, orange 218

soups 51-71
    beef & vegetable noodle soup 57
    chicken soup with almonds 69
    Chinese cabbage soup 54
    clear chicken & egg soup 68
    crab & ginger soup 63
    curried chicken & sweetcorn soup 65
    fish soup with wontons 60
    lamb & rice soup 70
    mixed vegetable soup 52
    mushroom & cucumber noodle soup 59
    noodles in soup 58
    Peking duck soup 67
    pork & Szechuan vegetable soup 71
    prawn soup 66
    seafood & tofu soup 61
    shrimp dumpling soup 62
    spinach & tofu soup 56
    three-flavour soup 64
    vegetarian hot & sour soup 53
    wonton soup 55
Southern Chinese cooking 10
soy sauce 13
    barbecue spare ribs 35
    chicken chop suey 107
    Chinese leaves stir-fried in soy & honey 166
    deep-fried pork with a soy dipping sauce 132
    honey & soy glazed duck 114
    lamb meatballs in soy sauce 118
spare ribs:
    barbecue spare ribs 35
    deep-fried spare ribs 32
    spare ribs with chilli 131
special fried rice 183
special fried rice with cashew nuts 186
spiced scallops 81
spicy aubergines 159
spicy beef & broccoli stir-fry 125
spicy mushrooms 161
spicy peanut chicken 103
spinach:
    garlic spinach 171
    green fried rice with spinach 179
    noodls in soup 58
    spinach & tofu soup 56
    spinach meatballs 24
    spinach with straw mushrooms 172
    steamed snapper with fruit & ginger stuffing
    80
    stir-fried greens 152
    wonton soup 55
spirits 19
spring greens:
    crispy seaweed 23
spring onions 13
    chicken with celery & cashew nuts 110
    Chinese fried rice 176
    pork dim sum 34
    pot sticker dumplings 37
    prawn stir-fry with lemon grass 86
    rice paper parcels 29
    sizzled chilli prawns 85
    spring onion sauce 17
spring roll skins 12
    pork pancake rolls 26
    spring rolls 25
squid:
    fried squid flowers 92
    seafood combination 83

squid in oyster sauce & vegetables 91
steamed cabbage rolls 28
steamed duck buns 38
steamed snapper with fruit & ginger stuffing 80
steamed vegetable cabbage rolls 167
steamers 14
steaming 15
stir-fried beansprouts 147
stir-fried cucumber with ginger & chilli 146
stir-fried duck with broccoli & peppers 111
stir-fried greens 152
stir-fried lamb with sesame seeds 120
stir-fried mixed vegetables 142
stir-fried mushrooms, cucumber & smoked tofu
   155
stir-fried pork with vegetables 136
stir-fried prawns & vegetables 82
stir-frying 15
stock, Chinese 16
strainers 14
straw mushrooms, spinach with 172
sweet & sour cucumber 43
sweet & sour pork 130
sweet & sour prawns 89
sweet & sour sauce 17
   lentil balls with sweet & sour sauce 167
sweet & sour tofu salad 42
sweet & sour vegetables 141
sweet fruit wontons 210
sweet rice 213
sweetcorn:
   curried chicken & sweetcorn soup 65
   money bags 162
   see also corn cobs
Szechuan chilli chicken 106
Szechuan cooking 10
Szechuan hot sauce 79
Szechuan peppercorns 13
   salt & pepper sauce 17
Szechuan prawns 84
Szechuan preserved vegetable 13
   pork & Szechuan vegetable soup 71

T

tarts, Chinese custard 217
tea 18
techniques 15
three-flavour soup 64
toasts, sesame prawn 31
tofu 13
   braised pork & tofu 137
   braised vegetables with tofu 157
   deep-fried tofu with Chinese five spice 156
   seafood & tofu soup 51
   spinach & tofu soup 56
   stir-fried mushrooms, cucumber & smoked
      tofu 155
   sweet & sour tofu salad 42
   tofu & vegetables with black bean sauce 153
   vegetable & tofu casserole 154
   vegetarian hot & sour soup 53
tomatoes:
   fried noodles with mushrooms & pork 206
   fried rice with pork, tomatoes, peas &
      mushrooms 189
   red spiced beef 134
   roses 17

transparent noodles with prawns 197
transparent noodles with yellow bean sauce 195
trout with pineapple 74

V

vegetables 139-173
   beef & vegetable noodle soup 57
   braised fish fillets 77
   braised vegetables with tofu 157
   chinese braised vegetables 145
   fried vegetable noodles 193
   homemade noodles with stir-fried vegetables
      196
   mixed pickled vegetables 46
   mixed vegetable chow mein 194
   mixed vegetable soup 52
   oyster sauce beef 123
   special fried rice with cashew nuts 186
   spring rolls 25
   steamed vegetable cabbage rolls 163
   stir-fried mixed vegetables 142
   stir-fried pork with vegetables 136
   stir-fried prawns & vegetables 82
   sweet & sour vegetables 141
   tofu & vegetables with black bean sauce 153
   vegetable & nut stir-fry 150
   vegetable & tofu casserole 154
   vegetable chop suey 140
   vegetable fried rice 177
   vegetables in black bean sauce 149
   see also Szechuan preserveed vegetable;
   salads and individual vegetables
vegetarian hot & sour soup 53
vermicelli:
   Oriental salad 45
vinegar see rice vinegar;
   wine vinegar

W

water chestnuts 13
   fried rice with prawns 184
   hot & sour duck salad 47
Western Chinese cooking 10
wine 19
wine vinegar:
   vegetarian hot & spicy soup 53
woks 14
wonton wrappers 13
   crispy wontons with piquant dipping sauce 22
   fish soup with wontons 60
   sweet fruit wontons 210
   wonton soup 55
wood ears 13
   fish-flavoured shredded pork 133

Y

yellow bean sauce:
   chicken with celery & cashew nuts 110
   chicken with yellow bean sauce 99
   Szechuan chilli chicken 106
   transparent noodles with yellow bean sauce
      195
Yunnan cooking 10